THE CLASSICS
OF WESTERN
SPIRITUALITY

THE CLASSICS OF WESTERN SPIRITUALITY
A Library of the Great Spiritual Masters

Menahem Nahum
of Chernobyl

Upright Practices, The Light of the Eyes

TRANSLATION AND INTRODUCTION BY
ARTHUR GREEN

PREFACE BY
SAMUEL H. DRESNER

PAULIST PRESS
NEW YORK • MAHWAH

Cover Art:
The drawings of MARK PODWAL appear regularly on the Op-Ed page of the New York Times and he has exhibited in numerous museums, including The Louvre and, in New York, The Jewish Museum. He has published several books, including *Let My People Go: A Haggadah, A Book of Hebrew Letters,* and the forthcoming *The Golem: The Legend of a Legend* with a text by Elie Wiesel. Since no portrait of Rabbi Menahem Nahum of Chernobyl exists, the artist painted a bearded figure immersed in prayer wearing phylacteries and prayer shawl, surrounded by Hebrew letters.

Library of Congress
Catalog Card Number: 82-81633

ISBN: 0-8091-2374-6

Published by Paulist Press
997 Macarthur Boulevard
Mahwah, New Jersey 07430

Printed and bound in the
United States of America

Contents

PREFACE

We live in a time of divine eclipse. Darkness shrouds our age. One strains to make out the Image, so bold has man's bond with the beast become. Lord of the computer and splitter of the atom, human beings are forgetting how to be human, much less how to be holy. Some of this arrogance has been shattered by two world-wide catastrophies that have ground our gadgets to dust and turned our idols into demons. Having exhausted the substitute faiths of culture and science, we are beginning to understand what Abraham Heschel taught: that unless man is more than man, he is less than man. A craving for the whole wheat of the spirit gnaws at us. Therefore, the searching out of holy saints from the past; therefore, the claiming of holy books from days gone by. Such is the grand task of this series of publications. What else to do in an age when tyrants rule and charlatans beguile, when pornography is dignified as literature and aestheticism is paraded as the highest goal?

Wonderfully rich in holy men and holy books was Hasidism, the Jewish mystical movement which Martin Buber considered the most significant phenomenon in the past 250 years of religion. No wonder scholars are ransacking its hidden treasures and students are pondering its teachings.

Around the time of the creation of the Bible and the destruction of the Temple in Jerusalem, the people of Israel were driven into exile. They seemed lost to history, tolerated at best as a fossil from the distant past. But the ancient fires had not gone out. From time to time these fires would flare up as of old, producing new songs of love to God, new dreams of redemption for man. The last great light to be kindled in the history of the Jewish soul was the Hasidic movement. Emerging in the remote and parochial towns of eighteenth century

PREFACE

Eastern Europe, it swept the hearts of the people into a great surge of piety, offering lessons of love and joy and humility. To do the proper deed was not enough; one had to do it with the proper intention: the heart was as important as the hand. Hasidism taught the startling message that God is in every place and can be served through every thing, and established that rarest of historical phenomena, the truly religious community of brethren (Hasidim) and master (Zaddik).

Hasidic literature presents special problems. "It is a tragedy," writes Heschel, "that this great movement is essentially an oral movement, one that cannot be preserved in written form. It is ultimately a living movement. It is not contained fully in any of its books."* The Hasidic Masters felt it more important to "be" Torah than to "write" Torah. Writing books was often felt to be a sign of pride. Rejecting the way of the recluse and struggling with the daily needs of community, who had time to write? Few Masters left finished works; most are the notes of disciples or the edited writings of their teachers. Further, the literature itself is often obscure and archaic, requiring a comprehension of the previous layers of Jewish literature, which the authors assumed and built upon. The oral tradition of Hasidism, however, has virtually come to an end, and the vibrant Hasidic communities in Poland and elsewhere are no more. The Holocaust has obliterated all this. What remains is but a faint reflection of what was. The literature of Hasidism, consequently, takes on added significance.

Despite obstacles, the library of Hasidic books is a highly significant addition to mystical literature. So powerful was the energy generated by the new movement and so remarkable the circle of Masters, that works of genius were inevitable. They emerged with the force of a thunderbolt. The very first Hasidic book, for example, (*Toldot Yaakov Yosef,* 1780), was a declaration of war against communal corruption, private asceticism, and rabbinic arrogance. It projected the blueprint of a new type of leader, the Zaddik, who was marked by humility and concern for the people and around whom the new community would rally. Opponents put the book under ban and into the flames. These early Hasidic books, with their prevailing message of the proximity of God and the preciousness of man, were eagerly awaited by the people who so devoured their pages that few copies survive today. In describing the difference between Hasidic writings

---

*"Hasidism," *Jewish Heritage* (Fall/Winter 1972): 64.

x

PREFACE

and the other Jewish literature of the time, one sage remarked: With other books, we must turn many leaves to find the Lord. Here we meet Him on every page.

Readers will welcome this volume as the first successful attempt to render one of the classic works of Hasidic literature into English. Rabbi Nahum of Chernobyl was a formidable figure of early Hasidism. His book, *Light of the Eyes*, occupies a place of honor among Hasidic works. The translator and editor, Arthur Green, has already contributed significantly to the sparse studies on Hasidism with his important study on Rabbi Nahman of Braslav and his translation of Hasidic teachings on prayer. The virtue of the present volume is twofold: the felicity of the translation of a difficult text; and the introduction, prefaces and notes which serve to lead the uninitiated—and many of the initiated as well—through theological and literary complexities, which otherwise might cause one to stumble. As the reader becomes familiar with the directional signs and absorbs the terrain, what may have seemed a thorny confusion will be transformed into an orderly garden on whose paths he will delight to walk.

For some time now those who have been reading about Hasidism have sought to examine a major Hasidic text in the vernacular. This volume should go a long way toward answering that need, and, what is more, open the way for others to come.

FOREWORD

The Light of the Eyes or *Me'or 'Eynayim*, as it is called in Hebrew, is one of the true favorites of Hasidic literature. In an approbation prepared for the first edition of the work, published in 1798, Levi Yizhak of Berdichev said of the *Me'or 'Eynayim:* "All its words are words of the living God, arousing the human soul to rise upward, setting the heart aflame in service of the blessed Creator". That edition was the first of eleven published in the nineteenth century, to which must be added several reprints and photocopies attesting to the work's continued popularity in Hasidic circles down to our own day. A Jerusalem *yeshivah* called by the name of this book was responsible for a fine new edition in 1966, the version that serves as basis for the present translation.

Rabbi Menahem Nahum of Chernobyl, author of the *Me'or 'Eynayim*, was privileged to hear in person the teachings of both Israel Ba'al Shem Tov and his successor, the Maggid of Miezrich. Possessed of considerable rabbinic erudition and blessed with a fine homiletic skill, the disciple became one of the new movement's leading preachers and an important disseminator, first orally and then in writing, of his masters' teachings. His work combines learning and enthusiasm in a manner that exemplifies Hasidism at its best: neither does the abstruseness of an exegetical point allow him to lose the sense of spiritual wakefulness that so pervades the volume, nor does the passion of religious enthusiasm lure him away from the careful reading and weighing of earlier sources that is the hallmark of Jewish theology, even in its most mystical garb.

The translation is presented in the hope that these twin traits of Jewish spirituality will be joined again in the readership of this volume, that the scholar and the worshipper will meet again in its pages.

INTRODUCTION

Hasidism, the spiritual revival movement that sprang up in the Ukraine and Poland in the eighteenth century and played a decisive role in the history of East European Jewry on the eve of modernity, has left behind it two major sorts of written records. The *tales* concerning the lives of the various *zaddiqim* or Hasidic masters are rather well known to the Western reader. Beginning with the pioneering work of Martin Buber during the early years of this century, translation and re-telling of the Hasidic tales has been characteristic not only of works mostly inspired by Hasidism, but of the most diverse sorts of religious and humanistic writings throughout the West. Not so the other chief literary genre of Hasidism, the *homilies*. These have remained chiefly the property of the *hasidim* themselves, reprinted frequently in Hebrew and read or studied over the generations, but hardly at all made available to those outside the Hasidic "universe," either through translations or through modernized versions for the less adept Hebrew reader. While a number of modern scholars, particularly in Israel, have shown great interest in this literature, few other outsiders have been able to approach its gates.[1]

This situation is particularly detrimental to a proper understanding of Hasidism because the less accessible materials are those most

---

1. The only major Hasidic text currently available in English translation is the *Tanya* by Shne'ur Zalman of Liadi, founder of the *HaBaD*/Lubavitch school within Hasidism. The *Tanya*, one of the very few systematic rather than homiletic works of early Hasidic writers, is a most important document, but one that represents a very distinctive tendency within the movement. The translation is available through the Kehot Publishing Company, associated with Lubavitch headquarters in Brooklyn. A number of anthologies of Hasidic writings are available, including *Your Word Is Fire* (Paulist, 1977), compiled by the present editor and Barry W. Holtz. That volume deals specifically with the theme of contemplative prayer.

1

valued by both *ḥasidim* and critical scholars as the basic texts of the movement.[2] The homiletical literature, generally written by the masters or collected by their early disciples from the masters' oral sermons, began to appear in print rather early in Hasidism's history[3] and was recognized from the beginning as its contribution to the ongoing sacred literature of Judaism. The books were printed in Hebrew, the sacred tongue (the "originals" are thus all abbreviated translations of Yiddish sermons—for the holy tongue was not spoken, even in such seemingly appropriate circumstances), were treated as holy volumes, and were themselves so revered that several of the Hasidic masters are generally called by the names of their books rather than by their personal names. The tales, by contrast, were long borne by oral tradition rather than by the printed page; most did not begin to appear in print until the 1860s, over a hundred years after death of the movement's first central figure, Israel Ba'al Shem Tov (1700–1760), and in a time when Hasidism was already clearly in a state of relative decline.[4] The tales were often published in Yiddish, intended for consumption by "women and ignorant folk," and were printed in such hopelessly poor-quality chapbooks that many of their original editions have by now entirely vanished. Clearly *as a literary genre* these were regarded from within the movement as being of secondary importance.

It is easy to see, even setting Buber's preferences aside, why the situation reversed itself when the question became one of presentation to the modern and the non-Jewish reader. The tales, like pious

---

2. Martin Buber has taken well-known exception to this point of view, claiming that the tales are in fact the most authentic witness to that which was original and alive in Hasidism, and dismissing the theoretical writings of the movement as mere leftovers of the old "gnostic" Kabbalah that Hasidism had began to outgrow. The polemical exchange between Buber and Gershom Scholem on this and related points is itself a classic in the annals of modern literary/historical methodology. See Scholem's essay in his *The Messianic Idea in Judaism* and Buber's in Commentary 36 (1963):218ff.

3. These lines are written in the two hundredth anniversary year of the appearance, in 1780, of the *Toledot Ya'aqov Yosef,* the first Hasidic volume to appear in print. The *Toledot* has been studied by Samuel Dresner in *The Zaddik* (London, 1960 and repr.), an important work written in a style quite accessible to the non-expert in the field. On early Hasidic bibliography see M. Wender, "The First Decade in the Printing of Hasidic Works" (Hebrew), *Tagim* 1:31ff.

4. The publication of the tales, including the reason for their appearance only at such a late date, has been studied by Joseph Dan in *The Hasidic Tale* (Hebrew) (Jerusalem, 1975). See also the critical comments by Gedalyahu Nigal appended to his edition of *Sippurey Qedoshim* (Jerusalem, 1978). A great deal of basic work, including a comprehensive bibliography of Hasidic tales, remains to be done in this area.

INTRODUCTION

stories from many cultural contexts, have an immediate and broad appeal. Their heroes, given some bits of omission or clarification here and there, are familiar even to readers who know rather little of Judaism: like the Zen monk or the Sufi master, the Hasidic *zaddiq* is readily available through the tales to provide moral examples and spiritual uplift to those who stand at a great distance from both his inner symbolic universe and his socio-historical context. Not so the homilies: here the door is seemingly barred before all those who come from outside the universe of that rabbinic Judaism of which Hasidism so desperately tried to remain a part. While not written in code or indecipherable shorthand, as were the works of many earlier teachers in the Jewish mystical tradition, Hasidic homilies are highly dependent upon exegesis of Scriptural text and are interwoven with seemingly endless quotations from Talmudic and later literature. Such a homily will typically begin with mention of a verse, spoken aloud in awe and trembling by the preacher, and then meander, sometimes without apparent aim, through a broad field of other biblical and rabbinic passages until slowly, seemingly out of nowhere, a thread begins to emerge that in fact will bind them all together, explaining all the seeming contradictions while at the same time making the moralistic or spiritual point that was the preacher's goal. No wonder that translators have steered clear of this material![5] Tales and simple directions will inevitably be more accessible to the reader than homilies of this variety.

If this volume has not followed that seemingly obvious counsel, it is because the translator believes that an appreciation of the homilies is vital for a true understanding of Hasidism as a spiritual move-

---

5. The division of Hasidic literature into these two broad genres can be misleading. Within the tales a good deal of sifting and subcategorization can be done: Some collections carry classic wonder and folk-tales, only loosely related to Hasidism and known from earlier sources, whereas others are much more nearly historical memoirs in recording biographical tales and brief teachings ((*sihot* as distinct from *torot* or *derashot*) of the various masters. The most extremely, but by no means uniquely, historical among these are the various biographical and autobiographical writings of Nathan of Nemirov, the leading disciple of Rabbi Nahman of Bratslav. Among the theoretical writings, too, certain distinctions should be made. *Hanhagot*, or rules for personal conduct, are a distinct subset of this literature. The first text to be translated here belongs to this genre; the literature of *Hanhagot* has been the subject of a recent Jerusalem doctoral dissertation by Ze'ev Gries. One might also distinguish full-blown homiletic works of single authors (*Me'or 'Eynayim, Qedushat Levi*) from the semi-anonymous and partly aphoristic collections (*Liqqutey Yeqarim, Kitvey Qodesh*) that play a rather large role in the early literature.

ment. The words of the preacher, by their very nature, are not merely speculative, abstracted from the ongoing reality of life. However masked, it is issues current in the community he addresses that stir the homilist to speak. It is in this literature that the agenda of Hasidism is formed and its central concerns are expressed: Descent for the sake of uplifting, the raising of "sparks," the transformation of sinful and distracting thoughts, the centrality of prayer and the denigration of elitist intellectuality, and all the rest. Above all, the ever-new discovery of God's presence, even in those places one had least expected to find Him, and the re-assertion of His unbounded love for His world and Israel His children, breathe life into page after page of the homilies for the one who has learned how to read between the lines of fanciful interpretations of Scripture. The more profoundly mystical teachings of the masters, including those considered closest to "dangerous" or heretical teachings (those most infused with the spirit of pantheism, those tending toward the utter spiritualization of the commandments, and so forth), come out only in this literature. The place of Hasidism as heir to the entirety of rabbinic, theological, and Kabbalistic Judaism, while at the same time exercising a carefully selective reading of the tradition to express its own spirit, is seen only through a study of the homilies. As several recent scholarly works in Hebrew have shown, the uniqueness of Hasidism can only be discussed through a comparison of its teachings with the many published homiletical collections of contemporaries who directly preceded Hasidism or who chose to remain outside its orb. Translation of the homiletical material into English is particularly important in order to make Hasidism accessible to the student of comparative religion or of mysticism in the context of various traditions; it is only here that the theoretical contributions of this movement, including its views on such basic issues as language and symbol or history and redemption, will become apparent.

* * *

Facile talk of Hasidism as a unified and undifferentiated religious movement should be avoided as thoroughly as should such talk with regard to any other complex religious phenomenon. Though its period of significant creativity lasted for less than a hundred years (1750–1840, insofar as such abstractions can be dated), Hasidism produced a number of discrete schools and a vast array of distinct and idiosyncratic religious types. The writings associated with such communities as Bratslav, HaBaD/Lubavitch and Zydachov are at least as different from the spirit of the Ba'al Shem Tov as is he from many a "non-Hasidic" thinker of his generation. The movement produced folk heroes, such types as Zusya of Anipol and Aryeh Leib of Shpola, who left little or nothing by way of theoretical writings but are central to the oral tale tradition, and heady intellectuals like Rabbi Aaron of Starroselje, who composed several tomes of significant mystical teaching but whose life and image as a person have all but faded from collective memory.

Among the schools of Hasidic theory, it is generally accepted that the group around Dov Baer, the Maggid ("preacher") of Miezrich (Miedzyrzec), has a place of particular importance. Dov Baer was one of the leading disciples of the Ba'al Shem Tov, and at the master's death in 1760 he achieved leadership (as the result of a certain struggle) over most of the Hasidic groups. "The *shekhina*," as Hasidic lore has it, "moved from Medzhibozh to Miezrich." That city became the intellectual capital of the Hasidic world for the following twelve years, until the Maggid's death in 1772. A mystic who was at the same time a skillful community organizer, the Maggid attracted to his court a group of extraordinarily brilliant and religiously sensitive young disciples, many of whom were to become important theoreticians and propagandists for Hasidism in the decades following his death, and several of whom were to serve as founders of the leading Hasidic dynasties. Though not all of those who had seen themselves as the Ba'al Shem Tov's followers accepted the leadership of the Maggid, it may be fairly said that nearly all the significant later schools of Hasidic thought trace their roots in one way or another to the Miezrich circle.[6]

The Miezrich period in the history of Hasidism represents a reappropriation of earlier Jewish mystical terms and symbols and their integration into the new religious experience that lay at the core of the Hasidic world view. The Ba'al Shem Tov, though far from be-

---

6. The major exception to this is Bratslav. Rabbi Nahman, a great-grandson of the Ba'al Shem Tov, had close relations with a number of figures who had studied in Miezrich, but may not be considered a disciple of that school. On Bratslav see my *Tormented Master: A Life of Rabbi Nahman of Bratslav* (University of Alabama Press, 1979).

ing the unlettered peasant that both detractors and later romantic interpreters have made him out to be, was not an intellectual in his
religious approach.[7] His teachings are cast in pithy aphorisms, often
based on a radical new twist given to a single verse of Scripture or
saying of the rabbis. The personality that lay behind them was one
deeply infused with the presence of divinity throughout the world, of
a God potentially discoverable in each moment of human experience,
and of a reality that could always be uplifted and transformed into a
Godly one, no matter how bleak or evil it might seem to outer appearance. He had a moderate level of that rabbinic learning typical to
householders of his day, combined with special expertise in the area
of "practical Kabbalah" as it is euphemistically called, the magical art
of healing through holy names, amulets, and herbal medicines.
Though he attracted a number of men of learning to his circle of disciples, it was clearly the force of his personality and the freshness of
his religious vision that attracted them, not his knowledge of Kabbalah as a literary/religious tradition. The Maggid was otherwise: an
educated Kabbalist before he came to the Ba'al Shem Tov, his
strength was that of giving clear and rich intellectual expression to
his inner life as a contemplative. His homilies, collected in three volumes,[8] are filled with terms and phrases that echo of every earlier era
in the history of Jewish spirituality. It was he who first began to see
that if Hasidism was to claim its place as a significant religious movement within Jewry, it would have to establish itself, as had philosophers and mystics in previous generations, by offering a particular
reading of the ongoing legacy to which the Jewish people is heir. The
aims of the movement and the theology of its leaders would best be
stated through its selective rereading and interpretation of prior tradition.

As might be predicted for a popular movement of mystical piety
within postmedieval Jewry, the three elements of the literary tradition that served as chief objects for this effort of reinterpretation
were the Pentateuch, the Aggadic teachings of the early rabbis, and
the Zohar. While the influence of many other texts and genres can be

---

7. See Joseph Weiss, "The Study of Torah according to R. Israel Ba'al Shem
Tov" (Hebrew), in *Essays Presented to Chief Rabbi Israel Brodie* (London, 1970).

8. *Maggid Devaraw Le-Ya'aqov* (1781); *Or Torah* (1804); *Or ha-Emet* (1899). The first
of these has been published in a critical edition by Rivka Schatz (Jerusalem, 1976). The
Maggid's teachings have been collected in an extremely useful (though unscientific)
manner by Israel Klapholtz in *Torat ha-Maggid*, 2 vols. (Tel Aviv, 1969).

felt within Hasidic literature,[9] none approaches the centrality of these three as a *recognized literary* source. A few words on each of these as they are treated in the Maggid's circle, with special emphasis on the Zohar and the treatment of Kabbalistic themes in early Hasidism, is essential to any understanding of the texts before us.

The written Torah stands at the base of that great inverted pyramid known as the Jewish exegetical tradition. Always the best known book, along with the prayer book, even among relatively unlettered Jews, the entirety of its text is kept freshly in mind through the annual cycle of synagogue reading. From earliest rabbinic times, the weekly reading formed the basis for most of Jewish homiletics. To this Hasidism is no exception; the vast majority of the published volumes of Hasidic teaching follow the weekly cycles of the public reading.[10] As is natural for homiletic literature (as distinct from Scriptural exegesis), it is most often the opening verses of a section that will serve as the basis for a preacher's thoughts. Only incidentally will the homily shed light on the meaning of the verse with which it opens; the purpose is rather the opposite, for the verse of Scripture to shed light on some other issue that is the chief object of the homilist's concern. In Hasidism this issue will frequently be a devotional one: the technique of "raising sparks," the problem of distracting thoughts during prayer, the transformation of inner (and cosmic) darkness into light, and so forth. The nature of the Hasidic authors' concerns, combined

---

9. We do not speak here of the influence of Lurianic Kabaalah and the remnants of Sabbatianism on early Hasidic thought. These were tremendous, but of a different character than that of the works here mentioned: no text of the Lurianic or Sabbatian sources serves as an object for Hasidic commentary. References to the Lurianic literature are most frequently of a general sort: "It is found in the holy writings of the ARI, of blessed memory" and the like. Most often these turn out to refer to such later Lurianic compendia on the liturgy as *Peri 'Ez Hayyim* or Jacob Koppel's *Qol Ya'aqov*. These were the most readily accessible sources of Lurianic teaching in Eastern Europe, and it is natural that they were used in Hasidic circles (see below, Noah number 1, and *Tormented Master*, pp. 78f). This was done in total innocence of any awareness that the authors of many of these later Lurianic compendia were themselves secretly sympathetic to the spirit of Sabbatianism. On Jacob Koppel see Tishby, *Netivey Emunah u-Minut*, pp. 204ff.

10. To these are added, at the appropriate point in the yearly cycle, sermons for the holidays and other significant events of the liturgical calendar (special Sabbaths, etc.). Many Hasidic volumes will also have appended selected comments on the latter portions of the Hebrew Bible, particularly the Psalter, and sometimes passages from the Talmudic *aggadah* as well. The recitation of psalms was a common act of popular piety among Ashkenazic Jews, and the Psalter therefore has a major place in the religious consciousness of Hasidism: after the Torah it is clearly the Biblical book most quoted in Hasidic literature.

INTRODUCTION

with the penchant for discussing them chiefly in this homiletical context, often leads them to an extreme spiritualization of the Biblical
text, one that some will be surprised to find within so traditionalist a
Jewry. Thus the ark of Noah (thanks to a fortuitous play on words)
becomes the word of prayer, the descent into Egypt becomes the exile
of the soul, the tabernacle in the wilderness becomes the holy place
within the heart, and all the rest. While this in no way sacrifices their
belief in either the external authority or the historical accuracy of the
text, it is quite clear that the chief object of the Hasidic preachers'
concern is an eternal message of the struggle for spiritual attainment,
a Torah that applies "in every time and to every person," as their frequent admonitions would have it.

The basic store of rabbinic teachings to which most Hasidic
works refer is a rather limited one. Bits of exegesis quoted in RaSHI's
universally known commentary to the Torah, aggadic statements collected in certain well-worn pages of the Babylonian Talmud, and the
basic Midrashic collections (Rabbah and Tanhuma) on the Torah cycle would supply the seeker with by far the larger part of them. Of
course no homilist was perforce restricted to these, and the greater
his knowledge the wider his range of potential sources of inspiration.
The very first printed book of Hasidism, the *Toledot Ya'aqov Yosef,*
shows a particularly broad range of rabbinic erudition. Most of the
authors, however, restricted themselves to those sources mentioned,
perhaps not only out of their own limitations but out of those of their
anticipated hearers. A homiletic point made by a new and forceful
stringing together of sources familiar to the listener's ear is potentially of greater power than one that has to turn to proof-texts that he has
never heard before. Since most of the homilies were intended, first
orally and then in writing, to have a broad-based popular appeal (*Ha-
BaD* and Bratslav are again both exceptions here), it was best to remain close to the RaSHI passages that much of the audience was sure
to remember from study in childhood.

Hasidism remained, throughout its history, deeply faithful to the
authority of rabbinic *halakhah.* Whatever flirtations it may have had
with radical spiritualization of the commandments, in fact its enemies
could find only the most miniscule legal objections to Hasidic behavior when they sought to describe it in bans and letters of denunci-
ation. But while the life-style of the Hasidic community remained
totally within the law, *halakhic* sources provide but little of the inspiration for the movement's thought. Essentially there is no reason why

8

INTRODUCTION

an originally legal text of the Talmud could not provide a departure point for the spiritual homily just as well as could *aggadah*. Most of the early leaders seemed to eschew such a mixing of realms, however, perhaps out of deference to a certain disdain Hasidism had originally felt toward the ivory-tower legal learning of the contemporary rabbinic world. This lack is particularly noted when the writings of the Maggid's circle are compared with those of such later figures within Hasidism as R. Yehudah Leib Eiger or R. Zadoq ha-Kohen of Lublin, both of whom taught in the latter years of the nineteenth century and whose works are filled with typically Hasidic comments on those legal portions of the Talmud that form the bread and butter of a traditional rabbinic education.

The use of Kabbalistic materials in Hasidism is particularly problematic. Like any group of latter-day pious Jews inclined toward mysticism, the Hasidic authors greatly revere the Zohar, which they hold to be the second-century composition of Rabbi Simeon ben Yohai. Numerous phrases of the Zohar's Aramaic had crept into the Hebrew sacred vocabulary by the time of Hasidism, and in many of the homilies one can see that the author had prepared his words by looking into the Zohar text (or at least the opening paragraphs of it) for the particular sabbath on which he was speaking. It is said of Rabbi Pinhas of Korets (one of those who stood outside the Maggid's camp) that he thanked God for having created him in that era when the Zohar was already known to the world, "for the Zohar had kept me a Jew." Both the Kabbalistic system of the Zohar, in its rudimentary outlines, and the religious *ethos* of the Zohar had a great influence on all of Hasidic theology.

The *content* of Kabbalistic teaching, however, underwent drastic change as it entered into Hasidism. The Maggid and his school, despite their own intellectuality, had little use for the latter-day Lurianic Kabbalah as they had received it, with its baroque overgrowth of heavenly realms and meditative techniques of access to them. Their rejection of cold and distant rabbinic erudition as a value had its parallel in the rejection of an arcane and inaccessible Kabbalism: Both were equally alien to the simple nearness of God that the Ba'al Shem Tov and those around him had known.[11] To a certain extent this rejection applied to the theoretical concerns of the Zohar as well; the

---

11. See the treatment by Joseph Weiss in "The Kavvanoth of Prayer in Early Hasidism," *Journal of Jewish Studies* 9 (1958).

emphasis that work places on an esoteric theosophy and cosmogony could hardly find a comfortable home in a popular movement of religious enthusiasm. There is a single-mindedness about the devotional focus in which Hasidism views the religious life that does not permit such "idle" speculation. Where the constant striving for nearness to God is the only legitimate value, even extended discussion of His nature and deeds, when lacking that devotional focus, may be depicted as distraction.

*   *   *

The central symbol of Zoharic thought, indeed the key to all symbolism in the older Kabbalah, is the system of the *sefirot*, those ten inner emanations that represent progressive stages in the unfolding of life within God. Portrayed through a myriad of symbols and described in countless patterns of pairing and unification, the *sefirot* have the effect of transforming the God of static oneness, as portrayed in most of Western theology, into a diety of vibrant and dynamic unity, manifest in ever-changing patterns. Though the *sefirot* no doubt to some extent represent stages in the unfolding of human consciousness, and particularly of the reemergence of consciousness as one returns from the mystical heights, almost all discussion of them takes place on the theosophical, rather than the psychological, plane. First and foremost the *sefirot* were said to exist in the mind and person, as it were, of God. The Kabbalist, characteristically shy about speaking of his own inner life, felt more free when discussing the realms above than those within. Indeed it is only by attempting to translate back from theosophical projection, or by peering behind the speculative language of the Kabbalists, that we can hope to gain some sense of that inner experience which motivated their speculative life.

All this has changed in Hasidism. Here, in a world where true worship and attachment to God are the only valid goals, talk of the stages of the *human* inner life has become essential. Claims of experience and assertions of expertise in the cultivation of inwardness that many an earlier Kabbalist would have found audacious have become commonplace in Hasidism. So too the *sefirot:* Their value as cosmology has given way to their psychological use; rather than realms within God, they now describe stages and qualities of human personality that are essential to the religious life.

The *sefirot* are divisible, for our purposes, into two groups: an upper triad and a group of the lower seven, called the seven "qualities" or "days." The upper three *sefirot* represent the life of the mind or the world of abstract contemplation. They are called (according to the Hasidic count), *ḥokhmah*, *binah*, and *da'at*, "wisdom," "contemplation," and "mind."[12] *Ḥokhmah* is the first point of emanation, the moment at which the "nothing" of boundless and undifferentiated divinity first crosses the threshold into the "being," and thus the primal stuff of existence in this world. Since external existence is to some degree (this varies from homily to homily and from writer to writer) illusory, true being is in fact being-in-*ḥokhmah*, or a being that lies directly in touch with the divine *nihil* that dwells within all things and gives them life. *Binah*, thought or contemplation, represents a second stage in the movement toward existence: the paradoxical existence of recognizable entities while yet within the mind of God. Traces of the maternal symbolism associated with *binah* in the older Kabbalah are still evident in the Hasidic sources, even though *binah* here serves more as the stage of the reuniting of opposites and the purging/transformation of evil in the human mind than it does as a step in the cosmic birth process. The fact is that these cannot be separated from one another: Just as the earlier Kabbalah, in speaking the language of cosmogony, reflected dimly the inward stages of the devotee's mental life, so does the Hasidic material, in its attempt to re-psychologize the language, maintain the aura of cosmic mystery that earlier generations had lent to these symbols. *Da'at*, the dialectical resolution of *ḥokhmah* and *binah* in the triad of intellectual forces,

---

12. It should be emphasized that the names conventionally assigned to these symbol-clusters are by no means exhaustive, nor even significantly descriptive in some cases, of their meaning. The names are derived from certain Scriptural associations (cf. Exod. 31:3; 1 Chron. 29:11) more than they are from any real attempt to describe, though the terms themselves in turn become sources for mystical reflection. The latter is particularly true in the writings of the *HaBaD* school, the name of which is an acronym for the upper three *sefirot*, indicating its contemplative focus. The translations offered here attempt to represent the usage of these terms in the present volume: *binah*, elsewhere translated "understanding," here mostly represents that "World of Thought" to which the forces of evil must be uplifted in order to be "sweetened" in their "root," i.e., the world of pure contemplation that exists—in man as in God—beyond that stage where categories of moral judgment have any meaning. *Da'at*, a key concept in early Hasidism, is often misleadingly translated "knowledge," based on its etymological origins in the root *YD'*. Here it is generally translated either "awareness" or "mind," the former in the sense of religious awareness or concentration ("Study Torah and keep the commandments with *da'at*") and the latter meaning referring also to mental powers, particularly those needed for apprehending God ("the secret of Egyptian bondage is that *da'at* was in exile").

serves as a channel for the flow of awareness from the contemplative life out into the more external reaches of human existence, emotional, moral, and physical. A proper balancing of mental forces and a constant state of watchful awareness allow *da'at* to function properly, a function that lies at the very root of the religious life as seen in Hasidism. Expounding on older symbolic sources, our present author sees *da'at* as personified both in Jacob, the third member of the patriarchal triad, and in Moses, who embodied "the mind of all Israel" in the moment of revelation on Sinai. *Da'at* in the individual plays a role parallel to that of Moses in the receiving of Torah: It is through the single channel of *da'at* that the mystical forces above (within) are given the opportunity to influence that which happens in the world (person) below.

The seven lower *sefirot*, associated by the Kabbalists with the seven days of Creation, culminate in *malkhut* or the *shekhinah*, the bride of both God and Israel and the Sabbath among the *sefirot*. The six "weekdays," seen in the Kabbalah as further stages in the emanation process, have in Hasidism been relegated almost entirely to the realm of human emotional and moral life. The lead in this change is taken by the first two of the six, *hesed* and *din*. The "right hand" and "left hand" of God in the Kabbalah, representing the forces of grace and rigor respectively. Here the two are assumed primarily to speak for love and fear as the essential emotions of the religious life.[13] The authors of this work and of several other early Hasidic classics speak tirelessly of the need to beware of improper love and fear and of their dangers to spiritual life, and the need to uplift these and restore them to their root in the love and fear of God. The same is true for the following four *sefirot*, as will become clear to the reader of our author's *Upright Practices*.

Malkhut, the last of the emanations, has a role of particular significance in Hasidic thought. The essentially feminine imagery associated with *malkhut* is preserved in Hasidism; it is an all-embracing maternal figure, loving even in the moment of chastisement, that the *hasid* seemingly is to have in mind. The term *malkhut* means "kingship" or "dominion"; it is used to refer to the indwelling presence of

---

13. The centrality of love and fear is itself not original to Hasidism, but characterizes Jewish moralistic literature through much of the late and post-medieval periods, especially those works written in the Kabbalistic spirit. The association between these aspects of the religious life and the *sefirot hesed* and *din* also goes back to the Zohar period.

God in the world. For a religious movement that receives its impetus from the intoxicating consciousness that "the whole earth is full of His glory," the indwelling *shekhinah* is central both to the devotional life and to a proper understanding of the world. Here cosmology does come back into play; the psychological meaning of *malkhut* is decidedly secondary to a real sense that the outer world embodies the *shekhinah* or lies totally within it and that all created things are but the varied garb of her Presence.

In fact what seems to have transpired in Hasidism is that the sefirotic system, while formally maintained, has been emptied of all its intermediary content. The second through the ninth *sefirot* have been transferred primarily to the psychological and devotional realms, leaving the beginning and the end, *ḥokhmah* and *malkhut*, alone in the cosmological scheme of things. The primal point of origins and the fullness of divine Presence in Creation now face one another in an unmediated way, and by a classic of *coincidentia oppositorum* turn out to be one and the same. The terms *ḥokmah* and *malkhut*, opposite ends of the spectrum for the earlier Kabbalist,[14] are here used almost interchangeably: His *ḥokhmah* fills the world, *ḥokhmah* equals Torah equals *malkhut*, and various other such formulations are taken for granted. This seemingly drastic change is entirely appropriate to the purposes of Hasidism. The older Kabbalah, puzzled by the mystery of the one and the many, sought to overcome the difficulty of the emergence of multiplicity and otherness from the undifferentiated One by graduating the process. Hence the rungs within rungs that emerge once the Kabbalistic diagram is expanded beyond its original tenfold core. Hasidism, discovering the joys of simple and direct relationship with God (both with the "father in Heaven" of rabbinic theism and with the "Nothing" of mystical religion), no longer had use for the arcane and alienating cosmic diagrams it had inherited from the Kabbalah. A radical simplification of cosmology was needed to reflect the new experience, as well as to render it accessible to those who could never master the complex secrets of Kabbalistic intellectuality. Since the

---

14. Of course the earlier Kabbalists too were aware of the potentially circular nature of their ten: the pre-Kabbalistic *Sefer Yezirah*, the first document to speak of the *sefirot*, announced at once that "their beginning is tied to their end and their end to their beginning." The Kabbalistic incorporation of "the last in deed was the first in thought" (a saying of the Aristotelian commentators; see Stern in *JJS* 7:234) is further evidence of this. The extent of this association, however, and its proclamation as a commonplace, is new in Hasidism.

INTRODUCTION

option of denying venerable Kabbalistic terms and symbols was one not open to the *ḥasid*, their transference to the realm of religious psychology, where they could indeed serve a useful purpose, made rather good sense.[15]

Two other terms central to the prior Kabbalistic legacy of Hasidism should also be mentioned here, as their use in Hasidism is distinctive and at times misleading, especially to the reader who sees them in their original Kabbalistic context. These terms are *zimzum* ("contraction," "reduction") and *shevirah* ("breaking," as in "breaking of the vessels"), both inherited by Hasidism from the mythic language of the Lurianic Kabbalah.

Zimzum is a central notion of the cosmogonic myth laid out by Isaac Luria (1534–1572) and his followers. The sixteenth-century circle of Kabbalists seems to have been interested in two questions, both of which received an answer in *zimzum:* (1) If God is boundless and all-filling, how can the non-God come to exist? (2) If the good God fills all the universe, whence the roots of evil? These questions, variations of the classic Creation and Theodicy questions of Western theology, are now answered in a stunning and original manner: God's Creation in fact began with an act of withdrawal. God had to retreat into Himself, as it were, and leave an empty space within which the world could be created. Were it not for this divine self-withdrawal, there could be no non-God, and thence no universe. At the same time, as God vacates the primal space in which Creation is to happen, the vacuum left allows room for the original growth of those demonic forces that could only be born in a place from which God has been removed.[16]

---

15. On the emphasis on religious psychology in Hasidic thinking, see the remarks by Gershom Scholem in *Major Trends in Jewish Mysticism,* (New York, 1954) p. 341. An expanded treatment of this theme is to be found in Siegmund Hurwitz's "Psychological Aspects in Early Hasidic Literature," in *Timeless Documents of the Soul* ed. James Hillman (Evanston, 1968). The simplification of the sefirotic system in Hasidism has been discussed briefly by Rivka Schatz in *Ha-Ḥasidut ke-Mistiqah* (Jerusalem, 1968), p. 45.

16. It is not our place here to discuss the pre-Hasidic history of Lurianic concepts in any detail. The question of whether evil originates only in God's absence or whether *zimzum* might not represent an intentional purging of the roots of evil from *eyn sof* is a central issue addressed in the major scholarly work on the subject, I. Tishby's *Torat ha-Ra' weha-Qelipah be-Kabbalat ha-ARI.* The English reader should follow the summary treatment in Scholem's *Major Trends,* seventh lecture, and the brief but entirely readable discussion in Louis Jacobs' *Seeker of Unity* (New York, 1966), pp. 49ff.

INTRODUCTION

The Maggid and his school used the motif of *zimzum* in a rather different way. The religious revival of which they were a part did not have need for a radical doctrine of the origins of evil. In the spirit of early Hasidism, evil was either the illusion of those who had not yet seen the all-pervading light of God's presence or else the lifeless and necessarily ephemeral trap into which the sparks of divine light (see below) had fallen. The existence of the non-God remained a problem, but primarily in the realm of mystical psychology: does the God to whom I am joined in mystical union so overwhelm me that I no longer have a consciousness of my own? Or, phrased somewhat less directly, does the all-pervading character of divinity in the world leave room for the reality of my separate mind? It was to respond to these questions that Hasidism turned to *zimzum*, almost always interpreting it in a way that might better be rendered as "reduction" or "concentration" of divine Presence than anything smacking of "absence" or "withdrawal."[17] God reduces the intensity of His light, in both Creation and Revelation, so that man will not be "blinded" by His presence. God so concentrates His Presence in the heart of Israel that it never departs throughout the tribulations of exile. The loving Father so phrases His abstruse teachings that even the most simple of His children will be able to comprehend them. *Zimzum* in the Hasidic reading takes place for the sake of man, particularly for the sake of the mystic, that he might attach himself to God without reservation and yet remain human, alive, and sane.

Shevirah, the breaking of the vessels, is preserved in a form closer to its Lurianic intent. After *zimzum*, God sent forth into the empty space that ray of His light which was to create both the *sefirot* and lower worlds. The light was too intense, however, for the lower sefirotic vessels to bear, and they were tragically smashed. Shards of the broken vessels and sparks of light were scattered together throughout the universe, the former now transformed into *qelipot* ("shells") or demonic forces that prevent the rising of the sparks and thus the resto-

---

17. The uses of *zimzum* in both *HaBaD* and Bratslav are somewhat different from that which we are to describe here. On the former see Jacobs, *Seeker of Unity*, especially in reference to the second section of the *Tanya*, the treatise on Unity and Faith. This remarkable document exists in English translation (see n. 1) and should be read by anyone seriously interested in Hasidism. With regard to Bratslav, see especially *Liqqutey MoHaRaN* 64 and my translation/discussion of that text in *Tormented Master*, pp. 310 ff.

ration of divine wholeness.[18] The world as we know it is a cosmos already on the mend from this cataclysmic event, and man's essential task is that of seeking out the sparks, uplifting them from their fallen state (the metaphor often subtly switches from one of "breakage" to one of "fall"), and thus participating in the ongoing process of redemption.

Hasidism personalized this notion, speaking of particular sparks that belonged to each individual Jew, sparks that only he could raise up. In doing so, it necessarily added a certain degree of fatalism to the idea. The sparks belonging to your soul are constantly awaiting you and you alone to uplift them. Because God is gracious and wants the work of redemption to proceed, He will send you to those places, or will bring to your hands those objects, in which are contained the particular bits of divinity that are yours to uncover. All of life is thus a sacred mission, and whatever it is that the course of your life seems to bring you, be aware that it may contain the highest degree of urgency in the hidden but sacred task. The author of *Me'or 'Eynayim* is much preoccupied with the redemption of sparks, and much of his preaching is aimed at reminding the hearer that no matter how simple and seemingly ordinary the encounter—and this includes encounters with the non-Jewish world as well as with objects in space and moments in time—he may never be sure that it is not just this that all the worlds await from him as the fulfillment of his most urgent mission.

*   *   *

There are two other matters characteristic of the literature of Hasidism that are in need of some words of prior explanation, particularly for the reader who does not come bearing some familiarity with the movement. These are the centrality of the *zaddiq* and the attitude of the literature toward the non-Jewish world.

Hasidism, like many a popular religious movement, is built on the foundation of charismatic leadership. The Ba'al Shem Tov, along with a number of other teachers and holy men of his day, was

---

18. The motif of the broken vessels has been discussed by L. Jacobs in a Hebrew article to be found in the same collection referred to in note 7. The motif of "shells" has its origins in much earlier literature, involving mystical reflection on the nut as a sacred symbol. The history of this speculation has been traced by A. Altmann in the *Journal of Jewish Studies* 11 (1960): 101ff. and by J. Dan in *JJS* 17 (1968): 73ff.

INTRODUCTION

thought to be possessed of more than an ordinary measure of divine presence. This belief was also held with regard to those who came after him, the Maggid and the generation of his disciples. By the third and fourth generations of the movement (c. 1790–1820), the position of holy man had become institutionalized, the charism supposedly passing upon the death of a leader to his designated son or, in some cases, chief disciple. This remains true throughout the history of the movement; Hasidism in its historical sense is unthinkable without the belief in the centrality and the special powers, in one form or another, of the *zaddiq*.

Spiritual leadership was manifest in Hasidism in as many ways as there were varied personalities among the leaders. The Ba'al Shem Tov, it should be recalled, was originally a folk healer and master of amulets by trade. Here, as throughout the history of Jewish mysticism, the lines between mystical and magical teachings are not so clearly drawn as some would hope. If the latter-day tales of the Ba'al Shem Tov reflect any degree of historical reality (a complicated question, to be sure) it would appear that he was a clairvoyant, and that reverence for this special gift was a part of the esteem in which he was held. The Maggid, as we have said, was more of an intellectual, one closer to the contemplative than to the "practical" side of Kabbalistic teaching. Of the many other truly remarkable figures who peopled the Hasidic landscape toward the end of the eighteenth century, some saw themselves primarily as teachers, others as intercessors in prayer, still others as spiritual guides or as moral examples, and at least one (Nahman of Bratslav) as a proto-messianic redeemer. The literature they and their disciples left behind is filled with reference to the *zaddiq*, abstract and theoretical discussions often serving as masks for very practical discussion of his role.

The idea of charismatic religious leadership has a long history in Judaism prior to its appearance on such a grand scale in Hasidism.[19] The association of the term *zaddiq* (literally "righteous one") with this figure is also not altogether a Hasidic innovation. Even within the Hasidic sources, one can trace a certain historical (though not necessarily chronological) development. The earliest published works, those of Jacob Joseph of Polonnoye, employ the term rather seldom. They are concerned with the preacher and his role in creating a

---

19. I have discussed this matter in "The *Zaddiq* as *Axis Mundi* in Later Judaism," *Journal of the American Academy of Religion*, 45 (1977).

bridge between the lofty demands of the religious life and the abyss into which most of his hearers are sunk. His is the delicate and frightening task of holding fast to both of those worlds, in order that by his person—as well as by his message—he might effect an uplifting of the community before him. It generally remains true, however, in Jacob Joseph's writings, that it is the role, rather than any essential transforming divine bestowal, that puts the preacher in a position to accomplish this awesome goal. He must be, of course, a person of "form" (Torah and spiritual concern) rather than one of "matter" (corporeal pursuits), but this too is a result of personal attainment rather than of divine gift.

There are others among early Hasidic authors, the writer of the present volume among them, who refer to the *zaddiq* and his unique role in the world order, but do so in a somewhat marginal and non-institutional way. It is not quite clear in the *Me'or 'Eynayim* whether *zaddiq* refers to a particular small core of designated leaders, or whether it might not function, as it does in much of earlier rabbinic literature, as a goal hopefully to be attained by anyone who follows the ways of Torah and avoids sin.[20] There are places in the book (see particularly homily number 3 in *wa-yeze*) where the unique charism in connection with the term is clearly present, but where we do not yet have a sense that this *zaddiq* is a known fellow to whom the reader is expected to turn as his guide and leader. There is certainly almost nothing in this volume that parallels the very definite preachments in favor of the *zaddiq*'s necessary role in one's spiritual and even prayer-life as taught in the writings of the author's contemporary and fellow-student in the Maggid's school, Elimelech of Lezajsk. Whether this obvious difference has to do with differing bents of personality, historical circumstances or different interpretations of the Maggid's teaching remains an open question; in this area as in others, even the Hasidism of Miezrich is far from being of a single mind.

It is difficult not to turn to apologetics when discussing the atti-

---

20. S. Dresner shows a similar complexity in the use of the term *zaddiq* where it does appear in the *Toledot*. See the sources quoted in *The Zaddik*, pp. 275f., n. 18. In addition to its Kabbalistic associations discussed in the aforementioned article, the term *zaddiq* has a rather specific place in certain documents of the Sabbatian movement. See the important discussion by Y. Liebes in *Da'at* (Bar-Ilan quarterly on Jewish philosophy and mysticism) 1 (1978) and the sources cited there. These sources were unknown to me when I wrote the *Axis Mundi* piece; their relationship to the Hasidic use of *zaddiq* bears careful consideration.

tude of Hasidic thought toward the non-Jewish world. The identification of the gentile, his religion, and his nation-state with the cosmic forces of evil is quite total in this literature. There are, to be sure, sparks of holiness to be found amid the nations. Indeed, it is only these that give them life, just as the demonic forces themselves are sustained only through energy generated by the sins of Israel. The goal of discovering and uplifting these sparks is central to the *Me'or 'Eynayim,* and forms the subject of quite a few homilies in this volume. The end of such redemptive activity, however, is generally seen as the downfall or disappearance of the wicked nations, which cannot continue to exist once the sustaining sparks have been uplifted from their midst.

This view of Israel's role among the nations, reaching back to the traditions of ancient apocalypse, was greatly reinforced by the attitude of the Zohar, which painted as boldly mythic a portrait of the human world as it did of the worlds above. Whatever traces of ambivalence might have been present in the old rabbinic portraits of such personifications of the nations as Esau and Balaam had been quite wholly swallowed up by the viciously demonic character of these figures as portrayed in the Zohar. The dualism of the classical Kabbalah, in which the forces of evil battle the good and the godly until the end of time, is played out in this world by the struggle of Israel against the heathen. The drawing of such battle lines leaves little room for moral ambiguities. Written in thirteenth-century Christian Spain, it is no apology for the Zohar to say that its world view simply mirrored back the world view of the larger society: If the Jew was demon and sorcerer to the mind of medieval Christendom, the Christian (or the gentile per se; no distinction between Christians and others is made in this literature) was the embodiment of evil and violence in the eyes of the Jew.

The socio-historical situation of the Jew in Eastern Europe gave free rein to such a fantasy portrait of the world around him. The horrendous atrocities of the Chmielnicki massacres were well remembered in Hasidic times, as were the more recent and equally bitter memories of the renewed Ukrainian pogroms of 1768. What little contact Jews had with churchmen was at best hostile and disputatious, and more than a few clergy were seen by Jews as among the most active agitators to pogroms. Even aside from the specific fear of persecution, the small-town Jew of Eastern Europe, in sharp contrast to his compatriot in the urban centers of the West (Venice, Amster-

INTRODUCTION

dam, Prague), had contact with only the lowest level of gentile society, the peasant who came to market to sell his wares. On the basis of such contacts alone it is not difficult to see how fertile was the soil for the growth of the notion that the gentile was simply not endowed with the same divine soul as the Jew. The reader who is, however rightfully, repelled by such formulations as they appear in this text— and the translation has not deleted them—will do well to recall how much of Jewish historical experience in the world of the nations has tended to confirm them.

There is a certain subtlety with which the teachings on the presence of holy sparks amid the gentiles must be read. To be sure, the myth of heathen wickedness is fully maintained by these preachers. Nonetheless, the fact that an important part—perhaps the central part—of Israel's sacred task lay in the raising up of such fallen sparks served functionally to justify both the fact of the disapora as a whole and specifically those contacts Jews did have with the surrounding culture. Strong elements of East-European folk culture are to be found in the cultural life of the Hasidic communities: melodies, occasionally even with their Slavic words, folk tale motifs, wise sayings, and recipes for herbal healing were all parts of the common folk-store that Hasidism, by this theory, encouraged Jews to claim as their own. There are ways in which Hasidic society as a whole may be shown to reflect the general Polish/Ukrainian culture. Such emulation could be well justified by this theoretical need to constantly be turned outward for the sake of the redemption of sparks. Loud proclamation of the nations' wickedness would thus serve to screen the large-scale adaptation of elements from without by a movement that clearly had to present itself as one of entirely native Jewish piety.

*　　*　　*

The author of the present volume, Rabbi[21] Menahem Nahum of Chernobyl, is a well-known figure in the history of Hasidism. He was

---

21. In the case of Hasidic masters, the term "rabbi" does not necessarily indicate formal rabbinic ordination and legal authority, i.e. it is used to translate *rebbe* as well as *rav*. There is no evidence that Menahem Nahum was an ordained rabbi. The later legends (*Bet Nahum*, [Warsaw, 1927, reprinted in *Bet Chernobyl*, Israel, 1968], p. 25) claim that he was town rabbi as well as preacher in Chernobyl, but there is no historic confirmation of this. Had he been officially appointed rabbi, that fact would certainly have been indicated in the *haskamot* to his book.

the father of Rabbi Mordeacai of Chernobyl, whose eight sons were in turn the progenitors of many Hasidic dynasties that held sway in various cities and towns of the Ukraine until the destruction of that Jewry, partially in the wake of the first world war, and finally by both Soviets and Nazis. The Twersky family, as the descendants of Rabbi Menahem Nahum are called, continue today to count among themselves a number of leaders of Hasidic communities, both in the United States (most prominently the Skvirer rebbe of New Square, New York) and Israel.[22]

Given the fact that he was both *pater familias* of an important Hasidic clan and author of one of the recognized classics of Hasidic literature, surprisingly little is known about the life of Rabbi Nahum (as he is usually called), and no sustained effort has yet been made to gather together those few documentary sources that do exist. As would be expected, R. Nahum is a favorite of the later legendary tradition within Hasidism, but the historical reliability of this material is much in doubt.

Tradition designates 1730 as the year of Rabbi Nahum's birth, and records his birthplace as either Nurinsk or Gurinsk[23] in the province of Volhyn. He was the son of a rabbinic family of some means, and though orphaned of his father in childhood he was given a good rabbinic education, culminating in study at one of the traditional academies of Lithuania, the stronghold of rabbinic learning. As a young man he visited the Ba'al Shem Tov, and came to be considered a follower of the first leader of Hasidism. At the Ba'al Shem's death in 1760 he joined with those disciples who accepted the Maggid's leadership, and was one of the eldest among the circle of disciples in Miezrich.[24]

Thus far traditional biography, or at least the sum of what can be

---

22. Unlike the Polish and Byelorussian dynasties, the Ukrainian tradition was to divide the legacy of religious authority among all or at least several of the sons and sons-in-law of each deceased *rebbe*. One son retained the title of his father (e.g., Chernobyl rebbe, Sadegora rebbe, etc.) while other sons became *rebbes* of still other localities. This constant subdivision made for numerous impoverished Hasidic "courts," most having but a handful of disciples after the turn of the twentieth century. These stood in sharp contrast to such unified religious establishments as the courts of Belz or Lubavitch.

23. See Horodezky, *Ha-Hasidut weha-Hasidim*, vol. 2, p. 59 and A. D. Twerski, *Sefer ha-Yahas mi-Chernobyl we-Ruzhin*, p. 2. Nurinsk seems to be correct. Such a place is found between Berdichev and Kiev; neither can be located in Volhyn.

24. Along with Aaron of Karlin and Menahem Mendel of Vitebsk.

culled from the mostly legendary sources. Significant is the fact that he is not portrayed as stemming from those lower or less educated classes that Hasidism is often said to represent; at very least it can be said that the movement took special pride in the presence of members of the rabbinic elite within its ranks.

Whatever means his family did have, his life as an adult did not reflect their support. He worked as a teacher and lived a life of poverty.[25] Legend depicts him as having lived as a wandering preacher for some years; even after he was given the office of town preacher by the Jewish community of Chernobyl, north of Kiev, his economic situation was not good. The single historical document we possess that offers some glimpse of his life is a letter sent by Rabbi Shne'ur Zalman of Liadi to his followers, asking financial help for the destitute and ailing Rabbi Nahum.[26] The letter will afford the reader a glimpse into the particular charm and unique formal style of old rabbinic letter writing:

> After greetings appropriate to those who love His name, I stretch forth my request and entreaty, to arouse the pure and generous spirit of their pure hearts to a tremendous good deed: the support of the holy Torah [through the person of] that pious and holy man, that other-worldly *ḥasid,* "chariot of Israel and its horsemen,"[27] the man of God who is called holy, glory to the sanctity of his name, our teacher Rabbi Menahem Nahum, the son of our teacher Rabbi Zevi Hirsch, may his peace be great, the preacher of the holy community of Chernobyl. Afflicted by the hand of God for quite some time, his expenses have been in the thousands. Even now he bears the suffering of love;[28] may God heal him, "give him life after two days," and "renew his youth like an eagle."[29] Because of this [situation] his holy hand is stretched forth to us through his letter borne by his faithful messenger, the pure man who bears this letter, may his

---

25. Correcting my unfounded statement in *Tormented Master,* p. 124, n. 3.
26. The letter is published by Horodezky in *Ha-Ḥasidut weha-Ḥasidim,* vol. 2, p. 66.
27. 2 Kings 2:12.
28. Meaning that he bears his burden lovingly, but also hinting that his love, i.e., his relationship with God, is one that often brings suffering in its wake.
29. Hos. 6:2; Ps. 103:5.

peace be great, [requesting that you] be to him of aid and
help, supporting him with your "righteous right hand."[30]
Thus have I come to fulfill his holy words [asking that you]
"fill your hands for the Lord,"[31] doubling and redoubling
the portion with a full and broad hand, for "one raises upward in holiness."[32] This almsgiving will do much to bring
near our redemption and the deliverance of our souls. "Silence is praise for it"[33] and for this reason I have written
briefly. I am certain that in your great and faithful kindness
you will hear these words of mine. "May the words of my
mouth be acceptable,"[34] and for the sake of this may the
Lord doubly bless you. "May this act of righteousness bring
about peace and life for eternity,"[35] doubly so for the sake of
the one who loves your soul and seeks your well-being,
Shneur Zalman the son of our teacher Rabbi Baruch, the
memory of that righteous one be a blessing unto the life of
the world to come.

In another letter, also undated, Shne'ur Zalman appeals to Rabbi
Nahum for aid in a favorite project of his own: the support of the
small and struggling Hasidic community in the holy land.[36] With
dates lacking, it is impossible to know whether the two letters, one
indicating great poverty and the other access to significant means,
might reflect a drastic change in the course of Rabbi Nahum's financial fortunes during the course of his years in Chernobyl.

Rabbi Nahum's teachings were published in three volumes, two
in the year of his death and a third, much slimmer, some twenty years
later. His collected homilies on the Torah, *Me'or 'Eynayim* [The Light
of the Eyes] appeared in Slavuta in 1797/1798 with the approbations
of six important figures in the Hasidic community, the best known

---

30. Isa. 41:10.
31. 1 Chron. 29:5.
32. The money that you offer for the sake of this man will be dedicated to a "higher" cause and thus uplifted. The Talmudic phrase is derived from a legal context: Items
dedicated to sacred purpose may not again be made profane.
33. Ps. 65:2.
34. Ps. 19:15.
35. Is. 32:17.
36. The letter is published in the collection appended to Abraham Kalisker's *Hesed
le-Avraham*, Jerusalem, n.d., 75b, letter 77.

among them being Levi Yizhak of Berdichev and Zusya of Anipol.[37] Levi Yizhak's letter is a particularly grand one, and stands out in contrast to the much briefer notes he wrote for the publication of various other Hasidic works that appeared in his day. *Yismah Lev* [The Heart Rejoices],[38] published in the same year and place, is a further collection of homilies, these written around Aggadic passages in the Talmud rather than around verses from the Torah. In fact the distinction is somewhat arbitrary; the former volume contains any number of *derashot* that concern themselves chiefly with one or another Talmudic passage, and are tied to a Biblical verse in only a rather secondary or artificial way. The disciple Elijah ben Ze'ev Wolf of Yurevich served as editor of both of these volumes.[39] The third volume, *Hanhagot Yesharot* [Upright Practices], was first printed somewhere in the Ukraine in 1816/1817, and contains a list of recommended personal practices and a brief credo.

Rabbi Nahum died in 1797, and did not live to see his works published.[40]

---

37. The others were Jacob Samsom of Shepetovka, Aryeh Lieb of Walchisk, Asher Zevi of Ostrog, and Judah Leib ha-Kohen. Jacob Samson had already settled in the Holy Land, but was passing through on one of his several fund-raising journeys for the Jewish community there. See A. Yaari, *Sheluhey Erez Yisra'el*, p. 623. See also the several mentions of him in *Tormented Master*, index s.v. Jacob Samson. Aryeh Lieb of Walichisk, whose son later married the daughter of Rabbi Nahman of Bratslav, was a disciple of the Maggid. Asher Zevi, preacher and later also rabbi of Ostrog, is the author of *Ma'ayan ha-Hokhmah* [The Fount of Wisdom], an important and little known volume of Hasidic teachings. Considerable biographical information on him is found in M. Biber's *Mazkeret li-Gedoley Ostrog*, pp. 260ff. Judah Leib ha-Kohen, like the others, was a disciple of the Maggid; his teachings are collected in *Or ha-Ganuz* [The Hidden Light]. Very little is known about him. See Walden, *Shem ha-Gedolim he-Hadash*, p. 80.

38. The two titles are taken from Prov. 15:30—"The light of the eyes causes the heart to rejoice." The title of the second volume should thus properly be *Yesamah Lev.*

39. In later editions the two are printed together. The best edition for use is that of Jerusalem, 1966, in which many of the rabbinic references have been supplied, though not in an entirely reliable fashion. This edition forms the basis for the present translation.

40. There is some question as to the date of his death and the approbations (*haskamot*) to the *Me'or 'Eynayim*. His death date is listed by A. D. Twerski and others as 11 Heshvan, 5558 (1797). The three haskamot that are dated, however, were all written on the 23rd of that month, and show no indication that the author had died. The identical date on the three documents indicates that an assembly of Hasidic leaders took place on that day. (We do not know where or for what purpose such a meeting took place, but it may well have had to do with the renewed conflict over Hasidism that occurred following the death of the Vilna Gaon, a month earlier.) The *haskamah* of R. Zusya in particular makes it clear that it is Menahem Nahum himself who plans to publish his teachings. In fact the hand of the disciple is mentioned in only two of the undated *haskamot*, those of Jacob Samson of Shepetovka and Aryen Lieb of Walchisk. The matter is

INTRODUCTION

*　　*　　*

As a part of the Classics of Western Spirituality series, the present translation has been executed with the serious but nonspecialist reader in mind. The aim was to produce a *readable* text, while remaining entirely faithful to the intent of the author as preserved in the Hebrew. Perfect literalism has thus frequently been sacrificed for the more readily comprehensible gist of a phrase or sentence; this translation has sought *not* to be what one present-day Hasidic author proudly called his work, "a Hebrew book with only the words in English."

The present volume contains the homilies of *Me'or 'Eynayim* to the book of Genesis (about one quarter of the entire work) and the brief *Hanhagot Yesharot* in its entirety. The choice of Menahem Nahum of Chernobyl as a candidate through whose works to make the literature of early Hasidism available to the English reader was not an arbitrary one. Given the inherent difficulty of all this literature for one who stands outside its orb, a writer of some prominence, but one who did not compound the already significant difficulties, had to be sought. Some classics of Hasidism, the *Degel Mahaneh Ephraim* of Rabbi Ephraim of Sudilkov, for example, were disqualified because they spoke too briefly. The aphoristic style in which they are recorded depends so fully on the exegetical play, often obscure to the reader in translation, that their brevity would translate as excessive obscurantism. Other works, the *Toledot Ya'aqov Yosef* and the *Or ha-Me'ir* among them, were disqualified for the opposite reason: The homilies are so long, the associations within them so abstruse, and the style so repetitive as to scare off all but the most dogged reader. Such a work as the *No'am Elimelekh* was disqualified for excessive concentration on a single theme (the *zaddiq*), while the works of the Maggid himself were again felt to be too difficult. The choice finally lay between the *Qedushat Levi* of Levi Yizhak of Berdichev and the *Me'or 'Eynayim* of his friend Menahem Nahum. It is my hope that the readers will be pleased with the simplicity and wholeness of vision to be found in this work, the product of the Maggid's school that to this reader's mind remains closest to the original teachings of the Ba'al Shem Tov.

---

in need of further investigation. One is further surprised to find, in Horodezky's chapter on Rabbi Nahum, a letter written by him and dated the 3rd of Heshvan, 5560 (1799)—all the more surprising since Horodezky himself, two pages later, confirms the death date in 1797. We can only assume that the date on the letter represents a printer's or copyist's error.

25

INTRODUCTION

The choice to limit our selection of *The Light of the Eyes* to Genesis alone was determined partly by the exigencies of time and the size of the planned volumes, partly by the desire not to offer too much of a good thing. Since the connection to Scripture is often a rather loose one in these homilies, themes tend to repeat throughout the work, and these readings of the first book of the Bible will give the reader a fairly good sampling of the content of the work as a whole.

The *Hanhagot Yesharot* is part of an extensive literature of lists compiled by disciples of the various masters, each comprising a number of personal practices the master was said to emphasize in his own religious life. Speaking a direct and practical language, the *Hanhagot* were extremely popular among *ḥasidim*, and played the role of devotional manuals for the conduct of personal life. The present collection of practices was published some nineteen years after the author's death, and we cannot determine whether they were edited in his lifetime or result from a student's recollection of his master's ways, set to writing only after the master's death.

Bearing the reader and his needs in mind, I have tried to leave the text relatively unencumbered by notes of a purely technical character. The notes to the text are intended to help the reader follow the discussion, understand a new term, or, occasionally, to reflect more generally on a theme that has come up in the work. They assume a reader who neither knows Hebrew nor has much prior familiarity with the literature of Hasidism, but one who does, on the other hand, know how to read a homily and who has both respect and patience for the style of traditional religious literature. It is precisely for this reader that I have sought, in the works of Rabbi Nahum, to make accessible the theoretical literature of Hasidism.

The plays on words that dot such a text are alluded to briefly in parentheses. The reader who does not know Hebrew will see that such an association has taken place in the text, but will not per force be burdened by the cumbersome task of trying to figure it out. In such references, capital letters are used to signify those letters of the Hebrew stem that are involved in the wordplay. Because our intent in this case is practical rather than theoretical, the capitals may or may not indicate the actual Hebrew word stem involved; they point rather to the author's intended usage. The same is true with translations of Biblical passages. While frequently aided by the Jewish Publication Society versions, I have often chosen to translate according to the author's use—or intentional misuse—of Scripture, rather than fol-

26

INTRODUCTION

lowing what contemporary scholarship tells us to be the plain meaning of the Biblical text.

Inevitably, there are key Hebrew terms for which any single English rendering is inadequate. I have not sought in this volume to remain utterly consistent in the rendering of any term, but rather have always followed the contextual principle. There are terms for which no translation will suffice: *qelipot*, though literally "shells," here usually comes out as "evil forces"; *dinim*, also containing some degree of evil, or at least of divine punishment, is here usually rendered "judgment forces." *Da'at* is sometimes "mind" and sometimes "awareness," while *sekhel* can be either "intellect" or "mind," and so forth. One significant change I have permitted myself is the frequent usage of the second person, while the Hebrew is written almost entirely in the third. Both Yiddish and the Yiddishized Hebrew in which Hasidic works were written have much more room for the third person impersonal ("one") than does English. To have translated more literally in this regard would have been to give the texts an awkwardness that they do not have.

This translation of Rabbi Nahum's works is dedicated to two of his descendants: to the memory of the late Abraham Joshua Heschel, my revered teacher and the one who introduced me to this writer, and to my very young friend Tamara Twersky Reimer, a gift of that which by legacy is already her own.

27

UPRIGHT PRACTICES

I

1. "The beginning of wisdom is the fear of the Lord" (Ps. 111:10); keep this ever before you. Believe with full faith that the Creator, blessed be He, the King of Kings whose glory fills all the earth, stands before you in each moment and sees all your deeds, both those that are public and those hidden in the depths of your heart. This should lead you to a constant sense of shame, of which Scripture says: "So that His fear be on your faces and you will not Sin" (Exod. 20:20). On this verse the sages asked: "How is the fear of God present on a person's face?" And they answered: "In shame."[1]

2. Purify your mind and thought from thinking too many different thoughts. You have only to think about one thing: serving God in joy. The word *Be-SiMHaH* ("in joy") has the same letters as *MaHaShaBaH* ("thought"); all thoughts that come to you should be included in this single one. Of this Scripture speaks in "Many are the thoughts in a person's mind, but it is the counsel of the Lord that will stand" (Prov. 19:21). Understand this.

3. Our rabbis say: "Sanctify yourself within the realm of that which is permitted."[2] In the moment of sexual union turn your thought to the sake of heaven. Recite the prayer of the RaMBaN as it is printed in *The Gates of Zion*. [Before the sex act] say: "For the sake of the union of the Holy One, blessed be He, with His *shekhinah*. . . ." See further what is written in the *Shulhan 'Arukh, Orah Hayyim*, section two hundred forty, concerning holiness before the act of union. Remember how careful the sages sought to be concerning this holiness.[3]

---

1. "Shame" (*bushah*) as spoken of here has the sense of "embarrassment" rather than of "guilt." The sense of *bushah* as described in Hebrew ethical literature is usually the result of awareness of God's greatness, rather than response to a particular sin.

2. Do not limit yourself to literal observance of the law that forbids, but add to holiness of your own accord by the way you do that which is permitted.

3. *The Gates of Zion* is a collection of penitential prayers and supplications edited by Nathan Hanover and first printed in 1662. It contains a prayer for this occasion ascribed to Nahmanides. The *Shulhan 'Arukh*, Joseph Caro's law code of the sixteenth century, serves as the basic guide to Jewish religious practice. "For the sake of the union . . ." is the formula of Kabbalistic intent to be recited before the fulfilling of each

4. Give as much in alms as you are able, as Scripture says "You establish me in righteousness" (= almsgiving; Isa. 54:14). How good and pleasant it is to have a box for alms and to place three coins in it (or at least one) before each prayer. Before eating too you should set aside a coin.

5. Fast one day in each week. Be alone with your maker on that day and confess explicitly all your sins against Him, even those of your youth. Be ashamed and ask forgiveness; cry, for "all the gates are locked except that of tears." Then turn back to rejoicing over the fact that you have attained full repentance.

6. Keep away from depression to the utmost degree. Thus you will be saved from several sins, especially those of anger and pride. Be intelligent and judicious in the matter of worry over your sins.[4] Depart from them with a whole heart, ask God for forgiveness, and then serve him wholeheartedly. Have complete faith [in the effectiveness of your repentance], following the rabbis' teaching: "If a man betrothe a woman on the condition that he be a righteous person, that woman is considered betrothed, even if he had been completely wicked. He might have had a thought of repentance."[5]

7. Fulfill the teaching of the *Saying of the Fathers*[6] that taught: "Be of very very humble spirit before every person." When you see a wicked person, say in your heart "Even he is greater than I." "The more the knowledge, the greater the pain" (Eccles. 1:18).

8. Pray and study with fear and love.[7] Know that the letters [of

---

religious commandment. The commandment to be performed is thereby dedicated to the union of the upper divinity with the *shekhinah*, symbolically represented as the male and female potencies within God. The point that the sex act is the fulfillment of a Biblical commandment ("be fruitful and multiply") is here overshadowed by the vision of human coupling as evocative of the great union above.

4. The Ba'al Shem Tov taught that excessive brooding over sin left a dangerous opening for the evil forces that abound in the human mind to become dominant and keep one from further religious devotion. He taught rather the uplifting of sins or, as the author here suggests, quick and full resolve to depart from them, followed by an immediate turn to worship of a more positive character. Brooding over sin, as can be seen from the language of the following sentence, keeps one from that wholeness of heart required for true worship.

5. The rabbis' willingness to render a legal decision in this way (Qiddushin 49b) shows how much stock they put even in single thought of repentance.

6. Avot 4:4.

7. Fear and love, held in their proper balance, are taken to be the central emotions of the religious life. This is a commonplace in later Jewish literature, particularly that written under the influence of the Zohar. See further discussion in *Me'or 'Eynayim*.

the text before you] are called heaven and earth, and that all the worlds and all creatures great and small are given life by His word. "This is the whole of man" (Eccles. 12:13). Understand this.

9. Keep yourself from being cross toward your household in any matter. Let your speech be pleasant, for "the words of the wise are heard when pleasant" (Eccles. 9:17).[8]

10. Cleave to the wise and to their disciples; learn always from their deeds. Keep away from people who do not have good qualities of character. This is the main thing: good qualities.[9]

11. Study books of moral teaching each day, something on the order of the *Beginning of Wisdom*. That work is filled to overflowing with wisdom, fear of God, and praiseworthy qualities.[10]

12. Keep away from having your head turned; accept not a drop of human praise. Praise that you receive from people is to be considered a great liability. Those who speak ill of you are in fact doing you a great favor. Your intent should be only for the sake of His great name, to do that which is pleasing to Him.

13. Accept whatever portion the Lord gives you in love, whether it be for good or for ill and suffering. Thus did our rabbis teach on "with all your might" (Deut. 6:5)—thank God for every portion that He gives you, whether good or ill.[11] "Evil does not come from the mouth of the most high" (Lam. 3:38), but only good. Compare this to those bitter medicines that are needed to heal the body. The same are needed for healing the soul.[12]

14. If you find yourself unable to study or pray with fear and love, continue in any case to study and pray to God with complete faith. This is what the rabbis have taught: "A person should ever involve himself with Torah and the commandments, even if not for

---

8. The verse may also be translated: "It is pleasant to listen to the words of the wise."

9. Heb.: *middot tovot.* The popular and Yiddish usage refers to decency of character and proper human values: generosity, concern for others, respect, etc. In Hasidic usage, as will be seen frequently in this work, these "qualities" refer specifically to the seven qualities of the emotional life parallel to the seven *sefirot.*

10. Elijah De Vidas's *Reshit Hokhmah* was first published in Venice in 1579. It was frequently reprinted and exercised great influence in the later devotional life of Judaism, both in Hasidism and elsewhere. De Vidas's *Tractate on Love*, a major portion of the *Reshit Hokhmah,* is to appear in this series.

11. The rabbis' statement here plays on *me'od* ("might") and *middah* ("portion").

12. Thank God even for that which seems to you a curse rather than a blessing; in some way that you cannot presently understand, it is given you for the ultimate healing of your soul.

their own sake." "Not for their own sake" means that even if he has no fear or love, he should keep doing them for the sake of heaven. They also said: "From doing not for their own sake he will reach the stage of doing for their own sake," that is, he will attain to fear and love. Of this the prophet speaks when he says, " 'Are not My words like fire?' says the Lord" (Jer. 23:29).[13]

15. Do many acts of loving-kindness: dowering poor brides, visiting the sick, and all the other things of which the sages spoke. This is one of three things that stand at the very pinnacle of the world order.[14] Praise no one and speak ill of no one. The Ba'al Shem Tov has already said it: "If you want to praise anyone, praise God, if you want to speak ill of anyone, speak ill of yourself" and know your lowly state. If you possess some good quality, it belongs not to you but to God. Thus Scripture says: "Let not the wise man praise himself for his wisdom, nor the rich man for his wealth" (Jer. 9:22). All this was given you by God. Your bad qualities—those are indeed your own.

16. Remember God always: "I place YHWH ever before me" (Ps. 16:8). If you fail to do so even for a moment it is considered a sin. Thus the Ba'al Shem Tov taught on "Blessed is the man for whom God does not think of a sin" (Ps. 32:2). "Does the Lord give up on sins?" he asked. Rather interpret this way: When a person does not think of God—when God is out of his thoughts—that is sin. Consider this to be a very grave sin: Thus you will take care and not forget Him. In such a case, "blessed is the man."

17. Each day study from the Torah, Prophets, and Writings, from the Mishnah and the Gemara, each in accord with his abilities.[15] Do it all for the sake of His great name, and for no other purpose. "Then you will walk surely on your way."

18. Take care, insofar as possible, not to speak before prayer [in the morning]. Do so only for very great need. Consider your deeds

---

13. "Not for its own sake" is here interpreted to refer to religious action performed without those "wings" of emotional intensity that will enable it to rise upward. The word of study or prayer, even if spoken in an offhand manner, will ultimately communicate its own inner fire to the speaker and will lead him to the higher form of religious life; "continue to *do*" is the constant Hasidic counsel, "and the spirit will inevitably follow."

14. Along with Torah and worship. The author refers to Avot 1:2.

15. The Hasidic masters followed the Kabbalists in viewing Torah study not only as a religious obligation but as a *ritual* act. The structure of one's daily regimen of studies took on a great importance for the mystics, who saw correspondences between the order of materials studied and the divisions of the human soul.

before you pray, and repent of them. Humble your heart by considering your own smallness and lowliness. Thus will you prepare all the rungs of your soul to receive some bit of the fear of heaven as you stand before Him. Of this Scripture says: "Prepare to meet your God, O Israel" (Amos. 4:12).

II

Know first that God exists. He was first, and He created all things, both above and below. His creations are without end!

All began with a single point—the point of supernal wisdom, *hokhmah*. The power of the Creator is present in all of His creations; the wisdom of God fills and takes on the garb of every thing that is. Of this Scripture speaks in saying: "Wisdom gives life to those who possess it" (Eccles. 7:12).

Believe with a whole and strong faith that the Creator is one, single, and united.[16] He is the first of all causes and origins, utterly endless, blessed is He and blessed is His name. He created many worlds, higher and lower, without limit and without end. Of these Scripture says: "Worlds without number" (Cant. 6:8; *'alamot/'olamot*).

Believe with a whole and strong faith that He both fills all the worlds and surrounds them,[17] that He is both within and beyond them all. He created the lower world for the sake of the Torah and Israel, that His blessed divine Self might be revealed. There is no King without His people Israel.

Believe with a whole and strong faith that "the whole earth is full of His glory" (Isa. 6:3) and that "there is no place devoid of Him." His blessed glory inhabits all that is. This glory serves as a garment, as the sages taught: "Rabbi Yohanan called his garment 'glory.' "[18] His divine Self wears all things as one wears a cloak, as Scripture

---

16. The phrase *'ehad yahid u-meyuhad* has its origins in the philosophical poetry of the Middle Ages. It is not intended as a precise theological formulation, and should not be read as such. "United" is in fact quite inadequate for *meyuhad*, the meaning of which is not clearly distinguishable from *yahid* in this formulation.

17. The terms "fills" and "surrounds" to describe God's immanence and transcendence originate in the Zohar. See Zohar 3:225a (R.M.). In the spirit of mysticism, Hasidic authors seek an end to this duality, a way to point out that *sovev* and *memale'* are in fact one.

18. Shabbat 113a.

teaches: "You give life to them all" (Neh. 9:6). This applies even to the forces of evil, in accord with the secret of "His kingdom rules over all" (Ps. 103:19). All life is sustained by the flow that issues forth from Him. Were the life-flow to cease, even for a moment, the thing sustained would become but an empty breath, as though it had never been.

Believe with a whole faith that the slightest motion of your little finger can move great spiritual worlds above, as the Ba'al Shem Tov has taught.

Believe with whole faith that man contains all the worlds within him, as the ARI, the holy Zohar, and various Midrashim have taught. This being the case, God must be proclaimed King through every single deed we do, through study and prayer as well as fulfilling the commandments [for thus is His kingdom proclaimed] over all our limbs. Even ordinary conversation must be made holy.

God's sight should be brought into our daily words and thoughts. With every word and with each thought we must cleave again to their root in God, since it is only by His power that we think or speak.[19] When you have full faith in this, you will come to realize that all the events of your life have come about through God. Whether or not they have turned out as you wanted, you will consider them all to be for the good, since "evil does not come from the mouth of the most high" (Lam. 3:38), but only good. Of this I have spoken earlier. Within every bad thing there dwells His power of good, that which gives it life. This can be seen only by the one whose eyes are properly directed; otherwise the veils of sin tend to intervene and blind the human eye. To purify your sight, do not look beyond your own four ells; these will be the four letters of the name YHWH, that which calls all being to be. Mend all your bad qualities by means of goodness; subsume the left within the right, as the holy Zohar has taught. [Cultivate] all those qualities of which the pious authors speak. Then the good will gain in strength and lift itself out of the evil in which it had been enshrouded. Once evil is left on its own it will vanish altogether, and then our righteous messiah will arrive—speedily and in our day! Amen. Selah.

You must believe all of the above with a whole faith, and at every

---

19. In these sentences lies the essential core of distinctively Hasidic teaching. "Know Him in all your ways" (Prov. 3:6), for all things and all moments, no matter how seemingly ordinary, are but "garb" for the all-pervading presence of God.

single moment be prepared to give your life for it. Do not let your mind wander off amid passing vanities. Cleave rather to the praise of God, and join together His three names: 'eHeYeH, YHWH, and 'aDONaY.[20] Human thought is derived from the World of Thought, identical to the name 'eHeYeH. Everything is purified by means of this thought. Within all things are contained [sacred] letters in a broken state; through this binding of the mind to its source in the Thought of God you raise them up.

This too is the meaning of the *miqweh.*[21] It similarly is drawn from the *miqweh* above, the name 'eHeYeH, the world of *binah.* It is there that the forces of evil are transformed or "sweetened." These forces were made by the sins of man; as you enter the *miqweh* and repent thoroughly of them, departing from your sins with a whole heart, the one who confesses and leaves them will find mercy. Surely then you will be forgiven.

The human being represents the name 'aDONaY, also called *shekhinah* or indwelling, for it dwells within the lower world. Thus a person's thought, when turned to good and aimed toward repentance, contains within it the unification of all three names, 'eHeYeH, YHWH, 'aDONaY.[22] By concentrating on this you will be able to draw unto yourself sublime holiness and great purity.

... By holding fast to the praise of God, by singing the hymns of Israel's sweet singer,[23] you will be able to destroy the accusing and evil forces. Indeed King David prayed that his songs would be sung

---

20. Many sorts of meditation on the names of God have characterized Jewish mysticism in every period of its history. From the time of the Zohar, the association of particular names with the various *sefirot* became a commonplace. Here the point seems to be that 'eHeYeH represents the upper triad, the world of pure contemplation; YHWH refers to God as Being, the God of theistic religion; and 'aDONaY refers to the God who dwells within the human self. It is the union of these three, the God of theism serving as a bridge between the other two, that forms the content of mystical contemplation.

21. The ritual bath, originally ordained for purification from states of bodily taboo, but used by *hasidim* especially as preparation for the Sabbath, holidays, or daily morning prayer. It is to this latter usage that the passage here refers: *miqweh* as a purification from sin before the daily prayers.

22. While incorporating a desire to retain the power of meditation on the names, Hasidism also wants to claim that the unification of names is effected of its own accord in the person who is morally pious and upright. This renders the abstruse science of such meditation accessible to the ordinary Jew.

23. The Psalms play a particular role in Jewish popular devotion; recitation of Psalms was an avenue of religious expression open to even the simplest and most unlearned of the community.

in the synagogues and houses of study. By them we can restore the crown to its former place, and the lily will awaken.[24]

Be among those who take stock of themselves each night before they lie down. Give an account of your sins and repent of them. Even a thought of repentance will suffice. Since *teshuvah* was one of the seven things that preceded the world into existence, time does not apply to it, and thus a thought alone will do to "sweeten" all. In this way you can send forth your soul (all three of its levels) to rise upward to the place of contemplation.

Rise up from sleep at midnight, for that is a time when God's desire is especially to be found. Serve Him in the midst of night and perform the midnight vigil.[25] As that vigil is joined to your morning prayer, you will be unified and will attach yourself to that which is above; then you will be able to bring forth whatever it is that you seek from God. Midnight prayer and service is a great thing; it is this that brings about peace above. If not for this, God forbid, those who are joined together[26] would be separated.

Take special care when reciting the *Shema* to pronounce each word. See that you are not distracted, at least not during the *Shema*, but recite it in fear and love. Each letter you recite in this way will help to bring life to your limbs.[27]

See too that you honor the Sabbath as fully as you are able within your means. Do so with food and drink and in other ways as well. The letters of *SHaBbaT* are those of *TaSHeB*, to indicate that "he who keeps the Sabbath, even if he is as idolatrous as was the generation of Enosh, will be forgiven."[28]

Here is a basic principle: The root of all things is in almsgiving.

---

24. These are both metaphors for the final redemption, and a certain urgent messianic note is heard in their employment.

25. *Tiqqun hazot* is a series of penitences and prayers for the restoration of Jerusalem to be recited after midnight. These were instituted by the Kabbalists of the sixteenth century and, though commended by this and other early Hasidic writings, generally fell into disuse in Hasidic circles. Pious Jews of Near Eastern origin still recite them faithfully.

26. God and the *shekhinah*, or the transcendent God and His indwelling presence.

27. The two hundred forty-eight words of the *Shema'* are said to correspond to the number of limbs in the human body, fulfilling the Scripture, "All my bones shall say: 'Lord, who is like You?'" (Ps. 35:10).

28. Shabbat 118b. The generation of Enosh was that in which idolatry originated. See Midrashim and Targum Y. to Gen. 4:26.

By this deed you uplift the sparks from their broken state, and in this way you uplift your own soul as well. The letters of *ZeDaQaH* ("almsgiving") contain the letters of *ZeDeQ* ("righteousness"). In acting as a *ZaDDiQ* you are a holy spark of the cosmic *ZaDDiQ;* [by your righteous act you partake in that *zaddiq*'s uplifting of *zedeq-shekhinah*] from poverty and exile. Enough said.[29] Here is the rule: By any holy deed or by any life-sustaining alms that you offer to the poor, you uplift a holy spark that lay amid the evil forces, and thus you come to holiness. No "act of holiness" can take place, however, in the presence of fewer than ten, and those ten are in turn a hundred. In this way is *ZeDaQaH* formed, and thus is a soul uplifted from its broken state.[30]

This too is a basic principle: See that you bring your own negative qualities to submission. Hold fast to good qualities. In this way too you will cause sparks to rise from their broken state. This is why a person must recite a hundred blessings each day. The meaning of this is as follows: "Blessings" refer to the pond above (*BeRaKHaH/ BeReKHaH*) and the streams that flow forth from it. You have to bring about the flow of these hundred blessings upon you, these hundred that also represent the ten good qualities. Overcome your own bad qualities and cleave to Him, bless His name, and in every way bring down the flow of His bounty upon you.

When you stand up to pray, decide first that you will attach yourself only to pure and virtuous thoughts, rejecting this lowly world down to the very last degree. Thus you may bring yourself to the most sublime joy of spirit, becoming joined to Him in a wondrous way. In this you attain to *malkhut*, the "I" of God.[31] Thence you may bind yourself further and enter into a state of union, until you reach the Nothing, the World of Contemplation, that which is referred to as "Who?". Of this the sages say "Know before *whom* you stand"—

---

29. The double play involves three words derived from the root *ZDQ*. The union of the last two of the ten *sefirot*, often described particularly in conjugal terms, is sometimes called that of *zedeq* and *zedaqah*, masculine and feminine forms of the same word but often translate "justice" and "righteousness" or "almsgiving." The ninth *sefirah*, *zedeq*, is also frequently associated with *zaddiq*, the one who performs just acts of goodness.

30. The inner mathematical relationship between the single one, the decade, and the hundred is often discussed in Kabbalistic sources concerned with number. This is here associated with a play on the word *ZeDaQaH*, but in somewhat obscure fashion.

31. Zohar 1:65b.

you stand before the "Who?".[32] Unification means that you not separate mind from words, especially during the *'amidah*, when the true union and coupling takes place. In this way that union may come to be revealed in the lower world as well. Amen. May this be His will.

When you awake at midnight, as we have suggested above, be sure that your very first thought is that of attachment to God. How great is the Creator! He has just restored your soul to you! As you glorify Him, ask yourself for what purpose He has sent that soul back to you.[33] Realize that it is for the sake of His service, that you serve Him with soul through Torah, worship, and the commandments. As you begin to pray, accept the fact that you worship Him even though your soul may pass out of you in prayer.[34] Keep your thought fastened on your blessed Creator throughout the day.

Do the same with your emotions:[35] Should something like improper *love* or this-worldly pleasure be aroused in you, know that it stems from a spark of divine *ḥesed*. You have caused that spark to fall into the hands of evil; it alone gives life to those evil forces. It is within your power to uplift those holy sparks, to separate the proper food from that which is to be cast aside, to find the hidden good. The Creator has so made it that we might have a choice: "See that I place before you life and death, good and evil. Choose life . . ." (Deut. 30:19). Treat all other emotions and human qualities in the same manner: improper desire for glory, for praise, improper attachments and loyalties.

Fear no one but God. Scripture's words "The fear of the Lord is His treasure" (Isa. 33:6) are to be understood thus: [Our] awe before His greatness is God's own treasure. There are various types of fear, to be sure, but [the true treasure is] that sense of awe before His greatness, fear of the Lord because He is Master and Ruler, indeed the

---

32. Zohar 1:1b. As the most revealed level of divinity is called "I," for there God presents Himself as one available to human search, the most hidden reaches are referred to as "Who?", the place of the transcendent and unanswerable question.

33. The passage is built around the prayer of thanksgiving for restoration of the soul to life, an early part of the daily morning service.

34. The Ba'al Shem Tov was said to have spoken of the possibility that a person might die due to the intensity of prayer. It was he who originally offered the counsel of preparing for death before each prayer of the day. See the sources quoted in *Your Word Is Fire*, p. 33.

35. Here begins a list of the seven lower *sefirot*, each of them referred to some aspect of the spiritual/emotional life. The sefirotic references are here italicized to help the reader remain aware of the list.

very source[36] of all the worlds. Such awe will lead you to serve Him with all your strength and intensity. No longer will you be pulled away by the attractions of this lowly and despicable world. Day by day you will grow in the strength of His service. You will do this not for fear of death, of punishment, or of hell: all of these are nought in the face of your true fear of the Creator.

Further: Do not *glorify* yourself, however great your learning or your good deeds, your wealth or your fine qualities. Glory belongs only to God.

So too all the rest. Do not *triumph* over any person. Grant triumph only to Him, His alone is the only true victory. Yours is rather to triumph over your evil urge, that which leads you away from the good and into the path of evil.

Further: If people should come to *praise* you, do not let it lead you to self-importance. Rather give praise constantly to God, to Him who created you out of nothing and brought you into being. It is He who sustains you from your mother's womb unto the very day of your death. Were the Creator's concern to depart from you for but a moment, you would not survive that moment in the world.

Further: with regard to *attachment*.[37] Attach your thought always to the Creator; do not turn it away even for a moment to think of the vanities of this world. As soon as you turn your thought elsewhere you are considered as an idolator, as Scripture says: "You will turn aside and worship other gods" (Deut. 11:16).

Further: with regard to *kingship*. Proclaim God King over all your limbs; "Let there be in you no other god" (Ps. 81:10). On this verse the sages ask: "Who is the 'other god' that dwells in the human heart?" Their answer: "The evil urge and his retinue are called by this name."[38]

God has made everything in parallel form: As there are seven holy qualities, so are there seven evil ones parallel to them. It was so made in order to "grant reward to the righteous who sustain a world that was created by ten utterances," who triumph over the seven

---

36. Note how the language of theism and that of emanation are combined with one another: God is at once Master and Source!

37. "Attachment" is a somewhat unusual way to refer to *yesod*, the sixth of the seven lower *sefirot*. The point is that it joins together *malkhut* and the forces above; it is the instrument of attachment.

38. Shabbat 105b.

wicked qualities and cleave to God through their own qualities of goodness, breaking down the evil urge and those that support it. So too in order to "take leave of the wicked who destroy a world that was created through ten utterances,"[39] who spend all their days in pursuit of their own desires, seeking out the pleasures of this lowly and despicable world. In doing so they deny the One, Single, and Unified God. In the end they will have to give account to the King of Kings, the Holy One, blessed be He, for every single one of their deeds.

Should someone whisper to you, however, that he is so thoroughly defiled by the stain of sin that there is no repentance for him—God forbid that this be the case! There is *nothing* that stands in the way of repentance, for repentance was one of those seven things that preceded the Creation itself. No force of judgment has a place there, and just a thought—a thought of complete repentance and resolve never to return to that folly—will suffice to gain forgiveness for all one's sins. From that day forward, of course, you must cleave firmly to God and break down all your bad qualities. Of this the rabbis said: "Whoever gives up on his *middot* has all his sins forgiven":[40] Subjugate your evil qualities and rise above them. Join your mind to your body (for the upper three *sefirot* are like the seven lower ones), and rise above all these measured qualities to that place where there is no judgment at all.[41]

Raise everything to the level of *binah* and there it will all be "sweetened," as the Zohar says: Even though *binah* is the source of judgment-forces, it is only in their root that they can be transformed. Then are all your sins forgiven. Everything you have done up to that day, however, you will still have to weigh, all in accord with the pleasure you took in this world and its delights. The same will apply to all the other qualities. You must bring your self to sorrow over this, fasting regularly on Mondays and Thursdays, either those following Passover or those following Sukkot, during the weeks referred to as *shovevim tat*.[42] So too every eve of the new moon, considered to be a

---

39. Avot 5:1.

40. Yoma 23a.

41. To the rung of *binah*, beyond the differentiation between good and evil and hence beyond the origin of the *dinim*.

42. A period of eight weeks (the name is formed by an acronym of eight Torah portions, beginning with *shemot*) during the winter set aside by the Kabbalists as a time of penitence, particularly for sexual misdeeds.

small Day of Atonement. Fasting on that day has to do with the waning of the moon.[43] We have mentioned its meaning above: The *shekhinah* is in exile, as Scripture says: "I am with him in sorrow" (Ps. 91:15). You have to participate in the *shekhinah*'s suffering.

---

43. See the discussion of the waning of the moon below in *Me'or 'Eynayim, bereshit* 2. The designation of the eve of the new moon as a lesser Yom Kippur is also a Kabbalistic custom.

THE LIGHT
OF THE EYES

BERESHIT
Genesis 1:1–6:8

I

INTRODUCTION. The opening teaching of *The Light of the Eyes*, while not marked as an introduction to the volume, might indeed be said to serve that purpose. Rather than dwelling on Creation or cosmology itself, the homily uses this occasion to introduce the major themes that will preoccupy us throughout our reading.

Rabbi Nahum begins with Torah, designated here as the creative force in the universe. The notion that Torah or Wisdom had a role in Creation reaches back to the most ancient Jewish speculations; its relationship to the Logos idea has long been discussed. As received by Hasidism, Creation through Torah is a way of expressing the ultimate reality and power of language, and particularly of the word of God. In this way Creation is related intimately to the second great moment of divine giving, that of the Torah at Sinai. It is because God created the world through Torah that the commandments have ultimate and even cosmic significance; it is because Torah was there from the beginning that the study of Torah is the center of religious life and the appropriate locus for the best of man's ongoing creative energies.

For the mystic, however, a world filled with Torah is a world filled with God Himself; the earliest Kabbalists had already rendered it heresy to distinguish between the "name"—for all of Torah is God's name—and the One who bears it. Thus the entire world is fraught with the divine Presence. This message, more than any other, was the essential old/new teaching of Hasidism. It applied even to the "lower rungs," the humblest and most seemingly defiled earthly settings. The Ba'al Shem Tov and his followers sought to show that wherever (and this was meant psychologically in the first place) a person might be, there was the place to discover God. "Descent," they taught, "is for the sake of ascent"; "the light is greater when raised up from the darkness." While this notion did not lead the Hasidic masters to follow their Sabbatian predecessors into intentional sin, its dramatic rhythm remained essential to their spiritual life.

The presence of God in all things meant for the *hasid* a turn toward inwardness, away from the externals. Countless times in this and other volumes one finds it argued that "if mere external beauty can be so attractive, imagine the pull and joy of the true beauty, the presence of God that lies within." The ultimate in inwardness for the rabbinic Jew—and here Hasidism is at its most traditional—is *Torah li-shemah*, study purely for its own sake, or for the sake of God who is manifest in Torah. No greater joy and no more perfect reward exists for the Jew than the pure and selfless dedication of one's time and efforts to such study. What more appropriate way to open a book of homilies on the Torah?

The true beginning point of Hasidic mysticism, however, lies in the next step taken. If *all* was created by Torah, and the presence of God is indeed everywhere, how can there be any study that is *not* for its own sake? Suppose one studies out of pride, for careerist goals, or to impress others? Does God's presence truly lie in those seemingly improper motives as well? Can the God who is everywhere indeed be so great as to exist even in this seeming betrayal of His own Torah?

Rabbi Nahum's response to this question, posed as the center of his opening teaching, may be said to occupy him throughout this book. *The Light of the Eyes* may be seen as an extended treatise on the ways in which all externals lead back to the center, the ways in which all that seems far from God can be the very prod to finding Him again, and about the uplifting of all of human life, even the profane and the guilty, to His service.

*　　　*　　　*

IN THE BEGINNING GOD CREATED HEAVEN AND EARTH. THE EARTH WAS FORMLESS AND VOID, WITH DARKNESS OVER THE FACE OF THE DEEP. THE SPIRIT OF GOD WAS HOVERING OVER THE FACE OF THE WATER. GOD SAID: "LET THERE BE LIGHT"; AND THERE WAS LIGHT. GOD

SAW THAT THE LIGHT WAS GOOD, AND GOD
SEPARATED THE LIGHT FROM THE DARKNESS.
GOD CALLED THE LIGHT DAY AND DARKNESS
HE CALLED NIGHT. THERE WAS EVENING AND
THERE WAS MORNING, ONE DAY. (Gen. 1:1–5)

IN THE BEGINNING. It was through the Torah, called "the beginning of His way" (Prov. 8:22), that God created the world; all things
were created by means of Torah. Since the power of the Creator remains in the creature, Torah is to be found in all things and throughout all the worlds.[1] So too in the case of man, as Scripture says: "This
is the Torah, a man . . ." (Num. 19:14), as will be explained. And since
God and Torah are one, the life of God is present in all things. "You
give life to them all" (Neh. 9:6)—He reduced Himself, as it were,
down to the lowest of rungs, until a part of God above was placed
into the darkness of matter. The intent of this was that the lower
rungs themselves be uplifted, so that there be "a greater light that
comes from darkness" (Eccles. 2:13).

This was the meaning of Joseph's descent into Egypt, the lowest
of rungs, the narrow strait in the great sea (*MiZRaYiM/MeZaR YaM*).
Through him joy was to be increased and the light brightened, for joy
is greater when it has been lifted out of darkness. For that reason his
name was Joseph, which means "he adds." This also is the meaning of
"Jacob saw that there was produce (*shever*) in Egypt" (Gen. 42:1).
Shever may also mean "breakage"; the fallen fruit of supernal wisdom
is Torah, that which has fallen from above and become "broken."
Anything that has fallen from its original rung may be referred to in
this way. "In Egypt" here refers to the narrow straits: He saw in the
straits the fallen fruit of Torah, needing to be purified and uplifted.
Thus he said "Go down there," in order to raise them up. He went
down in order to restore them to their living root.

In this manner we should understand Joseph's death as well:
This descent of the Torah down to the lowest rung may be considered a death; we speak of one who has gone down from his rung as of
one who has died. [But then why does Scripture say] "And they em-
balmed him" (Gen. 50:26)? The Torah is called a Tree of Life, and "in

---

1. "All the worlds" is derived from the Kabbalistic notion of there existing several levels of Creation, one above the other. Here it is used in a broader sense of
"throughout the universe."

the case of trees we are concerned with their bearing fruit" (*wa-ya-ḤaNeTu/ḤaNaTaH*).[2] This means that even there, at the lowest of rungs, the Torah bore fruit. "And he was placed in a casket," for the rabbis have taught that "both whole and broken tablets were placed in the ark" (*aron/aron*).[3] Even the fallen fruits are raised up and placed in the ark along with the whole tablets, the Torah itself.

Now let us return to the first matter. Since it is the Torah in all things that gives them life, it behooves us not to look at their corporeal nature, but rather at their inner selves. Scripture says: "The Wise man has eyes in his head" (Eccles. 2:14), on which the Zohar asks: "Where else would a person's eyes be?" This means rather that a wise person looks at the head of things; he always tries to seek out the source and origin of whatever he sees. This then is the meaning of IN THE BEGINNING GOD CREATED: Through the Torah heaven and earth came into being, both in general and in each particular detail. Thus have our rabbis explained the fact that "heaven" and "earth" in this verse are both preceded by the particle *et*, to refer to all that would later be born of them.

THE EARTH WAS FORMLESS AND VOID. This refers to those who are sunk into earthly concerns; they indeed are "formless and void" for they do not look to the flow of life. And earthly objects taken for themselves are truly void and without form. Now RaSHI has explained this verse to mean that a person is astonished (*tohe/tohu*) over the formlessness (*bo hu*) that was there. He meant to say that one who is truly a person will be astonished at the fool, so busy with pursuits of matter, when in fact it is in him (*bo hu*), when the life of God is right there in his own self, and he fails to understand and keeps himself far off. But when a person looks in all things at the life that flows within them, he fulfills the verse: "I place the Lord (*YHWH*) ever before me" (Ps. 16:8), for in all things he places before him the Being (HWYH) that causes all being to be.[4]

---

2. He takes the root ḤNT here to refer to "bear fruit" rather than "embalm." Both meanings are possible; such plays on words will be found frequently in the text, and are common to most Hasidic writings.

3. As Joseph, representing the Tree of Life in broken or fallen form, was placed in an *aron*, so were the broken tablets, again Torah in broken pieces, in the days of Moses.

4. Ps. 16:8 was used by the Kabbalists as support for the practice of constant meditation on the letters of the name. Here our author suggests, in typically Hasidic fashion, that he who finds God in all things is in fact also carrying on this venerable practice. Note how even the most spiritual practices can be yet again "spiritualized."

BERESHIT

Our rabbis have said: "Whoever studies the Torah not for its own sake, better that the birth-fluids have turned around to destroy him." But elsewhere they claim that it is "always good for a person to study, even if not for its own sake, for improperly motivated study will lead to study for proper reasons." The contradiction may be understood if we ask whether there really exists a "not for its own sake" anywhere in the world, since all things receive their life through Torah. Who would give life to anything that was not ultimately "for the sake of," or derived from, the Torah? Study "not for its own sake" means study for some bad motive: to be glorified or exalted over others, for lust after money, or the like. These desires for glorification or money themselves are really forms of glory and desire in a broken state; their true roots are the glory of God and His desire. This person has taken those qualities for himself; when he understands that they are derived from the glory and love of God he will come to hold on to the root and origin of things. Then he is the "wise man with eyes in his head," of whom we have spoken. It is from his very self-centered thoughts of desire and glorification that he has returned to the root, and thus he has moved from "not for its own sake" to "for its own sake." This is why one should ever study Torah, even if for improper reasons, since the improper motive itself may lead one to do it "for its own sake." If this does not happen, however, and one continues to study only for the wrong reasons, then indeed better that he not have been born.

Now the Torah is called "light," but the fool who studies Torah not for its own sake walks in darkness, not kindling that light. He who sits in darkness needs to kindle the light. This is the meaning of DARKNESS OVER THE FACE OF THE DEEP: He is so enmeshed in corporeality that he does not kindle the Torah's light. Thus study not for its own sake does indeed exist in the world, but Scripture says of it THE SPIRIT OF GOD WAS HOVERING OVER THE FACE OF THE WATER. Because of this one may return and bring oneself back to true life and to God. GOD SAID: LET THERE BE LIGHT. When a person studies for its own sake, that is, for the sake of God, his words kindle that light. At first light and darkness existed together in a confused state; the "light" here is Torah and the "darkness" is the improper motive. But afterwards GOD SEPARATED THE LIGHT FROM THE DARKNESS.

This is why the rabbis ask: "Why is it that the goats ('*iZey*) walk at the head of the flock and the lambs follow behind them?" Israel are

51

considered the strongest (*'aZim*) among the nations; the rabbis are here asking as to the source of that strength, that which leads them directly to the head of the matter. And the Talmud answers: "The flock follows the order of Creation, dark first and then light."[5] This means that Israel begin in the darkest of levels and go from there to the light. As they climb into the light they "sweeten"[6] or transform their ordinary consciousness into an expanded state of mind. That is how they have this power [to reach the head of every thing]. Idolators, on the other hand, remain in the lower mental state, still being attached to corporeal things. Thus our sages say of Balaam that he did not even know his own beast's mind. This must be properly understood.

Now man was created in an ordinary state of mind, with a "small" consciousness. But surely God's intent in creating man was that he serve Him. Why then did He create him without the proper mind for such service? This was for the very same reason we have stated: Wisdom is greater when it arises out of folly; the darkness longs to be included in the light. Thus the lesser state of mind is considered the "wife" of expanded mind, of whom Scripture says: "Your desire shall be for your husband" (Gen. 3:16). It is the woman who first rouses desire in her bridegroom; thus a person is first in the lesser state. When his mind is expanded, however, the lesser state too is joined into that higher mind, and an act of coupling has taken place. This is the meaning of "As bridegroom rejoices over bride, so does God rejoice over you" (Isa. 62:5), as will be explained elsewhere. Now it is impossible to come to the light of that higher state too suddenly; for that reason the lower state must precede it. This is an explanation of the question concerning the goats; "goats" (*'iZey*) may refer to audacity (*'aZut*). The rabbis then ask: "Why is there so much of that at the beginning?" Why must a person begin in so low a state? And they answer that each person must follow the order of Creation: darkness first and then light. This is the meaning of GOD CALLED THE LIGHT DAY AND DARKNESS HE CALLED NIGHT. Just as there is no day without night, but rather THERE WAS EVENING, the lesser state of mind comes first, and afterwards THERE WAS

---

5. The Talmud speaks of dark-colored goats and white lambs; so does night precede the day. Our author takes the passage as a metaphor for the nature of Israel's particular strength of spirit, the bringing forth of light from the midst of darkness.

6. The term "sweeten," referring to the uplifting of evil or the transformation of judgment, occurs very frequently in this text. Its origin is in the old Spanish Kabbalah.

MORNING (*BoQeR*), then comes the expanded state, by which a person can examine (*meBaQeR*) his deeds. ONE DAY: The two form a single unity.

This is the general order of things, and should be followed by everyone. At the age of thirteen, a person acquires awareness of mind. This awareness (*da'at*) indicates an intimate union, that of the lower and upper rungs. This is what is meant by wholeness of mind, in the way of "Return, O backsliding children!" (Jer. 3:22). Those things that have slid away, as in "he went backsliding in the way of his heart" (Isa. 57:17), must be brought back and joined together. There are some, however, who have no awareness, even after thirteen years. Such people remain minors; a person who has no awareness is seduced by his own drives.

Such was the case of Potiphar's wife's seduction of Joseph, which is written in the Torah: a person must save himself as Joseph did. My teacher explained it in this way. The rabbis say that "the image of his father's likeness appeared to him" [and prevented him from submitting to her wiles]. Because "the clothes she wore in the morning she did not wear in evening" and she glorified herself in them, Joseph was able to look through them into the root of her beauty and self-glorification; he sought to know where those qualities came from, and he found that the root of even that glory was the life of God. "Glory" (*tif'eret*) in God is specifically associated with the aspect of Jacob; this is the meaning of "the image of his father's likeness." Every person has to act in a similar way.

This is also the meaning of "Esther was just plain earth" [she did not participate actively in sexual encounter with the king]. The name "Esther" is related to the word "hiding" (*hester*), as the rabbis derive Esther's name from the verse "I shall surely hide" (Deut. 31:18). This then was Esther: hiddenness down to the lowest of rungs. Just "natural ground"—the life of God all hidden and contracted there.

It is further said of Joseph that "he dug his nails into the ground" [to hold back from her enticements]. They mean that he "dug" into the innermost hidden "ground" of things. But he did so with his nails, a nonessential appendage of the body; through the nonessential he got to that which lies hidden deeply within it. Thus it also says of him that "he came home to do his work" (Gen. 39:11), upon which the Zohar comments: "The work of God: unification." This is what Joseph was doing: uniting the upper and lower rungs. This is the complete union.

THE LIGHT OF THE EYES

They also said that "Esther was of [an unattractive] greenish color, except that a thread of grace was drawn over her." Those things that come from the lowest rungs are in themselves repulsive . . . except that God has drawn a thread of grace over them. Thus a person should always attach himself still more to God, the grace of all grace and the joy of all joys. Indeed it is only logical: If a single thread of grace drawn into that which was formerly repulsive can occasion such desire, how much greater should one's desire be for the source of that life itself? Why then should one turn to things of the body?

This is the meaning of "How does one dance (*meRaQQeDin*) before the bride? The House of Shammai says: 'A bride as she is,' but the house of Hillel says: 'A beautiful and gracious bride.'" The word *RiQQuD* can also mean "sifting," as in the sifting out from food of that which has to be discarded. The House of Hillel means to say that she is beautiful because she is graced, because of that thread of grace which is drawn over her. For this reason one should not look at the outward body, but at the "food," at the life within. The House of Shammai says: "A bride as she is"; there is no argument between the two schools, merely a difference in way of expression. The *shekhinah* is called "bride" (*kallah*) because all is included (*kol kalul*) within her; she is the Ingathering of Israel since everything is gathered and included in her. The root of all is in her—thus should a person look to the root, as will be understood.

The rabbis' other statement about Joseph, that "he came home to fulfill his [bodily] needs," is thus also not in conflict with that which has been said [that he came to do God's work of unification]. Here too there is merely a difference in form of expression: This one meant to say that even in the fulfillment of our bodily needs we may turn inward.

It is known that God is esoterically represented as a bridegroom, and we are His bride. He has sent us betrothal gifts, all of the commandments, with which we are to adorn ourselves before the bridegroom, just as a bride must adorn herself to awaken desire on the part of her spouse. The lesser self must be included in the greater. These are "adornments which did not exist [previously]."[7] And this is called "whole knowledge" as in "Adam knew his wife Eve" (Gen. 4:1).

---

7. The point is that God Himself, as bridegroom, has provided the wedding gifts with which Israel is adorned. We seek to be joined to Him in love, and He provides the commandments so that we may, by fulfilling them, arouse His desire for us as well.

There were, as is known, two Eves.[8] The first was the temptress; only of the second does Scripture say: "This one shall be called woman" (Gen. 2:23). Adam, however, uplifted the temptress too and joined them together. Hence "Adam knew Eve"—the particle *et* in that sentence refers to the one who was less than Eve, as the rabbis have interpreted it. This "knowing" refers to being joined together, and it is this sort of knowing [that includes the uplifting of the temptress] that is considered whole.

This makes for the letter *shin* in its four-pronged form: intellect and understanding, but within mind both love and fear.[9] There is also a three-pronged *shin*, which is called the "lesser knowing." Our sages have inquired concerning the name of Jethro (*YiTRo*) and say that he was called thus for he added (*YiTTeR*) a section to the Torah. They mean to say that a person must have both love and fear; love without fear is nothing. Even though such a person thinks he loves God, it is not true. He only thinks so because he is so used to loving the world and various other forms of love that he assumes he has a desire for God as well, but such is not the case. First one has to fear Him and only afterwards may one come to love [as was the case with Jethro].[10] Then you will be able to transform the lower rungs as well, and the "knowledge" will be complete. He was called *YeTeR* (or Jethro) because of [his prior concern with] extraneous or "additional" matters (*moTaRot*); now when he came close to God he "added" something to the Torah and completed that four-pronged *shin*. Therefore Moses said to him: "You shall be our eyes" (Num. 10:31). The eyes see, and the heart lusts. Then the eyes are considered "fallen," for the eyes in the wise man's head have fallen from that rung. Now that he was coming near to God, the eyes would be restored to their place

---

8. Ancient legends recount that Adam was first tempted by Lilith, the demoness, and only afterward encountered the true Eve. The latter part of this teaching is difficult, primarily because the author is at once using several examples to make the same point. Joseph, Esther, Adam, and the bride each come to teach some variant on the theme of discovering the divine presence within the physical, or of using temptation toward sin itself as an occasion to return to God.

9. Kabbalistic tradition speaks of a mysterious four-pronged *shin* as a "lost" letter of the Hebrew alphabet. The reference veils the role of *da'at* as the meeting place of intellectual and emotional aspects of the religious life. Adam "knows" Eve in both of these ways.

10. The rabbis say that Jethro, Moses' father-in-law, was converted after he saw God's might in the destruction of Egypt. This tradition is rooted in the exegesis of Exodus 18:1.

and all would be united (*meYaHeD*) with God, as in "Jethro rejoiced (*wa-YiHaD*)" (Ex. 18:9). This will suffice.

II

INTRODUCTION. The moon and the lunar calendar have since ancient times played a major role in Jewish myth and imagination. It was in part by Israel's faithfulness to her ancient lunar calendar that she stood out in the Roman and later Western worlds; the major events of the Jewish year continue to be commemorations of either the new or the full moon, the entire calendar set by the phases of the moon's waxing and waning. No wonder that the rabbis compared Israel herself to the moon, her cycles of historic rise and fall parallel to the monthly cycle of lunar increase and diminution.

The teaching opens with reference (here supplied in full) to an ancient explanation of the moon's waxing and waning. The "two great lights" of Genesis 1:16 were not able to share dominion, and the moon, who protested this situation, was remade into the "lesser light" by God, and set into the monthly course of growth and decline. Sensing the injustice of this decree, God asked that Israel's new-moon sacrifice contain an element that was to atone for His transgression.

Whatever its original meaning may have been—and the interpretations abound—this striking mythic tale was used by later mystics as a symbol of one of their major teachings: the fall of the world into a lower state of being than that God had intended. Here the great cataclysm, rather than "breakage," is thought of as "waning," but a waning that so deeply affects the world that it shall not turn again until the arrival of messiah.

Typical of the Hasidic adaptation of these Kabbalistic motifs is their transfer from the realm of cosmology to that of *mind*. True exile, true "breaking," the true waning of the moon, are in fact states of the human mind as it lives without awareness of God. The redemption, then, is one of knowledge, of the realization that all Creation is fraught with His presence. "Earth will be filled with the knowledge of the Lord" is frequently quoted as a description of the world transformed. While full and unswerving awareness of God is reserved for the messianic future, life in the present is sustained by glimpses and foretastes of that unchanging reality.

Another central metaphor used to describe the intimacies of

spiritual life in Hasidism is that of conjugal union. Based on ancient interpretive traditions of the Song of Songs, the Kabbalists had been strikingly bold in their application of sexual language to the world of the divine. While earlier Kabbalah had been fascinated particularly by notions of union and coupling *within* God, the *ḥasid* returns the metaphor to its original intent of describing the love relationship between God and His people Israel. Various levels and degrees of such union are spelled out, the highest being that of "face-to-face," at once the way in which God spoke to Moses and the position generally associated with conjugal embrace.

*   *   *

["Rabbi Simeon ben Pazi found a contradiction in a verse of Scripture. First it says: 'God made the two great lights' and then it refers to 'the greater light and the lesser light' (Gen. 1:16). The moon said to God: 'Lord of the World! Is it possible for two kings to rule with a single crown (i.e., for both moon and sun to rule the world)?' He said to her: 'Go and make yourself smaller.' She replied: 'Because I said a proper thing am I to go and diminish myself?' . . . He saw that she could not be pacified. God said: 'Bring an atonement for Me for having diminished the moon.' Thus said Rabbi Simeon ben Lakish: 'Why should the kid-offering for the new moon be distinguished from all the sacrifices by Scripture saying of it alone "for the Lord" (Num. 28:15)? The Lord said: "This kid shall be an atonement-offering for Me, because I diminished the moon.' "]

In the Talmudic tractate Sanhedrin: "It is taught in the school of Rabbi Ishmael: If Israel merited to greet the face of their Father in Heaven but once a month it would suffice for them. Said Abaye: For that reason, the sanctification of the new moon must be recited while standing."[1] In order to understand this matter, we must first further quote our sages, of blessed memory, who said: "The face of Moses was like the face of the sun; the face of Joshua was like the face of the moon."

The secret of the diminishing of the moon is well known. All the rungs fell into a lesser state, and from this proceeded small-minded-

---

1. The sanctification of the moon is an ancient ritual performed outdoors, hopefully in view of the moon, on the Saturday evening preceding the moon's fullness. It is a joyous celebration of the restored light, and its liturgy embodies various messianic overtones.

ness, exile, and death; smallness of mind too is an aspect of the lessening of the moon. Israel (the chief intent of Creation), however, were made so that we might serve Him with wholeness of mind. Why not, then, create people with fully mature minds from birth, so that they have the power to serve Him fully? Rather the Creator brought about a world in which a person at birth has no fitness to serve Him at all. We keep growing in mental powers until we are thirteen years old; only then is growth complete and may one be called a "man." All this has to do with the diminishing of the moon, due to the accusation that was made against it. We Israelites count our months according to the moon and have been likened to it, as is known. For that reason the diminishing took place in all of human affairs. The mind especially has to begin in a lesser state, and exile too is a form of this diminishing of the mind or lessened awareness. Only afterwards may renewal or expansion of mind come to all Israel.

Today, however, there is no constancy to such expansion; we live in a pattern of waxing and waning. In future times, in the days of messiah (speedily and in our time!), the light of the moon will shine as brightly as that of the sun. Scripture's words "Your moon will no longer set" (Isa. 60:20) will be fulfilled, for then all the rungs will emerge from their diminution. Mind will be expanded to the fullest, and each expansion will no longer have to be preceded by smallness. Thus Scripture says: "Earth shall be filled with knowledge of the Lord" (Isa. 11:9). Mind and awareness will be so increased that "everyone will point with his finger and say: 'This is the Lord for whom we have hoped!' " . . . The world will receive new life and death will be abolished, since death too, as we have said, comes from the lessening of the moon. This state will then exist in constancy, and the high rung of consciousness we shall then attain will never be lost.

Now it is known that the moon has no light of her own, but only that which she receives from the sun. The closer she gets to the sun, the brighter her light. She is like the letter DaLeT, for she does not have (De-LeT) anything of her own. We children of Israel are compared to her; like the moon we have no light of our own, but only the light that shines from above like that of the sun. Moses and Joshua were like sun and moon; Moses had that wholeness of mind or expanded consciousness, while Joshua had only the light that was passed on to him, the light of Moses that shone on him. Thus did our sages, of blessed memory, say: "Moses received Torah from Sinai and passed it on to Joshua." Joshua did not truly *receive* it, but only had it "passed on" to him, unlike Moses. Thus it is said of Joshua: "a lad who would never leave the tent" (Exod. 33:11)—"lad" refers to his smaller state, and "never leave the tent" means that he would always stay close to Moses, in order to receive his sunlight. That is why he forgot three hundred laws in the period of mourning after Moses our Teacher's death: It was because he was distanced from the light of the sun, and forgetfulness too is an aspect of this same diminution.

So long as this diminishing goes on, even though the community of Israel unite themselves with their Creator, they may "couple" only back-to-back, as it were. Of this Scripture says: "He has turned His right hand backward" (Lam. 2:3), and further: "They went backward and not forward" (Jer. 7:24). At the time the Torah was given to Israel through Moses, the diminution of the moon was ended; through the giving of the Torah all Israel emerged from their lessened minds and came to full awareness. That generation is sometimes referred to as the "generation of awareness." They were able to come forth from Egyptian exile because mind itself came forth from the narrow straits. That is why it has been said: " 'inscribed (*HaRuT*) upon the tablets' (Exod. 32:16)—read not 'inscribed' but 'freedom' (*HeRuT*)"; freedom from all: from the angel of death, from political oppression, all that comes from the diminution of which we have spoken.

Scripture tells us that "the Lord spoke to Moses face to face" (Exod. 33:11), for he was always in that state of expanded mind, in accord with the root of his soul. In his case there was constant union and coupling, face-to-face. Of the hour when the Torah was given, before the sin of the Golden Calf, Scripture said of all Israel: "Face-to-Face the Lord spoke to your entire congregation" (Deut. 5:2). The entire congregation attained this face-to-face unity, the sort of coupling and union that take place where there is no diminution. Afterward, however, when they sinned with the calf, they fell back into their former lower rung, and the diminution spread forth everywhere, all of the rungs returning to their former state. We shall not again attain this state in constancy until our righteous redeemer comes, as has been said above. Moses, however, remained on his rung, and therefore even afterward it says of him, "The Lord spoke to Moses face-to-face," but following that "Joshua ben Nun was a lad who would never leave the tent," showing that Joshua too was affected by the lessening of the moon.

Face-to-face coupling may also be referred to as the inclusion of the female within the male.[2] Since the expansion is at its utmost, Israel long for the Creator so greatly that "each one points with his finger and says: 'This is the Lord for whom we have hoped' "; they become one with Him and are included within Him. This oneness is born of their intense longing for and attachment to God, but also because of the great longing that is aroused in Him, as it were, to cleave to the community of Israel, which has now reached so elevated a state. We Israel are like the female: We receive all the flow from Him, blessed be He. Thus it is written: "Moses has commanded us Torah, an inheritance (*MoRaSHaH*) of the community of Jacob," to which it has been added: "Read not *MoRaSHaH* but *Me'oRaSaH*, 'betrothed.' " When the Torah was given there was a face-to-face union, and it was said: "Go unto the people and sanctify them" (Exod. 19:10); this term "sanctification" can also refer to the betrothal (*qiddushin*) of a woman. They were then united, as it were, by being so included within Him that they too could be called "male," since the female is included in the male through her great love and longing for him, with full and undiminished awareness. This is parallel (despite a thousand differences) to physical coupling: Longing brings about the subsuming of the female within the male. It is through this that the birth process takes place and they form one flesh. This happens because they are joined together, a joining that must first take place in their spirits, without which there is no birth and no forming of one flesh. And therefore a man who is without woman is called "half a body." In the same way is His divinity joined to the community of Israel in that face-to-face coupling, to the point where Israel is considered a part of the male, since she is so included within Him.

Israel nowadays is in a lesser and diminished state, to be sure. Nevertheless, in the moment when we sanctify the moon the same union takes place that happened when the Torah was given, a face-to-face coupling in that expanded state, as the moon becomes full. That is why such joyous desire is at that moment awakened in a person of spirit; he feels at that time an inward delight and a nearness to God, to be sanctified/betrothed in is holiness. Then that which had been *DaLeT*, having nothing of its own, is uplifted "leaning on her beloved" (Cant. 8:5) in union, as she is included within the male. For

---

2. The point seems to be a psychological one, in obvious contrast to the physical act; the female is "included" or subsumed in the course of male domination.

this reason there is a tradition that from the time when the new moon is sanctified (between the ninth and the fifteenth of each lunar month) a person should not worry that he will die within that month. Since he has, in sanctifying the moon, come face-to-face with God and had his mind expanded beyond any diminution, he is above all things that come from diminution, including death, since it too is rooted there. This day becomes like the one on which the Torah was given, a time of liberation from the angel of death. This suffices for the entire month, so that a person will not die in any way related to diminution.

Now this is the meaning of Rabbi Ishmael's school saying: "If Israel merited to greet the face of their Father in Heaven but once a month . . ." Note that he says "*face*"; if Israel only manage in this time, when we are in the lesser state, "to greet the face of their Father," to attain face-to-face union, "once a month," as the moon is sanctified and they are face-to-face with one another, "it would suffice." Then they are fruitful in His service; through the commandment of sanctifying the moon they are included within Him, united with Him, and thus can they serve Him in a whole manner. And Abaye added, "For that reason, it must be recited while standing." Matters concerning the male, as is known, are referred to as "standing," while the female is described as "seated." In this moment when the moon is sanctified and the female is, as it were, joined to the male and considered male, the commandment is performed in a "male" way, that is, standing. Thus it is called the *qiddush*, "sanctification," of the moon, referring really to "betrothal," her betrothal, as it were, to her beloved. Of this Scripture says: "Who is this who rises out of the desert, leaning on her beloved" (Cant. 8:5)—joined to her beloved in a single union.

The same is true of the time spent in the study of Torah. Whoever merits to study Torah for its own sake—in fear and in love, in the higher state of mind—also merits by this to come forth from the lower mind and the lessening of the moon, entering a state of expanded consciousness and higher awareness, of great closeness to the Creator, blessed be He and blessed be His name. He feels in his soul a great sense of inclusion and is bound to God's love for the world; he is intensely attached to God in a way like in that hour when the Torah was given, a face-to-face union in which the female is drawn into the male, no longer in any way diminished. It was in this sense that they said: "There is no free person except the one who studies Torah"—he

61

attains freedom from political oppression or exile, for these are in turn derived from this (inner) diminution. Having now reached the higher state and the broadening of mind, one is no longer subject to exile. Thus the sages also said: "Whoever accepts upon himself the yoke of Torah has the yokes of empire and of worldly pursuits lifted off him." So too is he liberated from the angel of death, as we have found in the cases of various Talmudic sages and also of King David—while they were studying Torah the angel of death had no power over them. All this applies to one who studies in the way we have suggested; as he emerges from diminution, something of that which happened to everyone as the Torah was given also happens to him. He experiences something of that which will be always once messiah has come—speedily and in our day! In our times, however, such a state may exist only temporarily, while a person is busy at the study of Torah, in love and in fear.

Such study of Torah brings about a face-to-face unification, one in which there are no harsh or judging forces at all, since the one who studies has become one with God and may be called "male." The meaning of this is as follows. The Torah represents *binah* (in the sefirotic world), the place from which those harsh forces first arise. In order to "sweeten" these forces and remove their sting, they must be returned to their root. Thus Scripture says: "I am *binah* and *gevurah* is mine" (Prov. 8:14): Because I am *binah*, *gevurah* is mine.[3] "Bring these harsh forces to Me, bring them into the Torah" where they may be sweetened as they become part of that face-to-face coupling, becoming "male" along with Him, blessed be He, in true union. Once this union exists, no power can go to that harshness, all of which comes only from diminution and contraction. Once a person has reached expansion of mind there are no such judging forces at all. Therefore that which had been a mere *DaLeT*, having nothing of its own, has now been united with Him. Such an act may be considered one of *GoMeL DaLim*, of bestowing grace on the poor, since all the lower rungs have been graced as the *DaLeT* is joined to the Life of Life, the True Good, so that she is called by His name and is considered "male."

This is what the sages perhaps mean when they say in the tractate Shabbat: "Children come along to the house of study nowadays and say things the likes of which were not heard even in Joshua's day.

3. *Binah*, the third *sefirah*, is the "mother" or womb out of which emerge the seven lower manifestations. It is particularly the source of *gevurah*, the harsh and judging aspect of divinity.

'Alef Bet means *'alef binah,* learn understanding. *Gimel Dalet* means *go-mel dalim,* be gracious to the poor." Their intent was that which we have said here. The "children" refer to the lesser state, also called the "lad," still in a lesser state of mind like a child. "Now" such a one "comes to the house of study"—from a state of small-mindedness one turns to Torah, called the house of study or *midrash,* since the inner aspect of Torah is called the *midrash* of the sages. All smallness and harsh judgments, all the "children," now come to Torah and are sweetened there, since Torah is their source. Thus "learn *binah,*" *'alef* meaning "learn" as in "I shall teach (*'a'alefekha*) you wisdom" (Job 33:33). By learning *binah* (= Torah) you act graciously to the "poor," you sweeten the harsh forces that derive from the lesser state, and you attain to the full expansion of mind. Then indeed you are gracious to the *DaLim,* raising up the *DaLeT* who had nothing of her own and bringing her into union with the male, where there is no judging but only freedom, from death and from oppression. This is what they meant by saying "the likes of which were not heard even in Joshua's day"—the lesser mind's coming to Torah and being transformed into expanded mind in face-to-face union like there was at Sinai and like there will be in the future—this was something that did not happen in Joshua's time, one of lower mind and diminution of the moon. Joshua's face was described as "the face of the moon," indicating the widespread smallness of consciousness that existed in his day; the "lad who would never leave the tent." This was a time when male and female were not united, the female not able to be called by His male name.

It was because this "waning of the moon" had spread through all things that the Talmud explained the New Moon kid-offering as "an atonement for my having diminished the moon." All the distance that has come about between Israel and the Creator is caused by this smallness of mind. Whoever has a full mind, remaining bound to Him and coupling with Him face-to-face, surely will bring about no sin. All sin comes about only because of some lack in the mind, as our sages have said: "No one commits a transgression until a foolish spirit enters into him."

Now this is "bring an atonement for Me"; I am the cause, as it were, because I diminished the moon. In truth, however, Israel is still given a choice. Good and evil come to them all mixed together; they may still choose the good. Therefore the atonement is chiefly for them, but God takes it on Himself for having diminished the moon, without which there would have been no evil at all, and all would be servants of God as they will be when messiah comes.[4] In our time, however, everything has to be diminished, until all that smallness has been transformed. Then indeed will "earth be filled with the knowledge of the Lord."

Amen Selah unto eternity. Blessed is the Lord forever. Amen. Amen.

III

INTRODUCTION. The figure of the ẓaddiq is a dominant one throughout the literature of Hasidism. Usually thought of as "teacher" or "spiritual master" in Hasidic circles, the "righteous one" has a long history in the religious traditions of Israel. Our author opens this teaching by quoting a famous series of Talmudic statements concerning the ẓaddiq, statements that were often used in his day to describe or explain the role of the Hasidic leader.

The Light of the Eyes is surprising among Hasidic works for its relatively meager discussion of the ẓaddiq in this institutionalized form. When the term is used here, one frequently has the sense that its old pre-Hasidic usage is continued. *Ẓaddiq*, as described in the Talmudic passages around which this teaching is constructed, is a figure of righteousness, first in the sense of moral purity, and is one especially pleasing to God for his humane character. Some of the rabbinic sources, speaking of "a single ẓaddiq" for whose sake the world exists, or in identifying the ẓaddiq with the good that God saw in the first light of Creation, seem to point to a notion of unique charisma, one claiming that an individual ẓaddiq may bear within him the divine energy that at any time allows the world to be. Such a reading, however, is not emphasized in the present work, one that generally seeks to use the term as an accessible model for anyone's attempt to lead a life of righteousness.

Also apparent in this teaching, as frequently throughout the work, is the centrality of the Hebrew alphabet in the writings of the Jewish mystics. Ancient Kabbalistic doctrine, tied as much to magic as to theology, had seen in the letters of the alphabet—the building blocks of divine as well as human speech—a source of sacred energy.

---

4. While seeking to underscore the importance of the divine act as the origin of the world's diminished state, the author cannot abrogate the ascription of sin—and thus moral responsibility—to the community of Israel.

BERESHIT

It was by means of the *word* that God created, taught the Bible. Later interpreters took this to refer to the letters, combinations and permutations of letters seen as the root of all being. In Hasidism this belief is used most frequently and in any number of ways. Here the rungs of being are depicted as the successive letters of the alphabet, God Himself as the *aleph* and the lowest rung of being, that of death itself, as the *taw*. The task of the *zaddiq* is to remain at once tied to *all* the rungs, in order that he might raise up the lower levels and restore them to their place in God.

*   *   *

In the tractate *Yoma:* "Rabbi Eleazar said: 'From the blessings of the righteous you may learn how the wicked are cursed, and from the curses of the wicked you may learn how the righteous are blessed.' . . . He further said: 'The world was created for the sake of a single *zaddiq*. Scripture says: "God saw that the light was good" (Gen. 1:4) and "good" refers to the *zaddiq*, as in "Say that the *zaddiq* is good" (Isa. 3:10).' . . . R. Hiyya bar Abba said in the name of R. Yohanan: 'The world exists even for the sake of a single *zaddiq*, as Scripture says: "*Zaddiq* is the foundation of the world" (Prov. 10:25).' . . . R. Simeon ben Levi said: 'What is the meaning of "If it concerns the scorners, He scorns them, but unto the humble He gives grace" (Prov. 3:34)? He who comes to defile himself, the way is open to him, but he who comes to purify himself is given help.' . . . It was taught in the school of R. Ishmael: Sin dulls a person's heart, as Scripture says 'You will be defiled by them' (Lev. 11:43), spelled as though it meant 'You shall be dulled by them' (*we-niṭme'tem/we-niṭamtem*)." And the commentators add that these dental letters are interchangeable.

How shall we understand all these claims? First we must recall that the rabbis have said elsewhere, "There is a single pillar that reaches from earth to heaven. And who is it? *Zaddiq*." We know that the Creator, blessed be He, brought all the worlds into being through the Torah, through the Torah's twenty-two letters, into which He concentrated Himself. This process of concentration and emanation began with the letter *aleph*. Afterward He further concentrated the light-flow of His glory, bearing along with it the letter *aleph*, into the *bet*. Then both were taken into *gimel*, and so on through the letters was His divinity revealed, all the way down to the *taw*, the lowest of the rungs, containing both good and evil. *Taw* may stand for *tiheyeh*, "you shall live," or for *tamut*, "you shall die": It implies choosing.[1] The true *zaddiq* must always bind himself to all the rungs, even the lowest, the *taw*-rungs, which are in that place of choice, approaching each of them, step by step, until he returns from the end of the alphabet to the beginning. Even the lowest rungs were created by the letters of the Torah. *Taw* itself, the very lowest point into which God concentrated the revelation of his light, is part of Torah, far though it be from the *aleph*. The *zaddiq* who seeks to bind himself to God must be bound to *all* the letters, from *taw* to *aleph*, drawing all the rungs near to the One, to the cosmic *aleph*. This is the true goal of worship at its most whole: the uplifting of all the lower rungs. All this we have explained elsewhere as well.

This is the "single pillar": The *zaddiq* is called "single," since he unites all the rungs with his own self. "From earth to heaven": from the lowest of the rungs, the most earthly *taw*, up to the heavens of the highest *aleph*. For this reason the *zaddiq* is also referred to as "all," as Scripture says: "all that is in heaven and earth" (1 Chron. 29:11), rendered into Aramaic as "who holds fast to heaven and earth." He is joined to all the rungs and holds onto both earth and heaven. Thus the *zaddiq* is also called "foundation of the world." Just as a building must stand on a foundation, and when the building is to be lifted up it must be raised from that foundation, so too does that *zaddiq* who is bound to all the rungs raise up the entire "building" with him as he goes higher.

This is the meaning of "The world was created for the sake of a single *zaddiq*." For what reason did R. Eleazar say this? He taught that only for the sake of the *zaddiqim* who are "single" (literally "one"), united with all the rungs, was the world created. All the rungs are uplifted through them. Now surely such a *zaddiq*, one who can bind himself with even the lowest rungs of being, must bind himself also to all the other *zaddiqim*. Thus they may be referred to as "a single" *zaddiq*, even though there are in fact many, for they are so closely joined together, just as were Israel at Sinai,[2] with a single heart. . . .

They further said that the world exists for the sake of a single *zaddiq*, based on "*Zaddiq* is the foundation of the world." Were it not

---

1. The *taw* indicates the second person imperfect or future of the verb, hence: that which lies before you, or choice.
2. In Exod. 19:2 a singular verb is used to refer to the entire people of Israel. See RaSHI ad loc.

for the *zaddiq* the world could not exist even for a moment, due to the deeds of the wicked, who cause the world to fall and separate it from the One. Scripture refers to them in "a whisperer separates familiar friends" (Prov. 16:28) (*aluf/alef*); they bring about separation between the *taw* and the *aleph*. By the work of the *zaddiq*, who joins himself to all the rungs, the world is restored from this fall and unites again with *aleph*. As the foundation rises, so does the entire building. It is for this reason that the sages are called "builders," as in "read not 'sons' but 'builders' (*banayikh/bonayikh*)." They hold up the entire building of this world. . . . Through all that God measures out to the *zaddiq*, through all the events that happen to him, he raises himself higher and is joined to God. If God is good to him and shows him good fortune, he still fears Him greatly, lest he be too readily paid his due in this world.[3] This causes him to cleave ever more closely to his Creator. When such a man sees how the wicked are cursed, then too he rises higher, as our sages taught: "When God performs judgment upon the wicked, His name is exalted." Whatever he sees, whether in himself or in others, good or ill, it brings him near to his Creator and causes him to bind himself to all the rungs. Such is not the case with the wicked: When God brings blessing and good fortune into their lives they are drawn away from Him, as Scripture says: "Jeshurun grew fat and kicked" (Deut. 32:15), and further "Lest I be sated and deny" (Prov. 30:9). Only when the curse is brought down on them are their hearts broken and do they return to God.

This is the meaning of "From the blessings of the righteous"—when God showers blessing on the *zaddiq*—"you may learn"—from this the *zaddiq* learns to draw near to God. "The curse of the wicked"—it is like a curse to the wicked[4] that they are drawn near to God and repent. The *zaddiqim* too are drawn unto Him, due to the very blessings they have received.

"And from the curses of the wicked you may learn how the righteous are blessed." This means that the *zaddiq*, in seeing the curse that God brings down on the wicked, gains strength for his own life in God's service. Thus the sages say: "When God judges the wicked His name is feared and uplifted." The *zaddiq* becomes more strongly attached to his work of raising up the lower rungs. In this way much blessing and good come into the world; this is "how the righteous are

---

3. Foretelling punishment in the world to come.
4. Penitence seems to the wicked like a curse, forcing them to curb their wickedness.

blessed." Blessing comes to the entire world for the sake of the righteous who raise it up. They are properly called "the foundation of the world," since through them all the world is exalted and all the rungs are lifted.

It was for this reason that the rabbis said: "He who comes to purify himself is given help." The one who comes in search of purity draws himself, including that bit of divinity which is within him, near to God, the root of all. He enters into a state of attachment to God as that portion of God within him becomes one with the whole, with the Endless. The light of the Endless shines within him once that attachment of part to source has taken place. Then surely any act of worship he undertakes will be helpful to him, since God shines on him: There can be no greater "help" than that! But he who seeks defilement only has "the way open to him," for he is separating that *aleph* from the *shekhinah*, from that portion of divinity which dwells in the lower world. He is cutting that divinity off from its root in God, removing God from it, as it were. Thus his deed is called "transgression," for he causes God to pass by (*'aVeyRaH/'aVaR YaH*). The Word *MiZWaH* (commandment), on the other hand, contains the letters of God's name, WH in revealed form and YH in hidden manner. . . .[5] By means of the *mizwah*, which itself means "attachment," one becomes attached to God, even though His divine self remains hidden from the eye. No matter: The *zaddiq* is bound to God in the bonds of love. This comes about through His commandments and through the flowing light of His divine glory, which shines through them secretly and into the [divine] portion of the *zaddiq*. Not so with transgression: From there God has passed by, and the sinner is only given the opening to do as his heart desires, once the flow of God's light has departed from him.

But this requires further understanding. If we indeed say that transgression causes God to depart utterly from the person, how is repentance ever to be possible, once that good light is gone? If there is no good at all in him, how can that arousal of the good that leads to repentance ever take place? Scripture says: "The Lord is good" (Ps. 145:9), meaning also that the good is God. And now that good has disappeared from this one who has transgressed. Still further: We know

---

5. In the alphabet reversal system by which *aleph* becomes *taw*, *beth* becomes *shin* (therefore called *'at-bash*), etc., the first two consonants of *MiZWaH* represent the letters YH. Hence the *mizwah* or commandment *is* the name *YHWH*, but in half-hidden form.

that all things, even the most earthly and corporeal, contain His glory. If one were to imagine the departure of His light from anything,
great or small, that thing would simply cease to exist. How then can
transgression come to be? Does not His glory have to be there too? If
not, it would be as though it were not at all.

The truth of this matter lies, however, in that which we have
quoted elsewhere in the name of the Ba'al Shem Tov. On the verse:
"He looks in through the windows and lattice work," beaming His
fear in concentrated form upon the one who is about to go out and
commit a secret sin. Such a person's fearful imagination becomes
aroused; he keeps imagining someone looking at him, peering in
through some window or shutter. Fear thus falls on him as though he
were really within somebody's sight, for the divine fear has, as it
were, concentrated itself and come to him in order that he might return and turn away from sin. This is an act of God's great compassion, this bringing of His fear down to the very lowest rung.

It was with this in mind that R. Yohanan ben Zakkai said to his
disciples: "May it be His will that the fear of heaven be upon you like
the fear of flesh and blood." Know that when a person commits a
transgression and says: "I hope no one sees me!" it is really the divine
fear, now garbed in the fear of persons, that has come on him as he
sets out to sin. He keeps thinking that someone is looking in the window at him. If he only had the awareness that comes with faith to
know that it was God bringing this fear upon him, albeit in human
form, he would so easily come to hold fast to the fear of God. He
would then be able to penetrate the outer garments of this fear, to
draw near to God and away from sin.

Thus the Mishnah said: "He who walks in a dangerous place
should say: 'Save your people . . . in every time of crisis may their
needs come before You.' The Talmud explained: Even when they set
out to transgress (PaRaSHat ha-'iBBur/PoReSHim le-'aBeyRah) may
their needs be revealed to You so that you may have mercy upon
them." This is the true "dangerous place"—the place of going out to
sin. "Even when they do this, may all their needs be known to You!
May each one of them imagine that someone is watching him, so that
Your fear will be cast upon them. Thus may they be enabled to repent, fashioning out of that external fear a true fear of heaven which
will lead them back to You."

. . . In this way is a person sometimes brought to return to God:
It is that good which lies in the fear he feels in the very moment of sin

that leads him to repentance.[6] There too the divine presence is to be found, though in reduced form. Thus "the way is open" and a person is given a choice, because he has cut himself off from his root in God.[7] "The whole earth is filled with His glory! There is no place devoid of Him!"

Now the rung of *taw* is that of choice, of good and evil. The wicked are those who choose its evil side, calling the evil good. Of them Scripture says: "Woe unto those who call evil good" (Isa. 5:20). For them that lowest *taw*-rung, containing both good and evil, has been changed into a *tet*.[8] Thus the Talmud says: "It is a good sign to see a *tet* in a dream"; they think that the evil aspect of the *taw* is the good. All is the same to them, good and evil. Thus is formed the *tet*, that *tet* of *nitamtem*, "dulled," as in "read not 'defiled' but 'dulled,' " to which we have referred above. They bring about this dulling by making no distinction between evil and good. The heart indeed becomes dulled in that way, no longer a fit dwelling for the presence of God within the person, since there was no room for God in him when he was committing that sin. For this reason was *nitmetem* written without the *aleph*—for they separate themselves and the heart from the *aleph* of the world. And thus is transgression spelled as though to read: "God passes by"; the *aleph* disappears and the *taw* becomes a *tet*. And so *we-nitamtem:* They are dulled, without the *aleph*.

Not so the righteous. They bring themselves, bearing that *taw*, up to the rung of aleph, up to the cosmic One. May God, blessed be He, count us among those who serve Him in truth and in wholeness. Blessed is the Lord Forever. Amen. Amen.

IV

INTRODUCTION. The reader will by now have noticed the typical form in which Hasidic homilies are couched. A passage from Scripture or a teaching of the rabbis will be brought forth for exposition, one that is then shown to be hopelessly locked in inner contradiction or seemingly stands in direct conflict with another equally authorita-

---

6. Here the author expresses a relatively conservative view on the presence of God in the sinner. Unlike many other Hasidic statements on this matter, here it is not sin itself that contains God's presence, but rather the pangs of guilt that accompany that sin.

7. The *zaddiq*, who remains wholly with God, is above the realm of choice.

8. The two letters are identical in pronunciation.

tive source. It is in the course of resolving these conflicts that the essential points of the homily are made, until finally it is shown that the contradiction was nothing of the kind, but was intended from the first to illustrate precisely the point that our interpreter happens to find there.

The present teaching represents an extreme example of this method, taking as its text a passage that itself was a series of riddles. The fact that the ingenious solutions finally offered to the riddles seem to have little basis in the questions themselves need not deter us: Here as always it is the religious content of the homily and its exegetical ingenuity that draw us to it, rather than any hope for a simple answer to a possibly real contradiction in the ancient sources.

Central to the first part of the homily is the commandment of Deuteronomy 22:6–7 that concerns the finding of a bird's nest. This commandment was considered a particularly serious one by the rabbis, all the more so because it was typical of those Biblical admonitions that might lend themselves to being treated with frivolity. It is to the author's credit that he finds in these lines a rich and enduring spiritual message.

The notion of a spiritualized Temple is also of great significance in the course of this homily. Too often has it been claimed, both by defenders and detractors of Judaism, that the tradition of the rabbis did not allow for the symbols of Biblical religion to be reread in truly spiritual fashion. Hasidism provides the literature that gives the ultimate lie to this claim. Writing wholly within the rabbinic idiom, our author here makes it abundantly clear that the true sanctuary of God lies within the human heart, and that this inner Temple lay behind both the original command by which the outer Temple was erected and the destruction of that same shrine.

*   *   *

"Rabbi Paponai asked Rabbi Mattanah [the following riddles]: What if you find a bird's nest in a person's head? He replied: 'Earth upon his head' (2 Sam. 15:32).[1] He then asked: Where is the name of Moses

---

1. The question means: Is one obligated in such a case to fulfill the commandment (see below) of setting forth the mother bird before taking the young? The answer is affirmative: The bird's nest of the commandment is "upon the ground," and the verse from Samuel is here taken to show that a person's head is still a part of that "ground." These riddles were originally intended as wit-sharpening entertainments.

hinted at in the Torah?[2] He replied: 'He for his part [*Be-SHaGaM*, numerically = Moses] is flesh' (Gen. 6:3). And where is Haman mentioned? 'From (*Ha-MIN*) the tree' (Gen. 3:11). And Esther? 'I shall surely hide (*'aSTIR*) My face' (Deut. 31:18). And Mordecai? Scripture says: 'pure myrrh' (Exod. 30:23), rendered in Aramaic as *MaRey DaK-HYa*."

In order to understand the words and riddles of the sages, we should first present the verses "If you should happen upon a bird's nest before you along the way, in any tree or upon the ground, with fledglings or eggs in it and the mother bird upon them, do not take the mother along with her young. Surely send forth the mother bird and take the young unto you. Thus may it be well with you and your days be lengthened" (Deut. 22:6–7). Now it is known that all the worlds and all that grew forth from them were created with one true intent, the final product of all Creation: the human being. This refers particularly to Israel, who are called "Adam." Thus Scripture says: IN THE BEGINNING; for the sake of Torah, which is called "the beginning of His way" (Prov. 8:22) and for the sake of Israel, who are called "the beginning of His yield (Jer. 2:3). The Creator desires that His kingdom spread forth and become known throughout the corporeal world by means of Israel, His chosen ones. God takes greater joy in Israel's devotion to Him, so robed are they in matter, than He does in the devotion of all His sacred [angelic] hosts, as is known. Israel struggle against the corporeal that keeps them from His service; as they defeat corporeality and wickedness, they bring the left side into the right.[3] We know that there are two chambers in the human heart, the right-hand chamber, in which the good urge dwells, and the left-hand chamber, which contains the will to evil. By means of this goodly victory, the left is included in the right and evil is transformed into good, even helping in the service of God. Thus the rabbis said: "Were it not for the evil urge, there would be no joy in the study of Torah." Care and desire for worship come chiefly from the side of this "evil" urge that has been sweetened, from the accuser who has now become the defender. This is the meaning of "You shall love the Lord your God with all your heart" (Deut. 6:5), [on which the rabbis comment] "with both your urges." Thus Scripture also says: "His left hand is beneath my head as His right hand embraces me" (Cant. 2:6): The

---

2. Moses is of course mentioned frequently in the Torah. The question seems rather to mean: Where in Genesis, before Moses' birth, can you find a hint at his name?
3. Being incorporeal, the angels cannot uplift matter or transform evil into good.

longing and desire for devotion come from this transformed evil urge. God has no greater joy than this: That which had kept one from Him is now turned into good. Even though a person remains in the world of action and in the physical body, both of which might keep one back, he serves Him nonetheless! Indeed God's joy is very great.

All this is due to God's gift of the Torah to Israel, since Torah is the spice that seasons and sweetens the evil urge. It is by means of the Torah that God causes His *shekhinah* to dwell within a human being. Thus Scripture says: "Let them make Me a sanctuary that I may dwell within them" (Exod. 25:8). It is known that the light of the Infinite, blessed be He, shines forth and dwells in the letters of Torah. When a person attaches his inner life-force and his words to the Torah, that life within him is bound to the portion of divinity that shines forth from Torah's letters. Such is the case of one who studies with this intent, and has no ulterior motivations or extraneous goals. This person is himself also called a "sanctuary," for by means of the longing and joy that reach Him from such service, God contracts His *shekhinah* so that it may enter that man. Just as the Creator contracted His *shekhinah* so that it was able to be present in the collective Temple, coming down between the two staves of the ark (even though the very heavens of heaven cannot contain Him!), so does He do in the individual sanctuary within the person, because of His great longing for Israel. Such a one merits to be a "chariot" for the Creator, Who enables His *shekhinah* to be present in the two chambers of that person's heart, which are "thy two breasts," the two staves of the ark, and the two tablets, of which Scripture says: "Write them upon the tablet of your heart" (Prov. 3:3). This was God's chief intent in commanding both the tabernacle and the Temple: to cause His presence to dwell in that individual Temple which is man. The first and second Temples, once they were built, operated for all, through people's appearance there on festivals. Thus Scripture says: "All of your males will be seen" (Deut. 16:16). They would draw forth the holy spirit from their visit there, each one bringing the presence of the *shekhinah* into himself so that he would become a sanctuary and Temple. This was the true dwelling of the *shekhinah* between the two staves of the ark: the two chambers of the heart. Thus the left chamber too, by being included in the right, becomes a chariot for the Creator and a place where His glory dwells. The presence is found in the two chambers equally; therefore Scripture says "*between* the two staves."

All this comes about through the Torah, which is called *binah* or understanding. Thus Scripture says: "I am *binah* and *gevurah* is mine"; one has to bring to the Torah or *binah* all those *gevurah* forces of the left side,[4] so that they be sweetened and become good. For that reason the Torah is called a "spice"; it changes the spicing in that "evil" urge which comes from the left side. As the judgmental or negative forces reach *binah* they are transformed, for it is known that such forces may be mitigated only as they are returned to their root. All this happens by means of a person's firm attachment to the infinite light that shines in the letters of Torah, the root of all. Understand this. For this purpose were all the worlds created; "the last in deed was the first in thought." The intent was the world of physical being and action, so that even there His *shekhinah* might be found in contracted form.

Now it is impossible to attain to this rung except by means of humility unto the utmost, like that of Moses when he said: "And we are what" (Exod. 16:7). Even if one cannot be as humble as was Moses, the degree to which the *shekhinah* dwells in a person is all in accord with how much the person manages to humble himself. The closer you draw near to the bright light of God, the more humble you become; one who has seen His greatness is of course diminished in his own sight. That is why Moses, who saw so very much of God's greatness, was the most humble of all men. Therefore he said: "We are what," for he thought of himself as nothing in the face of God's greatness. As long as a person still thinks of himself as something, he will necessarily have limits, for everything that exists has some limit. God cannot dwell in such a person, since He is infinite and without limit, and that person is a bounded one. You have to be like the place of the ark, which took up no space at all, so fully humbled that you see yourself as nothing, not a being at all. Then you can be called "nothing," and the Creator who is called "no limit" or endless can contract Himself into you. Understand this.

This is the meaning of "I shall be unto them a small sanctuary" (Ezek. 11:16): Even after the destruction of the collective Temple I will be a sanctuary for those who make themselves small; for those who are humble "I shall dwell with the lowly in spirit" (Isa. 57:15). This also is the meaning of: "I have seen the worthy (literally those who rise upward), and they are few (*Mu'aTim*); those who rise up to the high rung of being chariots for the Lord attain this by being small

---

4. See above, *Bereshit* 2, n. 3.

(*Mu'aTim*) or humble in their own eyes. Matter should not be so prideful as to consider itself real being, since all of man's actions, his mind, and his good qualities are nothing but God, blessed be He, that portion of divinity which has been placed within him. Were this life-force from above to leave him, he would remain still as a stone or a clod. Everything is from God, as we have already stated. One who studies His Torah must make his chief goal one of service, of cleaving to Him and being a nest or a Temple where His blessed *shekhinah*, which is called a bird, may dwell. Thus "like a bird wandered from his nest, so is a man who wanders from his home" (Prov. 27:8) is interpreted by the Zohar that the "bird" refers to the *shekhinah* and the "man" to God. Since the Temple was destroyed, the *shekhinah* has wandered from her nest, and God Himself has no more than the four ells of *halakhah*, the lesser sanctuary in the person who has attained humility.

This is why the phrase "if you should *happen upon* a bird's nest" is written with an *'aleph* (*QR'* rather than *QRH*), as though it referred to "reading." When you read God's Torah, the verse means to say, you will see that "bird's nest" before you; your chief intent in study should be to become a nest for that bird, to fashion within yourself a dwelling place for the *shekhinah*. All this should be in your mind; this is the "bird's nest before you" of which Scripture speaks. Place this intention ever before you as you go "along the way" of Torah.

It is known, however, that the *shekhinah* does not actually dwell in any place where there are not at least twenty-two thousand of Israel. It is for this reason that the formula recited [by the Kabbalists] preceding the performance of a *mizwah* specifically states: "For the sake of the union of the Holy One, Blessed be He and His *shekhinah* . . . *in the name of all Israel.*" In Torah study and prayer or in fulfilling a *mizwah* one has to join with *all* of Israel, not only with the *zaddiqim*. The latter are called "trees" as in "Is there a tree in it or not" (Num. 13:20). You rather have to be included together with all Jews, even those who are on the lowest rung and most fully corporeal, for the bird's nest is "in any tree or upon the ground." To merit being a nest for that bird you have to be bound *both* to the *zaddiqim*, here called "any tree," and to "the ground," those people who are yet tied to earthly things.

"Fledglings or eggs." "Fledglings" refers to those who already have wings to fly, and can soar up to their root above by means of the awareness they have or by means of moral improvement. "Eggs" are those who have not yet come out into the air, who have not opened their eyes to see the light of God. The verse is listing various rungs in descending order: tree, ground, fledgling, egg. He who wants to be a nest has to join himself to all of these, to all the rungs, "in the name of all Israel." By joining himself to all of these, he raises them up and brings them under the dominion of Torah, so that "the mother bird" is "upon them." The light of His *shekhinah*, which is called "Mother," will then shine on them as well.

Now it is known that the higher the rung that a *zaddiq* attains, the more he will see himself as nothing, having seen so much of the greatness of God. He must not give any consideration to the high rung his service has reached, really that of infinity itself. The further he goes and the closer he brings himself to God's service, the more ever higher levels, filled with the presence of the *shekhinah*, appear before him. The intensity of that presence increases as he continues to reach upward. But finally he must realize that he has in fact attained nothing at all. And this is the meaning of "surely send forth the mother bird": set it out of your mind that you have reached a place where the *shekhinah* dwells. If you think such a thought you will surely fall, for you have then become a "something" and are no longer "nothing"; you will have taken on limits and will thus no longer be one into which God can place His infinite Presence. Surely such a one will not be able to bring the *shekhinah* to those yet below him; rather you must "surely send forth the mother bird." Think not about it, and then you may "take the children unto you," that is, you will merit to be united with all the rungs and to raise them up.

Thus were the rabbis asked: "What if you find a bird's nest on a person's head?" If you find a person so upright and faithful that the *shekhinah* hovers over his head, he having become the "nest" for that "bird," how has he reached this rung? And the answer was, "Earth upon his head." That is, the thought of earth, that he is but dust and ashes, is on his head; he is completely humble, thinking of himself as nothing at all, considering his corporeal self to be mere "earth." As for his service, it is the divine life within him that is really at his core as a worshiper; without that divine life he would be but a lump of clay. Therefore worship at its root is really performed by God Himself. This is what brings him to being a nest for that bird. And he goes on thinking of himself as nothing until "earth is *upon* his head," until he is even more humble than a clod of earth, which is higher than his head. This is the rung of Moses, that of "what." Abraham said: "I am but dust and ashes" (Gen. 18:27), but Moses [went further in humility and] said: "We are what." In humility too there are various successive rungs; you have to keep going in them, ever thirsting for that level of "what." And the further you go into humility, the more will the *shekhinah* be present to you.

For all this you have to begin with some awareness, something that will allow you to know His ways and not to be led astray by the evil urge. This prior awareness is the attribute of Moses, and the Zohar tells us that it is spread out through every generation, down to six hundred thousand [souls of Israel]. This spreading forth of awareness is the aspect of Moses in every Jewish soul, the six hundred thousand roots of souls [that were present in the generation of Moses].[5] The awareness that is present in each and every one of us is a presence of Moses in that soul, each to its own degree. The more of such awareness there is, the greater the rung of humility and thus presence of the *shekhinah* that soul will reach.

This is the meaning of "Moses from the Torah? Where?" How do you reach the rung of Moses, which is that of awareness, from the Torah? What helps you to acquire this awareness? The answer was, "He for his part (*Be-SHaGaM*) is flesh." "*Be-SHaGaM*" was numerically equal to Moses, meaning that you reach his rung of awareness by holding yourself lowly, thinking of yourself as "flesh," knowing that without God's own life-force flowing through you, you could do nothing in His service. By this realization you reach that rung of Moses, going step by step until you are sufficiently humble to attain the level of "what." And the letters of Moses' own name (*MoSHeH*) point to this, two of them being the same as "what" (MaH) itself, and the three-pronged *SH* pointing to the three patriarchs, the higher chariot, as is known,[6] which he reached by means of this absolute humility.

We have already explained above why the Torah is called a "spice" against the evil urge, for it is spiced and sweetened by the study of Torah. The Torah is *binah*, the very source of those negative forces, and they may be sweetened only in their root. Since everything has its root in the Torah, here the left side may be drawn into

---

5. The number of Jewish souls who lived in the generation of the Exodus is said by Kabbalists to remain constant, greater actual Jewish population in later times accounted for by subdivisions of soul-roots.

6. Abraham, Isaac, and Jacob are usually designated as the three upper "legs of the chariot," while David, identified with *shekhinah*, is the fourth. In this schema it is usual to place Moses together with Jacob, as inner and outer manifestations of *da'at/tif'eret*.

the right and made good, actually aiding in the service of God. We have explained this elsewhere in connection with the verse "a sacrifice to the Lord in Bozrah" (Isa. 34:6), which refers to the sacrificing of the evil urge that will take place in the future. This means that the evil will depart from him [the demonic one] and he will remain as a holy angel. In fact he was originally a holy angel, but he fell, and in the future that holiness will be restored to him and he will return to his angelic place. All of this taken place gradually, bit by bit. The *zaddiqim* in each generation lessen the evil in him and sweeten him by means of Torah, for that is his root.

And so the rabbis asked where Haman is mentioned in the Torah. What they meant was: "The evil one—where is his root in the Torah?" The answer was: "From (*Ha-MiN*) the tree" [of life]. Understand this.

Now it is known that whoever studies the Torah is a free person, as the rabbis said: "There is no free person except the one who studies Torah." And also, "Whoever accepts upon himself the yoke of Torah has the yokes of empire and of worldly pursuits lifted off him." This refers to the bitter yoke of exile, lifted off him because exile itself has come about due to the destruction of the Temple, both the general and the individual. Israel did wrong to the point where they caused the *shekhinah* to depart both from the collective Temple and from the temple within their hearts, that of which God had said: "I shall dwell within them." It was because He was banished from the individual sanctuaries [within the hearts of Israel], those of "I shall be unto them a small sanctuary" (Ezek. 11:16), that He also left the collective Temple, and thus the exile began. But even in our own times, he who succeeds in establishing his heart as a private sanctuary has done his part in the rebuilding of the great Temple. That is why sages are referred to as "builders," as Scripture says: "All your sons (*BaNaYiKH*) shall be taught of the Lord" (Isa. 54:13) and the rabbis comment: Read not "sons" but "builders" (*BoNaYiKH*). But the general Temple has not yet been built, because everyone would have to be such a person. Meanwhile, those who build their part of the Temple have the yokes of empire and of worldly pursuits, those of exile, lifted off them. They have a foretaste of something like that which is to come in the future.

And so: "Mordecai from the Torah? Where?" The name may be read as *MaR DaKHYa*, which may also be translated "bitter/pure." The bitterness of exile becomes pure and cleansed. And its source in the Torah was *MaR DeRoR,* which can mean "bitterness/freedom," or "bitter/pure" in the Aramaic translation. Since this is all mentioned in the Torah, it is through Torah study that exile is transformed and one is purified from its yoke.

They also asked: "Esther from the Torah? Where? [and answered from "I shall surely hide—*'aSTIR*]." Now it is known that harsh or troublesome things that happen either to individuals or to the whole come about because God's face is hidden. God hides His face from man, and then the harsh forces do their own work, God forbid. But now we have seen that the very root of those judging forces is in the Torah itself; by cleaving to that infinite light which flows through the letters, a person may bring those forces back to their root and sweeten them. So they were asking: "What is the source in Torah of those harsh forces by which God's face is hidden? The answer was "*I* (*'anokhi*) shall surely hide." Once you hold fast to the totality of the Torah [fully present in the word *'anokhi*, the first word of Sinai], that Torah which is all one (and if you hold fast to even a bit of a single unity you are attached to the whole), all those harsh forces will be sweetened, and good blessing will come on you. Amen Selah unto eternity.

V

INTRODUCTION. The notion that Creation took place for the sakes of Torah and Israel is already becoming a familiar one to the reader of this volume. Here the point of such statements is most clearly drawn forth. The world exists for the sake of revelation, so that God be recognized by His creatures and so that the lower world be uplifted through their devotion to Him. The "lower world" as it turns out in this teaching is itself filled with divinity; nowhere are the pantheistic leanings of Hasidism expressed more clearly. The human task, then, is not so much one of transforming bleak matter into something other as it is one of restoring God to Himself, or serving as a channel through which the indwelling God might reassert its unity with the God beyond. Herein lies the essence of mystical religion as the *ḥasid* conceives it.

The distinction made here between "upper" and "lower" wisdom is a widespread one in the literature of Jewish mysticism, and is parallel to a well-known motif in ancient Gnostic speculations. The terms serve a number of roles in the later Jewish sources: Most generally "upper wisdom" is associated with *ḥokhmah*, the utterly recondite and abstract beginning point of the emanation-flow within God, while the "lower wisdom" is *malkhut*, the end of that process. Here *malkhut* or *shekhinah* is seen in entirely immanent terms, and the union of the two wisdoms is thus the coming together of the God beyond with that divinity which inheres in this world. Because *shekhinah* dwells within the world, however, "lower wisdom" also has the sense of "worldly wisdom," that wisdom man must transcend in order to reach the higher wisdom that lies beyond.

*   *   *

IN THE BEGINNING GOD CREATED ... THE EARTH WAS FORMLESS AND VOID ... GOD SAID: LET THERE BE LIGHT ... AND GOD CALLED THE LIGHT DAY ... THERE WAS EVENING AND THERE WAS MORNING, ONE DAY.

God was from the beginning; nothing was there alongside Him. How then can Scripture say THE EARTH WAS FORMLESS? Once God was there, how is such a thing possible?

Creation took place for the sake of Torah and for the sake of Israel. Its purpose was that God be revealed to Israel, that we come to know of His existence. Even though His true nature lies beyond our grasp, once we recognize that God exists we will do everything for His sake. Thus will "Know Him in all your ways" (Prov. 3:6) become a reality, as we seek to be united with Him. There is no other and there is nothing without Him! There is no place devoid of Him; "the whole earth is filled with His glory!" (Isa. 6:3)

God's glory, however, is manifest in His many garments; the whole earth is a garbing of God. It is He who is within all the garments. This aspect of divinity is called *'adonay*, related to the word for "sockets" by which the tabernacle was held together.[1] This is God's presence as it has come down into the lower and corporeal rungs; our task is to unite it with the source from which it came, with YHWH Who calls all the worlds into being. In every act of worship,

---

1. It is the presence of God in all things that joins them to one another, that lends coherence to Creation. This play is on *'adonay/'adanim*.

be it study or prayer, eating or drinking, we bring about this union. All the worlds depend on this: the union of God within—'DNWY—with God beyond—YHWH. When these two names are joined together, the letters of each alternating with one another, the combined name Y'HDWNHY is formed, a name that both begins and ends with the letter *yod*. "You have made them all in wisdom" (Ps. 104:24), and *yod* represents that wisdom, the primal *hokhmah* from which all the other letters are drawn.[2] Just as matter is required for any creative act, the creation then working on the matter, so does Creation itself emerge from *hokhmah*. Hence it is called by the sages *hyle*, from the words *hayah li* ("it was with Me").[3] All things were in it; from it they emerged from potential into real existence. Even though the *aleph* is the first of the letters [and thus one might expect that it should be used to designate the first of all substances], *aleph* itself is constructed of two *yods* with a diagonal *waw* between them. That first *yod* refers to primal *hokhmah*, the prime matter in which all the worlds were included. The *waw* (shaped like an enlongated *yod*) represents a drawing forth and descent, the actualization of that potential. Thus were all the worlds created, forming finally the second *yod*, called the lower *hokhmah* or the wisdom of Solomon, the aspect of *'adonay*, divinity as garbed in all things and filling all the world.

When a person does all his deeds for the sake of God, he draws all things in the lower world (or the lower *hokhmah*) near to the upper font of *hokhmah*, the Creator Himself who calls all the worlds into being. By means of his awareness he fulfills "Know Him in all your ways." This "knowing" or awareness is a unitive force; it binds together the upper *yod* and the lower *yod* so that the entire universe forms one single *aleph*. That is why God is called "the cosmic *aleph*."[4]

This same unification takes place when a person studies Torah, since the Torah came from *hokhmah*. There it was "hidden from the eyes of all living and kept secret from the birds of the sky" (Job 28:21). There the entire Torah was contained in a single point. For this reason God spoke the Torah all as a single word, that which the human mouth could never speak nor the ear comprehend, until Israel said to

---

2. *Yod*, smallest of the letters, is said by the Kabbalists to be but a point, the infinitesimal point of divine nothingness—or *hokhmah*—out of which all being is to emerge.

3. Here the author seeks a Hebrew etymology for a Greek term, but one known to him only through its use in medieval Hebrew sources.

4. Or "prince of the world" based on a play of *'alef/'aluf.*

Moses: "You speak to us, that we may hear" (Exod. 20:16). Through Moses Torah was drawn forth from that upper wisdom and came down to form the entire holy Torah as it is in our hands, broader than the sea, the oral law containing all the statutes and commandments. This is the lower wisdom.

A person who has truly learned the entire Torah realizes that he knows nothing. The end of knowledge is the awareness that we do not know. Thus the Zohar says: "Once you reach there, what have you examined? What have you seen? Everything is just as hidden as it was in the beginning." When a person has learned and known that he has attained nothing, he joins together the upper and lower wisdom, forming that single *aleph*.[5] If, however, he thinks that he knows some particular thing, he has not attained to wisdom at all. Then he is called the "whisperer who separates the *aleph*" (Prov. 16:28).

This is the meaning of *be-reshit*: IN THE BEGINNING. The Tiqquney Zohar says that this refers to two beginnings,[6] the two rungs of wisdom, above and below. One is the beginning of the downward flow, while the other is the beginning point for one who ascends. This lower *hokhmah* is called "the gateway to the Lord" and he who seeks to enter must come through here. HEAVEN AND EARTH refer to the upper wisdom and the lower wisdom. THE EARTH WAS FORMLESS AND VOID: After it all comes forth it yet remains formless, "just as hidden as it was in the beginning." GOD SAID: This (name) refers to *zimzum*, the process of divine contraction. That which came down did so in contracted form. LET THERE BE LIGHT: The Torah is called light (Prov. 6:23). AND THERE WAS LIGHT: The Zohar comments that this light already was. It refers to the upper *hokhmah*, which spread forth and downward, forming the lower *hokhmah* [i.e., the "light" of Creation came from a light that already was, within God]. THE SPIRIT OF GOD HOVERED OVER THE FACE OF THE WATERS: "Water" refers to Torah, and the "spirit of God," according to RaSHI, is the throne of glory. This means that if a person studies Torah in the way we have indicated, he forms a throne of glory for the Lord.

---

5. When he has gone through the Torah, the totality of knowledge that exists in the lower world, and realizes that it is no-thing, he is ready to restore the unity of that no-thing with the nothingness of *hokhmah*, out of which all things emerged. Thus is lower *hokhmah*, manifest both as *shekhinah* in Creation and as Torah in revelation, joined again to its source above.

6. The letter *bet*, with which *be-reshit* begins, has the numerical value of two.

Further, he who studies Torah, uniting the upper wisdom with the lower, also defeats his own evil urge. Thus the sages have said: "If that wicked one attacks you, drag him off to the house of study." This is the meaning of GOD SAW THAT THE LIGHT WAS GOOD. [He saw that such study of Torah leads also to moral goodness.] And thus GOD SEPARATED THE LIGHT FROM THE DARKNESS, for in a place where unity reigns, the evil one cannot be. But if someone should whisper to you: "What need was there of the evil urge at all?" know that he is wrong, for our sages have taught us: "Were it not for the evil urge there would not be any joy in learning." The root of desire and joy is with the evil urge. It has to be this way, as in "His left hand is beneath my head as his right hand embraces me" (Cant. 2:6). It is with the evil side that one has to start, as we are taught: "A person should always study and perform the commandments, even if not for their own sake." For example, a person may set out to study just for the sake of enjoyment, since Torah is the greatest of joys. This is not for its own sake—"his left hand is beneath my head"—but afterwards "his right hand embraces me." This is THERE WAS EVENING AND THERE WAS MORNING—the evil urge and the good urge. Both of them are needed to form ONE DAY.[7]

VI

INTRODUCTION. Following in the footsteps of the above teachings, here *The Light of the Eyes* again speaks of the rhythms of darkness and light, insisting that dark must precede the light, but also that the coming of the light will uplift it.

The important symbol introduced in this teaching is that of the two Torahs, the revealed and the esoteric. This pair has been spoken of by Jewish mystics of many ages, and associated with various sorts of meanings. For many, the hidden was the Kabbalistic Torah, or the Torah interpreted with reference to the terms of the sefirotic world. For others the hidden Torah took on more of a quasi-magical meaning, associated with mystical names of God, obscure numerical equi-

---

7. Once again he insists that all the rungs must be included, that evil must be uplifted, to allow for the wholeness of good. The psychological point that there would be no pleasure without the evil urge is well known to rabbinic sources; here the emphasis is on the greater pleasure that derives from the conversion of evil into good.

valences, and the like. Here, however, the symbol is used in an ancient but surprisingly uncommon way. The revealed Torah is synonymous with *shekhinah*, the revealed (or discoverable) presence of God in this world, while the hidden Torah, as *ḥokhmah*, is none other than God Himself.

The notion that God *is* Torah goes back to the rabbis' identification of Torah as the instrument of Creation, the one who was beside Him from the beginning, and His essential wisdom. Philosophers in the Middle Ages spoke of His "uncreated Word," and Kabbalists as far back as the thirteenth century became fond of such shocking formulations as "He is His Torah and His Torah is He." Here the point is that through study of Torah (with the proper intent, to be sure), one can effect that unification of which our author has spoken so passionately above. The unification of Torah with its root above in the upper Torah, the goal of all "study for its own sake," is nothing other than the joining together of *shekhinah* with its root in God.

*　　*　　*

IN THE BEGINNING GOD CREATED HEAVEN AND EARTH.

The twenty-two letters of the Torah as it has been given to us flow from those same letters in the Torah above, the secret Torah. When a person studies Torah for its own sake, to unite the two Torahs, he also unites heaven and earth, God and His *shekhinah*. It is the light within Torah that brings a person back to the good; of this it has been said: ["If a person tells you . . .] 'I have struggled and found it,' believe." He does not say: "I have struggled and *learned* it," but rather "found," for this refers to the light that is hidden within the Torah. You struggle and find the light that God has hidden in His Torah, a light not revealed except through struggle. After a person has truly worked at such searching, it comes to be called *his* Torah.

The particle *et* in the opening verse refers to the twenty-two letters, from *aleph* to *taw*.[1] HEAVEN refers to the secret Torah, followed again by *et*, the twenty-two letters, and then by EARTH: the

---

1. *Et* (properly *'t*) is composed of *aleph* and *taw*, the first and last letters of the alphabet.

revealed Torah. Torah study for its own sake unites these two, heaven and earth, God and *shekhinah*.

If, however, a person does not study Torah for its own sake and does not bring about this union, THE EARTH WAS FORMLESS AND VOID. AND DARKNESS. Then is the light hidden; as the two are not joined together, the upper Torah cannot give of its light. And yet THE SPIRIT OF GOD HOVERS; even when one studies for the wrong reason, there is something of spiritual life in the holy letters, hovering OVER THE FACE OF THE WATER. And since God would not want to keep the good from those who walk in the proper path, a call for His mercies will bring one from this poorly motivated learning into true study for its own sake: GOD SAYS: LET THERE BE LIGHT. On the phrase AND THERE WAS LIGHT the Zohar comments: "A light that already was"—the light that existed before God hid it away for the righteous. GOD SEPARATED THE LIGHT FROM THE DARKNESS: "He who studies for its own sake attains many things . . . and is prepared to be righteous (*zaddiq*)." This is the separation: If before such study he was composed of good and evil together, now he is separated from all evil.

This is the meaning of THERE WAS EVENING AND THERE WAS MORNING: ONE DAY. The Talmud speaks of the goats going at the head of the flock, following the order of Creation.[2] Darkness came first and was followed by light. Why should a person have been so created that for his first thirteen years he have no responsibility to fulfill the commandments? And how may the deeds [and misdeeds] of one's youth be set aright? Why are the "goats" first, that is, why are the young so prideful? The answer is that the order of Creation must be followed: The lack must precede [its fulfillment] in all things. As a person's deeds change, his childhood is set straight.

Think of this as a house that contains no light. A lamp is brought in and the whole house lights up. One might ask where the darkness that formerly filled the house has gone. Darkness too is a created thing, as Scripture tells us, "He forms light and creates darkness" (Isa. 45:7). But the matter is as the Zohar has told us: Darkness longs to be absorbed in the light. As the light was brought into the house, the darkness was drawn into it. This is the meaning of "Rejoice, O young man, in your youth . . . but know that for all these things God

2. See above, bereshit 1 and n. 5.

85

will bring you into judgment" (Eccles. 11:9). RaSHI says that the first
part of this verse is the voice of the evil urge [while the conclusion is
the voice of good]. The verse means that after you repent you will
bring all your deeds of youthful folly with you, "into judgment," setting them aright and including them too in the light of your good actions. This is the meaning of THERE WAS EVENING AND
THERE WAS MORNING: ONE DAY.

Sources*: *Bereshit*

In the case of trees	Rosh Hashanah 13b
Whole and broken tablets	Berakhot 8b
Where else should a person's eyes be?	Zohar 3:187a
Thus have our rabbis explained	Bereshit Rabbah 1:14
Not for its own sake	Berakhot 17a
Always good for a person to study	Pesahim 50b
Why is it that the goats	Shabbat 77b
Thus our sages say of Balaam	Berakhot 7a
The image of his father's likeness	Sotah 36b
The clothes she wore in the morning	Yoma 35b
Esther was "just plain earth"	Sanhedrin 74b
The name "Esther"	Hullin 139b
He dug his nails into the ground	Sotah 36b
The work of God: unification	Zohar 1:190b
Esther was of greenish color	Megillah 13a
How does one dance before the bride	Ketubot 16b
Adornments which did not exist	Zohar 2:95a
The name of Jethro	Mekilta Yitro 1

II

Rabbi Simeon ben Pazi	Hullin 60b
In the School of Rabbi Ishmael	Sanhedrin 42a
The face of Moses	Baba Batra 75a
Everyone will point with his finger	Ta'anit 31a
Moses received	Avot 1:1

---

*NOTE: Sources used in this volume are very frequently quoted from memory and
hence imprecise. An indication of source does not assure that the wording found in the
source listed will be precisely that of the *Me'or 'Eynayim*.

86

BERESHIT

He forgot three hundred laws	Temurah 15b
Read not "inscribed" but "freedom"	Avot 6:2
Read not MoRaSHaH but Me'oRaSaH	Berakhot 57a
There is no free person	Avot 6:2
Whoever accepts upon himself	Avot 3:5
The angel of death had no power	Shabbat 30b
Children come along	Shabbat 104a
The New Moon kid-offering	Shevu'ot 9a
No one commits a transgression	Sotah 3a

III

Rabbi Eleazar said	Yoma 38b
There is a single pillar	Hagigah 12b
So too in the tractate Hagigah	Hagigah 12b
Read not "sons" but "builders"	Berakhot 64a
When God performs judgment	Mekilta Be-Shalah 1
May it be His will	Berakhot 28b
To see a *tet*	Baba Qama 55a

IV

Rabbi Paponai asked Rabbi Mattanah	Hullin 139b
Were it not for the evil urge	? cf. Zohar 1:202a
With both your urges	Berakhot 54a
The last in deed	A Greek saying; quoted here from *Lekha Dodi* (see history by Stern in *JJS* 7:234)

I have seen the worthy	Sukkah 45b
The rung of Moses	Hullin 89a
This prior awareness	Tiqquney Zohar 69, 112a
There is no free person	Avot 6:2
Whoever accepts upon himself	Avot 3:5
Read not "sons" but "builders"	Berakhot 64a

V

Creation for the sake of Torah	Bereshit Rabbah 1:7
Once you reach there	Zohar 1:1b
Two beginnings	Tiqquncy Zohar 1, 18a
The Zohar comments that this light	Zohar 1:16b
If that wicked one attacks you	Qiddushin 30b
A person should always study	Sotah 22b

THE LIGHT OF THE EYES

VI

I have struggled	Megillah 6b
A light that already was	Zohar 1:16b
He who studies for its own sake	Avot 6:1
The goats at the head of the flock	Shabbat 77b
Darkness longs to be absorbed	Zohar 2:256b

NOAH
Genesis 6:9–11:22

INTRODUCTION. The figure of Noah is an important one in Hasidic exegesis of Scripture, not least so because it offers to the interpreter a certain tantalizing ambiguity. Noah is the only figure (other than God Himself) to be described as a *zaddiq* in the Torah text. This term for "righteous one," bearing a long history of charismatic overtone, was just to emerge as the technical term for "master" in the parlance of the Hasidic master/disciple–centered community. Noah then must surely serve as a model, or else the term as applied to him would necessarily jar the ear of the Hasidic reader. At the same time, there exists a long tradition, well known to the Hasidic authors, of doubt about Noah's conduct. The comparison to Abraham, featured so prominently in the homilies presented here, generally is taken to indicate that Noah was made of lesser stuff than his successor: Surely when seen in the bright light of the patriarch, the candle borne by Noah would appear rather dim. The chief objection to Noah, it would seem, is that he accepted the divine decree against his generation with entirely too much equanimity. He neither urged repentance on his contemporaries in the hope that God's harsh judgment might be rescinded, nor argued with God Himself in the face of a decision that to a true *zaddiq* would have had to seem terribly unjust. The Zohar contrasts this behavior with that of both Abraham at Sodom and Gomorrah and Moses after the Golden Calf, making it quite clear that Noah hardly behaved as the proper leader of his generation. For Hasidism, a movement in which the leader was about to reassume the old prophetic mantle of intercessor for man in the heavenly court, the failings of Noah were crucial.

THE LIGHT OF THE EYES

The opening teachings of our section proceed from a series of variations on these oft-found themes. In the first, Noah's attempts at reproving his generation are in fact defended. The failure to heed, as in the generation of the wilderness, was their own. The second teaching plays on the contrast with Abraham, interpreting it in typically Hasidic manner. We then encounter a longer teaching, built around the Tower of Babel story, that begins to spell out themes that will become central in later portions of the book: the meaning of Israel's exile, the contributions of the patriarchs to Israel's spiritual legacy, and the place of Torah study in effecting redemption.

The fourth teaching in this portion seems to take a somewhat unusual form for the writings of early Hasidism. Rather than a unified homily, it appears that what we have before us is a consecutive commentary to the opening verses of the reading. Closer examination will reveal, however, that here too there was a single homily, recalled imperfectly by those who recorded it. In this case it was the chain of textual interpretations that was remembered and thus became the written teaching; elsewhere we will find the framework preserved, while the specifics are consigned to forgetfulness.

The final teaching recorded here is also fragmentary. The reading was tied homiletically to a teaching about the Days of Awe, though that connection is now partially lost. Interesting, however, is the author's discussion of fear and its place in the religious life. God seeks that He be feared in order that He may demonstrate fear's ultimate transformation: Fear of heaven too will turn out to reveal itself as nothing other than God's love.

*　　　*　　　*

I

THESE ARE THE GENERATIONS OF NOAH. NOAH WAS A RIGHTEOUS AND WHOLEHEARTED MAN IN HIS GENERATIONS.

RaSHI says that some interpret IN HIS GENERATIONS in Noah's favor—"How much more righteous would he have been in a righteous generation!"—while others read it to his detriment—"In the generation of Abraham he would have been thought of as nothing."

But why would anyone interpret the verse to Noah's detriment if there is a more positive way to read it? Does the Torah not call him RIGHTEOUS AND WHOLEHEARTED? Is this not sufficient indication that he was a perfectly righteous man, lacking nothing? If, however, you say that in Abraham's time he would have been nothing, surely he cannot have been perfect.

The truth is this: When the *zaddiq* reproves his generation and they refuse to accept his chastisements, he takes from the good they contain. Of this the rabbis said: "If he merits, he takes his own portion and his neighbor's portion in paradise." This refers not only to the world to come, but also to the good a person embodies in this world; it is taken from him if he refuses to accept criticism. My teacher explained the matter in this way: The word comes forth from the *zaddiq*'s mouth and enters the hearer's ear. The word is a spiritual reality, representing the tenth rung on the ladder of the *sefirot*. Hearing too is something spiritually real, and the act of hearing represents a higher rung than that of speech. When the one who hears refuses to accept that which he has heard, something of his hearing is taken away from him; the word returns to the *zaddiq* bearing some part of the other's hearing along with it.[1]

This is why some of the rabbis interpret our verse to Noah's detriment: Actually it is a way of getting to his praise. They read RIGHTEOUS ... IN HIS GENERATIONS to mean that he tried to reprove them but they refused to listen, and Noah thus received some of their goodness as it was taken from them. He was RIGHTEOUS AND WHOLEHEARTED, all the more so *because of* his generation. Similarly the rabbis have taught that [at Mount Sinai] when Israel said, "We shall do and we shall obey" (Exod. 24:7), two crowns were placed on each of their heads. After the worship of the golden calf, however, these crowns were taken from them. And it is further taught that Moses was found worthy and took them all. This may be taken to mean that Moses took the good that dwelt inside each of them. And in the writings of the ARI, of blessed memory, it says that he returns them to Israel on each Sabbath. Thus he interprets: "Moses rejoices in the giving of his portion"—he gives the crowns back to

---

1. Refusal to accept chastisement dulls the heart and lessens one's power of inner hearing. With each such refusal defensiveness is increased and the ears are closed still further.

Israel as their extra Sabbath souls, for surely Moses has no desire to profit from what really belongs to others![2]

According to the secrets of reincarnation it may be added that Moses was Noah and the generation of the wilderness was that of the flood after they had been refined in Egypt. Thus is the matter explained in those holy writings.

II

NOAH WALKED WITH GOD.

RaSHI comments: Of Abraham Scripture says: "The God *before* whom I walked" (Gen. 24:40). He explains that Noah needed someone to support him, while Abraham was strong in his righteousness and could walk on his own. But this explanation leads to the same question we had raised previously: Are we not told that Noah was RIGHTEOUS AND WHOLEHEARTED? How whole could he have been if he lacked that which Abraham had?

It is known, however, that everything depends on the arousal from below, the feminine waters, since it is the woman who first longs for the man. We, the Children of Israel, are "woman" in our relationship with God. We arouse ourselves from below to cling to Him; then do we awaken in Him, as it were, a desire to extend to us His flow of all goodness. Then does the flow come down from above: blessing and compassion, life and peace.

We, the Community of Israel, and the Creator, blessed be He, are a single whole when we cleave to Him. Either without the other is, as it were, incomplete. Thus it was said: "My name is not whole and My throne is not whole . . ." We are called the blessed Creator's throne; He, as it were, is unwhole without us. Surely we without Him are also incomplete. Now when we begin the arousal by our feminine flow of longing for Him and desire to cleave to Him, we awaken His desire for us as well. When these two desires are brought together there is one whole being. This is the meaning of "You shall be wholehearted *with* the Lord your God" (Deut. 18:13)—you along with the blessed Lord are called one whole being!

---

2. Moses' true Sabbath joy consists in returning to each of Israel that extra measure of soul which they had at Sinai but lost as a result of sin. Having no desire to hold that which is not his own, his pleasure is in the act of giving.

NOAH

This was the chief purpose of Creation: that we arouse ourselves from below to walk to the Lord. When this does not happen, God forbid, and there is no arousal from our side, then it is God Himself who has to waken us. But in such a case we accomplish nothing. Noah was one in whom there was no arousal from below: God, because of His desire that the world survive, had to arouse him first. He had to give Noah the desire to cleave to Him. This is the meaning of "Noah needed someone to support him." Abraham our Father was strong in his righteousness, walking on his own, bringing about the arousal from below. Now we can understand why Noah could have been called RIGHTEOUS AND WHOLEHEARTED; he did in fact cleave to God, but it was not he who brought about the arousal. It was for those who walk as did Abraham, however, that the world was created, as Scripture says: "These are the generations of heaven and earth as they were created (Gen. 2:4). "As they were created" has the same letters as "through Abraham" (*Be-HiBaRe'aM/Be-'aBRaHaM*). For he was the one who aroused God from below.

III

THE WHOLE EARTH WAS OF ONE LANGUAGE. (Gen. 11:1)

Our rabbis taught that they all spoke in the holy tongue.

The point is that God created the world through Torah, and by means of Torah the world continues to exist. There is no place without God; His divine life is everywhere. And since He and His Torah are one, all the worlds and all the nations receive their sustenance only from the Torah. But what is this Torah by which all are sustained? After the tower of Babel, we are told, "the Lord did confound the language of all the earth" (Gen. 11:9).[1]

Even though the tongues were confounded, some bit of the holy tongue remains present in each language; each of them contains a few words of Torah. It is by these words that they are sustained for as long as the world has need of each nation. The rabbis exemplified this by saying that *TaT* means "two" in the Cretan language and *FaT*

---

1. How then can the nations be sustained by the Torah, which is in Hebrew, a tongue they do not understand?

means "two" in "African."[2] This is why Israel were exiled among the nations: to uplift, in the course of their contact and conversation with the gentiles, the holy letters of Torah that have been mixed in among them. Israel raise these words back up to their root in Torah. Were Israel to serve God with full consciousness, the Torah would be quickly made whole, all that had fallen being restored to it. It is only because Israel are small-minded that the exile has to last so long, all the way down to the (speedy and soon!) coming of the messiah. When he comes, the Scripture "Then I will turn to the peoples a pure language" (Zeph. 3:9) will be fulfilled.

In connection with Abraham we are told of "the souls he made in Haran" (Gen. 12:5). Onkelos translates this as referring to "the souls whom he made into servants of Torah." Abraham was the first one who had the faith; he made God known through the lower world. That was why God said to him: "Go forth from your land" (Gen. 12:1). He had to uplift the Torah and gather those bits that had fallen among the nations. It was they who in fact had brought the Torah into "servitude," [trapping those bits of] fallen Torah that existed among them. Thus it has been taught concerning the verse "to the sons of the concubines Abraham gave gifts and sent them away from the face of Isaac his son, while he yet lived, eastward unto the east country" (Gen. 25:6) that Abraham gave them a defiled name.[3] The seed of Isaac have the power to uplift and purify, but these, as it were, could only defile the words by their sins. The "name" here refers to the words of Torah, since all of Torah is the name of God. Understand this. They have their sustenance from this attachment to the holy. Therefore when Jacob came along Scripture said: "Jacob lifted up his feet" (Gen. 29:1); that of Torah which has fallen among the nations is called "feet," for it has fallen to the lowest rung. Jacob raised up those "feet," restoring them to their root, as he "journeyed to the land of the children of the east" (Gen. 29:1), the place where Abraham had sent the concubines' sons, away from Isaac.[4]

Of this Scripture says: "They have left Me, a source of living waters, to hew out for themselves broken cisterns that cannot contain

---

2. Thus did they explain the otherwise mysterious word *ToTaFoT* (commonly translated "frontlets"), which appears in connection with *tefillin* in Deut. 6:8 and elsewhere.

3. A magical incantation, allowing for access to God, but in a defiled way.

4. Isaac had to be separated from those defiling words, while Jacob was able to restore them.

the water (Jer. 2:13). The prophet reproves them for having become involved in the concerns of the nations and thus having distanced themselves from the true Torah, the source of living waters. We have explained something similar in connection with Rabbi Meir's Mishnah: "Whoever studies Torah for its own sake merits many things . . . and becomes a flowing fountain." True, the nations to whose rung Israel have fallen also have some Torah in their midst, but they are to it only as cisterns to gathered waters,[5] cisterns that will not be able to hold their Torah-water forever, since in the end it will be uplifted from among them until nothing remains. This is the meaning of "that cannot contain the water." In general, everything must be drawn in to the Torah, the cistern must be brought to the source of living waters, the Life of Life, blessed be He. This comes about through the study of Torah for its own sake: for the sake of showing a path that will lead one to keep and fulfill it, for it is in this way that the Torah becomes a "source."

This is the meaning of "The Torah of the Lord is perfect" (Ps. 19:8). When will the Torah, which is now as it were incomplete, become whole? When will this mixing end? The Psalmist answers: "Restoring the soul"—when the soul is restored through study of Torah for its own sake, which sets the soul aright. Now the wise man has eyes to see that the "study of Torah" spoken of here takes place in all things, including conversations with non-Jews, so long as one remains directed to the proper aim. All this is based on faith; you must have wholeness of faith in order to fulfill: "Know Him in all your ways" (Prov. 3:6). This also is the meaning of "they were comingled with the nations and they learned their ways" (Ps. 106:35). How could King David possibly have said such a thing about Israel? He wanted rather to explain why Israel are among the nations—so that they may fashion learning and Torah out of the nations' ways. Think about this.

This is why it was said that "the son of David [messiah] will not come until the last penny (*PeRuTab*) is gone from the pocket (*KiS*). It is known that the Torah contains general and specific (*PeRaT*) rulings; there are times when a general principle may require detailing or when a specific ruling may require a general rule. But the "general" Torah may also be taken to mean the "entire" Torah (*kelal*), both written and oral, including Mishnah, Talmud, and other teachings of

---

5. The water does not flow naturally from them as from a spring.

the rabbis. The "specific" may then refer to that which has fallen among the nations, as in "the gleaning of thy vineyard" (Lev. 19:10—*PeRaT/PeReT*). The general needs the specific—it needs to purify and uplift it, until the "penny," that is the gleaning, comes out of the "pocket," its place of hiding (*KiS/KiSSui*).[6]

Thus Scripture says: "Command Aaron ... saying 'This is the teaching (*Torah*) of the offering which rises up' " (Lev. 6:2). RaSHI says that "command" implies urging, and Rabbi Simeon tells us that special urging is necessary when the commandment involves some cost to the pocket. "The offering which rises up" here refers to Torah itself: That which is offered in awe and in love flies upward; this is true Torah study. You have to especially urge people to do this because it will make for a lessening of the "pocket" (*kis*), the hiding, each one by his own study bringing some bit of the Torah out from its hidden state. Thus we are told that the Torah was given "*well* explained—in seventy languages." That of the Torah which was contained in each of humanity's seventy languages has been given to Israel, so that they may draw it near to the great well (*be'er*); they do this by their good deeds.

We are told of our father Jacob:[7] "The sun shone for him ... and he limped upon his thigh" (Gen. 32:32). Just above that it says: "He saw that he could not prevail against him and he touched the hollow of his thigh" (Gen. 32:26). Jacob, who is one of the legs of the sublime chariot, was serving God with full awareness; of course the angel could not subdue him. All he could touch was "the hollow of his thigh"—his offspring, touching them in such a way that they would have to dwell for a long time among the nations, until they could affect the cosmic repair.[8] And so "the sun shone for him." We read elsewhere that "the Lord God is sun and shield" (Ps. 84:12). Jacob performed an act of redemption, bringing some Torah from darkness into light. Torah and God are one and they are called "sun"; thus did "the sun shine for him." And just as one cannot look at the sun except

---

6. This paragraph is based on an essentially untranslatable combination of puns, playing the opening Talmudic statement off against the hermeneutical principle of *ke-lal ha-zarikh li-perat*, "the general requires specification."

7. After he had wrestled with the angel.

8. The Kabbalistic Jacob represents *tif'eret*, the central male principle of the sefirotic world. The angel, already taken by the early rabbis to represent the cheated Esau, later comes to represent the evil force incarnate. Jacob's service is too pure for the Esau-demon to get back at him, so the punishment is taken out on Jacob's children through the course of exile.

through a shield or visor, so can the brilliance of the Torah not be gazed upon except through various garb and coverings. "The sun shone for him when he passed Penuel (= the face of God)"—he called that redeemed Torah by the name of God, returning it to its root. But "he limped upon his thigh"—his offspring were thereby weakened. Only in the end will the Holy One, blessed be He, take the sun out from its case. Then its light will be healing for the righteous but judgment for the wicked. Israel will be healed because the Torah will then be whole. The wicked, however, will have had the life-flow drained out of them.

Blessed is the Lord forever. Amen. Amen.

IV

THESE ARE THE GENERATIONS OF NOAH. NOAH WAS A RIGHTEOUS AND WHOLEHEARTED MAN IN HIS GENERATIONS; NOAH WALKED WITH GOD. NOAH BEGOT THREE SONS: SHEM, HAM, AND JAPHETH. NOW THE EARTH WAS CORRUPT BEFORE THE LORD; THE EARTH WAS FILLED WITH VIOLENCE.

The Torah is eternal and in every person. How [do these verses apply] in our time?

The *zaddiq*, by means of his good deeds, brings joy to the Creator, as Scripture says: "You are my servant, Israel in whom I am glorified" (Isa. 49:3). God is made proud before the heavenly hosts and says: "See my servant, how he worships Me in great desire and ecstasy!" That *zaddiq* causes God to bless all the worlds, including this lowly world and all its creatures, with goodness.

Now it is known that the word *hayah* ("was" as in NOAH WAS) generally refers to a joyous event, while its other form, *wa-yehi*, implies the opposite; we also know that the true "generations" or offspring of the righteous are their good deeds: NOAH's very name means "pleasant"—he brought about that which is pleasing both above and below. This RIGHTEOUS AND WHOLEHEARTED MAN was the source of joy to HIS GENERATION, bringing them blessing and good. That is the service of the *zaddiq*—to bring that flow of goodness down into the world. NOAH WALKED WITH

GOD: The *zaddiq* also has to mitigate the forces of divine judgment. Since the "whisperer separates familiar friends" (Prov. 16:28) and the cosmic *'Aleph* is taken away from the *shekhinah*,[1] suffering and judgment forces abound. The *zaddiq* brings all of these to the Lord of Compassion and they are sweetened. This is the meaning of WITH GOD:[2] It is with the suffering and trouble in the world that Noah goes to serve the blessed Lord. He serves by means of that very fear and sorrow which the wicked bring into the world. All this he brings to the Lord of Love and has it sweetened. Indeed through the service of such a *zaddiq* God's own name is enhanced. "David made a name" (2 Sam. 8:13).

And thus NOAH BEGOT THREE SONS. These then refer to three good deeds. SHEM was so called because NOAH enhanced God's name (*shem*). HAM (numerically forty-eight) has to do with the forty-eight prophets who existed in Israel, related also to the forty-eight drops that flow from Eden, the source of prophetic inspiration. The deeds of the *zaddiqim* bring near the advent of messiah, the time of which it has been said: "Your sons and daughters will prophesy" (Joel 3:1). This is HAM, the prophecy they will receive from those forty-eight drops. JAPHETH (*YaFeT*): The deeds of the *zaddiq* cause the "shells" to flee away, broadening the borders of the holy. "He will broaden" (Deut. 12:20) is translated at *ki YaFeT* in Aramaic. This is the meaning of JAPHETH.

NOW THE EARTH WAS CORRUPT: The earthliness and corporeality of man keep him from coming before God and cleaving to Him. The *zaddiq* breaks down these elements within himself. He "CORRUPTS" or destroys the EARTH within him so that he may come BEFORE THE LORD.

THE EARTH WAS FILLED WITH VIOLENCE: It is written: "He who robs his father and mother ... is a companion to the destroyer" (Prov. 28:24). He who takes pleasure in this world without blessing God is, as it were, one who robs his Father. He is a companion to Jeroboam,[3] the one who led Israel into sin. It is known that the taste in all food and drink is derived from the sparks of holy souls, which lie within them. The food and drink are but vessels to contain

---

1. See above, *bereshit* 3.
2. The divine name ELOHIM used in this verse is often taken to refer to judgment or negative forces within divinity.
3. The reference to Jeroboam here is derived from a Talmudic source, and should not be confused with other references to that figure in later Jewish mystical literature.

those souls. He who performs an act of eating or drinking that is directed to heaven, making his table "the table which is before the Lord" (Ezek. 41:22), is truly bringing an offering, drawing those souls again near to their source. If his eating is not of this quality, God forbid, he destroys those souls, just as Jeroboam destroyed Israel. Thus THE EARTH WAS FILLED: one who has not broken his material self and is still filled with earth robs his Father; indeed it is violence that fills him as he robs his own parents.[4]

V.

THE ARK RESTED IN THE SEVENTH MONTH, ON THE SEVENTEENTH DAY OF THE MONTH, UPON THE MOUNTAINS OF ARARAT. (Gen. 8:4)

Scripture says: "God has made it so that He be feared" (Eccles. 3:14). All of creation was for this purpose: that His creatures stand in awe of Him. Thus it was said: "Thunderbolts were created only to straighten out the crookedness in the heart." These are but one of His powerful creations, as it says: "The thunderbolts of his mighty acts" (Job 26:14). Since the heart is crooked and we have no straight heart with which to serve the Lord, thunder was created so that man fear his Maker and be set straight.

It is proper that man stand in awe of God [not only when His might is revealed, but] also when He gives him goodness and blessing. This is "the great and awesome God" (Deut. 7:21). This is also "the love of God all the day" (Ps. 52:3); it too should call forth awe. Such is not the way of the wicked: when they see the countenance of the Lord shining on them they lose their fear. In this way they cause trouble and bring about judgment. About those times when there is fear [of great disaster] in the world, God forbid, Scripture says: "Learn not the ways of the nations and be not dismayed at signs in the heavens" (Jer. 10:2)—since you are doing the will of God. The nations of the world fear only calamity; the *zaddiq* is not afraid of the thunder, however. He takes it as a sign to awaken and strengthen his fear of God. This is NOAH WALKED WITH GOD.

---

4. The rabbis interpret the crime of Noah's generation to have been that of robbery. In his somewhat obscure closing lines our author may also intend that one who does not fulfill the true purpose of life is a robber to those who bore him.

THE LIGHT OF THE EYES

It has been taught that God Himself needs the presence of the *shekhinah* in the lower world. *Shekhinah* may be taken to refer to the fear of God.[1] The whole earth is filled with this presence; there is no place devoid of it. There is nothing besides the presence of God; being itself is derived from God and the presence of the Creator remains in each created thing. Now "the beginning of wisdom is the fear of the Lord" (Ps. 111:10), and "wisdom" (*hokhmah*) is the primal undefined energy (*HoKHMaH/KoaH MaH*) of Creation. What is this force? Whence was it made? "Lift your eyes to heaven and see who created these" (Isa. 40:26). "These" refers to all that which is seen by the eye. Their existence implies a question: Who created them? The mixed multitude [at the golden calf] said, "*These* are your gods, O Israel*" (Exod. 32:4), not believing in a God who created all that is. Not so our own people, the folk of Abraham's God, faithful children of those faithful to YHWH, blessed be He, who calls all being to be and creates all that is. Thus *MI 'eleH* ("who [created] *these*") is consonantally equal to *'ELoHIM* ("God"). Even though this name *Elohim* represents judgment, once we have faith that YHWH, blessed be He, created "all these," we bring His presence into each thing. The Lord of Love and Desire seeks no death but desires only love; the judgment is thus sweetened.[2] Thus the *shekhinah* or the fear of God in the lower world is indeed divine need: It has to be uplifted to the Lord of Love.

This is the meaning of: "No goodness comes into the world except for the sake of Israel." "For the sake" can rather be read as "by the path" (*bi-shevil*) of Israel: their prayers form a path by which the blessing can descend. By mentioning the twenty-two letters of the alphabet in prayer, the flow of divine blessing is called forth. Now the words "Lift your eyes to heaven" may be read as an acronym for the three services recited each day, *shaharit, minhah*, and *'arvit*. It is by means of these three daily prayers that we bring about the flow of blessing in all the worlds. Since the *zaddiqim* transform the source of fear and awe into love and desire, they negate all judgment. God longs for this fear. He is called "man" as in "the Lord is a Man of war" (Exod. 15:3) and fear is called "woman" as in "a woman who

---

1. *Shekhinah*, the tenth *sefirah*, is derived primarily from the left side and thus tends toward the fearsome. The fear of the Lord is also referred to as the outer gate to God's kingdom; so is the *shekhinah* the first gate to the one who ascends into the *sefirot*.

2. The question "Who created these?" itself leads one to God, but only to God as judge. It is the answer spoken in faith that transforms creation and fills it with the loving presence of the source of life, a force beyond all judgment.

fears the Lord" (Prov. 31:30). It is the way of man to pursue a woman![3]

The word is called "kingdom,"[4] for through the word may kingship be seen; the king's word commands his people and tells them his will, which all of them obey. Throughout the year the deeds of the *zaddiqim* cause such ascent. . . .

But especially in the month of Tishrey, by means of the commandments of *shofar, sukkah,* and *lulav,* the judgments are sweetened. This is THE ARK RESTED: "ark" may also mean "word" (*tevah*) or the kingdom.[5] IN THE SEVENTH MONTH: Tishrey. UPON THE MOUNTAINS: The patriarchs and the divine qualities, these are the sublime chariot. That is the place where there is no judgment, from which judgment flees. ARARAT: *'aR* refers to curse; *RahaT* means to run: It is the place from which curses run away. ON THE SEVENTEENTH DAY: For the world exists in seven-day cycles, each followed by another. These are called the seven days of building. . . .

Sources: *Noah*

I

If he merits	Hagigah 15a
The rabbis have taught that (at Sinai)	Shabbat 88a
The writings of the ARI	Siddur Qol Ya'aqov 142b (yismaḥ Moshe)

II

My name is not whole	Tanhuma Ki Teze 11

III

All spoke in the holy tongue	Targum Yer. to Gen. 11:1
The rabbis exemplified this	Sanhedrin 4b
To the sons of the concubines	Sanhedrin 91a

---

3. God as YHWH loves to have fear brought before Him and transformed into love; only thus can the ever fearsome God of Sinai also be lover to His people.

4. From this point on the teaching is fragmentary.

5. *Malkhut,* the tenth *sefirah* (= *shekhinah*) is sometimes called the "word" or "the world of speech." THE ARK RESTED here is read to mean "the *shekhinah* is uplifted."

THE LIGHT OF THE EYES

The son of David will not come
until   Sanhedrin 97a
Command implies urging   Sifra Ẓaw 1
The Torah was given *well* explained   Sotah 32a
Israel will be healed   Nedarim 8b

IV
Noah means "pleasant"   Bereshit Rabbah 30:5
Jeroboam . . . led Israel into sin   Berakhot 35b

V
Thunderbolts were created   Berakhot 59a

LEKH LEKHA
Genesis 12:1–17:27

INTRODUCTION. The weekly reading begins with God's command to Abram to go forth from his birthplace and his father's house "unto the land that I will show you." Judaism, among the most tradition-centered of all religions, does not forget that its origins lay in a radical break with the past, in a lone search for new religious direction. The figure of Abraham, alone recognizing God and standing in defiance of the entire world, is a familiar one in the Jewish literary imagination.

For the Hasidic authors, Abraham's journey from his homeland, his wanderings across the desert, and especially his sojourn in Egypt take on special significance. A major theme of early Hasidic writing is that of "descent for the sake of ascent," meaning that a person must reach down into the lower depths in order to raise up those fallen sparks of divinity that seek their redemption through him. Some masters taught this in terms of the master/disciple relationship: The *zaddiq* must lower himself to his followers' level in order to be able to raise them up with him as he rises to the heights. Others spoke of it as an internal process: A person must reach down into his own lower depths before reaching upward to heaven. Only then will his ascent be one of an entire and unfragmented self. Following an earlier tradition, this uplifting was also seen as a historical process. It was Abraham who began the work of raising the sparks from below as he left Haran for the Land of Israel and as he ascended from Egypt. The work is continued by the righteous of each generation, and only its completion will allow the final redeemer to come.

More than any other person except possibly Moses, Abraham figures in the Hasidic imagination as the ideal type for the *zaddiq*, indeed as the ideal Jew. According to the symbols of the Kabbalah, Abraham represents the attribute of divine love (*ḥesed*) and the right hand of God. While formally the authors may have spoken of a need to balance all of the divine qualities, in practice it was that of love which they most sought to emulate. The Ba'al Shem was said to have taught that he had come into the world only for the sake of love: for the love of God, the love of Israel, and the love of Torah. No Hasidic teacher would have argued with this definition of his role. No doubt that it was in many cases the masters' unusual warmth and love for their disciples, including a loving acceptance of even the most seemingly wanting among them, that gave them their large following. For *ḥasidim* this love was completely natural, surely nothing other than a continuation of that love which father Abraham had shown to strangers as he welcomed them into his ever-open tent, fed them, and spoke to them of the greatness of the Lord.

*   *   *

I

THE LORD SAID TO ABRAM: GET YOURSELF OUT OF YOUR LAND, YOUR BIRTHPLACE, YOUR FATHER'S HOUSE, UNTO THE LAND THAT I WILL SHOW YOU. I WILL MAKE YOU A GREAT NATION; I WILL BLESS YOU AND MAKE YOUR NAME GREAT. YOU SHALL BE A BLESSING.

On GET YOURSELF RaSHI comments: "For your own benefit, for your own good." This surely is difficult to understand. Abraham, who is called elsewhere "Abraham My lover" (Isa. 41:8), served God for love alone, not for the sake of any "benefit" that might result.

We may answer as follows: Abraham is called doubly by God: "Abraham Abraham!" (Gen. 22:11). Similarly "Jacob Jacob!" (Gen. 46:2) and "Moses Moses!" (Exod. 3:4). This is because "God's people is a part of Him" (Deut. 32:9). While the *zaddiq* exists down here in this lowly world, his root continues to exist above. He was created here only so that even one who inhabits a lowly body might still choose the service of God and not deny the seal of the king.[1] He remains as much a *zaddiq* in this world as he is in his root above. This is "Abraham Abraham!"—Abraham the earthly *zaddiq* and Abraham above. So too the other righteous: Their names here are the same as their righteous names above.

The souls above bask in the light of the *shekhinah,* as is known. Even though they enjoy this light, however, it comes to them as the "bread of shame." He who eats that which is not his own is ashamed to look on it. That is why God, blessed be He, brought the soul down to earth: so that out of its own choice it could serve God and thus receive an earned reward, no longer having to be shamed by the bread it eats. This is the meaning of "GET YOURSELF—for your own benefit, for your own good": let pleasure and good come to you as reward for your deeds and not as the bread of shame.

Now even though the soul is dressed in the lowly garb of matter and therefore has bodily and earthly desires, these very desires themselves may lead her back to serve the Lord. This is OUT OF YOUR LAND:[2] It is out of your own earthliness that you may turn to His service.

So long as a person is not humble, however, he cannot serve God. [Of the proud one God says:] "He and I cannot dwell in one place." And how is a person to achieve humility? The rabbis have taught us this by saying: "Know where you came from—from a smelly drop [of semen]. And know where you are going—to a place of worms and maggots." When a person takes it to heart that he came from such a putrid place and that he will finally wind up in the dust, what does he have left of pride? If both beginning and end are so lowly, how much importance can we attach to that which comes between? This is YOUR BIRTHPLACE of our verse: If you remember whence you originated, in a smelly drop of semen, surely you will humble yourself right down TO THE LAND THAT I WILL SHOW YOU.

King David said: "I shall walk before the Lord in the land of the living" (Ps. 116:9). Corporeal things—eating, drinking, and the rest of human needs—if you do them just for the sake of fulfilling your de-

---

1. Man is made in the divine image and the human form is the seal or imprint of the King. The corporeal nature in which that form is manifest, however, might tempt one to denial for the sake of earthly pleasures in themselves.

2. The same Hebrew term *erez* can refer either to a particular land or to the physical earth itself, and hence by extension to corporeality or lowness.

sires, have no life. But if you eat to sate your *soul,* and raise up the eating, drinking, and other needs[3] to God by your good intentions, then you fulfill "Know Him in all your ways" (Prov. 3:6) and all your deeds are for the sake of heaven. The land then becomes "the land of the living," for in your very earthliness there dwells the Life of Life. This too is TO THE LAND THAT I WILL SHOW YOU: that it be the land of the living.

I WILL MAKE YOU A GREAT NATION. Scripture says: "Then I will turn to the peoples a pure language so that they may all together call upon the name of the Lord" (Zeph. 3:9). Because we who serve the Lord at the same time share our bodily nature with the nations of the world, as well as with the animal kingdom, our serving Him through the body can wipe out all the evil in the world. Of this Scripture says: "The wolf shall dwell with the lamb . . . they will neither harm nor destroy" (Isa. 11:6). There will be no more evil in the world and all the nations will then serve God. This will be because of us, because we have served Him in all ways, including service through our own earthliness. Since all share with us in this, we raise them up by our service; all their service of God will be on our account. Thus I WILL MAKE YOU A GREAT NATION: Because of your righteousness *all* the nations will come to serve the Lord.

I WILL . . . MAKE YOUR NAME GREAT. The ARI of blessed memory has written that every man of Israel has both a holy name—the name his father called him, the name of his soul and life—and another name, representing the evil side of him. This is so because we are all mixtures of good and evil. Therefore the wicked, after they are dead, do not know their names. Because they did not do good, it is the evil name that has remained with them. Not so the *zaddiq:* Having defeated his own evil he has wiped away that evil name and caused it to be included within his good name. Thus I WILL MAKE YOUR NAME GREAT: Your name will expand to include the evil that has returned now to good.

YOU SHALL BE A BLESSING: When you have done all this, all the blessing that flows into the world will come for your sake; you become a channel by which that flow comes down from the world above. Hence *BE* A BLESSING.

---

3. This oft-repeated phrase is likely a reference to the sexual.

LEKH LEKHA

II

SO ABRAM WENT AS THE LORD HAD SPOKEN TO
HIM, AND LOT WENT WITH HIM. (Gen. 12:4)

The righteous Abraham fulfilled all that we have said, but still LOT
WENT WITH HIM. The *Midrash ha-Ne'elam* teaches that Abraham
is the soul and Lot is the evil urge. As the *zaddiq* ascends from rung to
rung, the evil urge goes up along with him. Even though he has overcome his physical desires and reached a higher level, there too the evil
urge may seduce him. "The greater a person is than others, the greater is his evil urge." It may be some very refined matter that leads him
astray; up in those delicate places he needs all the more to be on guard
against evil. There it is easy to be seduced in some subtle manner, by
something he would not even feel in that rarified atmosphere. He
must remain on his guard not to sin, even in the most subtle of ways.

III

I WILL BLESS YOU.

The same term refers to "grafting" of trees (*BaReKH/biBRiKH*). The
Torah is called the Tree of Life. Since God and Torah are one, He too
is called by that name. Thus the great Tree and the lesser tree, which
is man, are grafted together. This is the meaning of I WILL BLESS
YOU: One tree is joined to the other.

IV

THE LORD SAID TO ABRAM: GET YOURSELF OUT
OF YOUR LAND ... I WILL MAKE YOU A GREAT
NATION; I WILL BLESS YOU AND MAKE YOUR
NAME GREAT. YOU SHALL BE A BLESSING.

RaSHI comments on A GREAT NATION: "Thus we say [in the lit-
urgy]: 'God of Abraham.' And on I WILL BLESS YOU: Thus we
say: 'God of Isaac.' MAKE YOUR NAME GREAT: Thus we say:

'God of Jacob.' Might we mention them all again in concluding? Therefore Scripture says: BE A BLESSING: With your name alone is the blessing concluded."[1]

The Midrash notes that *LeKH LeKHa* ("get yourself") is numerically equivalent to one hundred, indicating that by merit of this going forth Abraham was to bear a son when he was a hundred years old. Thus too RaSHI had said: "Here [in Haran] you will not merit to have children."

We must understand what God is telling Abraham when he says that not all the patriarchs will be mentioned in the conclusion to the blessing. Had God not previously told him that by him *and his seed* would the divine name be called? Surely the mention of his sons would be considered fulfillment by Abraham, since Isaac and Jacob were his own seed.

Before getting to this matter, however, we shall need to comment on a rabbinic understanding of Creation. Since the opening verse of Genesis mentions only the divine name *Elohim,* while later Scripture (Gen. 2:6) refers to *YHWH Elohim,*[2] the rabbis have said: "It first occurred in His thought to create the world by the attribute of justice alone. Seeing that the world could not survive that, he brought forth the attribute of compassion and joined it with that of justice."[3] A surprising text: How may one speak of changes in the will of God? He sees the end from the very beginning! How then could He have wanted to create with justice alone, surely seeing that such a world could not survive?

We further have to understand what the holy Zohar says about the verse "These are the generations of heaven and earth as they were created" (Gen. 2:4). *Be-HiBaR'aM* ("as they were created") is consonantally equal to *Be-'aBRaHaM* ("through Abraham"). This refers to Abraham, the attribute of *ḥesed;* it was by God's great love that the worlds were created. If so, why was this not written explicitly in the

---

1. In the *'amidah* prayer the opening blessing contains the phrase "God of Abraham, God of Isaac, and God of Jacob." The section concludes, however: "Blessed are You, O Lord, shield of Abraham."

2. The name *YHWH* is generally taken to refer to God's mercy, the name *Elohim* to His justice. These relatively straightforward rabbinic designations are much complicated by the Kabbalah. The references below will be to *ḥesed* and *gevurah* in the *sefirot.* See Introduction for explanations of these terms.

3. A central insight of the rabbis: Had God created the world by justice alone, all humanity would have been destroyed, since all are found wanting by the measure of His justice. It is only through divine compassion that we live.

Torah, with the letters in their proper order? What is being said by this reversal of letters?

We know, however, that Creation was brought about by contractions. The Creator, blessed be He, is whole in all ways and lacks for nothing; it was no lack that set Him to creating the world. A person who lacks some particular thing is called unwhole; he may be called whole only when he fulfills that which had been lacking. Surely it would not occur to any intelligent person to say such a thing of God! Past, present, and future are all one for Him; that which is to be in the future was already there in the "past," even before Creation. Even then He was whole in every way, and He had no need of His own for Creation. It is rather because He is so great a lover and has so much love and goodness, as it is said: "The Lord is good to all and His compassion is over all His works" (Ps. 145:9), that He created the world. It is of the nature of the good to do good; He desired Creation for the sake of His creatures, so that they know the power of His kingdom and enjoy the splendor of His glory. It was for this purpose that He created the worlds. Thus we say: "Lord of the world who ruled before any creature was yet made." He was fully king, *in potentia*, before anything was yet created. But as the worlds were created "when all was made according to His will, then was His name called 'King.'" He was so proclaimed by his creatures who recognized the power of His kingdom and His majestic glory, who took pleasure in His service, receiving reward in this world and the next.[4] Creation thus happened by God's great *hesed*, which shone down on His creatures.

The *hesed* of God, however, is a most brilliantly shining light, one so bright that His creatures cannot stand to look at it. Just as one may not look directly at the sun and enjoy its light, but only through some sort of veil that reduces the light and makes it bearable, so (though the difference is vast!) is it with the light of God's great *hesed*. His creatures would be completely obliterated if they received His light directly. The quality of *hesed* thus had to be reduced by means of *gevurah*, the attribute of justice. Justice measures out the divine love in limited ways, all in accord with the creatures' ability to receive it. Now all this had to happen before the light of His *hesed* could shine forth; the measuring had to take place first if the shining of *hesed* was

---

4. "Kingship" is an attribute of relationship. It is only because God has people who recognize His sovereignty and accept His rule over them that it is appropriate to call Him "King."

to bring about a world. Thus: "The world is built by *ḥesed*" (Ps. 89:3). And therefore this contraction of the light by means of divine justice may also be considered an act of *ḥesed*, since it too was for the good of His creatures. It is in this way that they are able to receive His light; in this He is called by the whole name *YHWH Elohim*, a single unity.

This is what they meant by saying that it first occurred to God to create the world by justice alone. But Creation in itself, you will object, was an act of *ḥesed!* The point is that he saw "the world would not survive"—creation by *ḥesed* alone would make a light so bright that the world could not stand it. Therefore "he brought forth the attribute of compassion"—the thought to create the world in justice was itself a compassionate one, as has been said. . . .

This is the secret of direct light and refracted[5] light. *Ḥesed* itself is a direct light; nothing prevents or limits its flow and the creatures have not the power to receive it. That which limits is called "refracted light," since it sends the light back, limiting and contracting it so that it will flow forth in such a way that it can be received. Both of these are considered *lights*, however; they are a single unity for the good of God's creatures. Together they are an act of love, for it is only by such limitation that *ḥesed* may be received. This is why Abraham is not mentioned directly in the Creation story, as we have mentioned above. A direct mention of Abraham [the embodiment of *ḥesed*] would indicate that by direct light alone was the world created. As the light had to be refracted for Creation to take place, so did the name of Abraham have to appear, but in distorted form.

Now just as things were in the general order of Creation, so are they always in the present and in the particular, even in the individual person. Before God desires to shine His great love on a person and do good for him, that person must undergo an experience of *zimzum* by God's justice. This too is for his good; through it he will later be able to receive the goodness of *ḥesed*. The brightness of love's light would be too much for him were it not preceded by such a contraction; the situation is the same as that which we described in regard to Creation. It was this the sages meant when they said: "A person is obligated to recite a blessing for ill tidings just as he recites a blessing over the good"—with joy. The blessing over evil tidings must also be said in joy. In truth all of it is for the good; even that ill tiding is ultimately for the person's good, causing a limitation of that love which

---

5. *or ḥozer* may have the meaning of either "reflected" or "refracted" light.

God desires to give him afterwards, making it the measure of love that he is able to receive. The greater the good God seeks to bring to the person, the greater must be the preceding *zimzum;* if the favor is a very great one, the contraction that comes before it may seem to be very harsh indeed. One who believes this will surely bless the ill event in joy, knowing it to be the beginning of the good; thus is judgment joined together with love and the name *YHWH Elohim* made whole.

A person who is aware and perceptive about his own life will see the good that comes to him afterwards. If such a one does not find it, surely it is for the atonement of his sins that the evil befell him, to bring him into the life to come. Thus the sages said: "Suffering purges a person's sins." Of course there is no greater good that God might give a man than this, since "a single hour of peace in the world to come is greater than all of life in this world," with all its joys. Or there is no greater favor than being brought closer to God in one's heart through all these punishments, having one's fear of heaven increased. He who has eyes in his head will understand that this is the case.

In the Talmud we find the story of Honi the Circle-maker who, when the world was in need of rain, drew a circle and stood in its midst, proclaiming: "Your children have looked to me as one who is of Your household. May it be Your will to have compassion upon them" and so forth. The rain began to fall fiercely and Honi continued: "Not thus did I mean, but desirable rains, bearing gifts of blessing." Then the rain began to fall more gently. Now why did God not cause the rains to fall gently in the beginning? Surely His desire was to do the *zaddiq*'s will! This confirms that which we have been saying: Before any good can come into the world there has to be a prior act of *zimzum,* coming from the constructing side of divinity, so that afterwards the good can be received. Thus are *hesed* and *gevurah,* divine love and divine justice, united into one: Both come only for the sake of the good.

Our father Abraham served God out of love. Scripture in fact calls him "Abraham My lover" (Isa. 41:8). He held fast to the attribute of *hesed* alone and taught his generation how to love the Lord. Later in his life he fathered Isaac, who held fast to the rung of *gevurah:* Scripture speaks of God as "the fear of Isaac" (Gen. 31:42). It was because God wanted these two to be included in one another that he commanded Abraham to bind his son to the altar. At the binding of Isaac there welled up in Abraham a cruelty toward his own son, caused by his love for God. Thus was the *ḥesed* of Abraham comingled with the *gevurah* of Isaac. The very word *'aqedah* or "binding" indicates this: Here love and judgment are *bound* together and form a single union. Then came Jacob, representing that compassion which includes them both. Since *gevurah*-forces themselves are acts of love, as we have said, coming to limit *ḥesed*, compassion can encompass them both.

The order of the patriarchs thus follows the primal order of Creation. Because of the great love God wanted to reveal, divine love itself was aroused to create. But when He saw that such a world could not exist, it entered His mind to create it with the attribute of justice, joining them together into compassion; it was the two of them together that wrought compassion. When His attributes were to be revealed by the patriarchs they followed the same order: First there was the direct light of Abraham, followed by the refracted light of Isaac. Through the two of them there came about Jacob, compassion, since justice or limitation itself was a compassionate act.

This is the meaning of THE LORD SAID TO ABRAM: GET YOURSELF OUT OF YOUR LAND. He indicated to him that by this going forth he would father a son at a hundred years. This "son," the attribute of justice, would spread forth through the world as God became known through Isaac. I WILL MAKE YOU A GREAT NATION; I WILL BLESS YOU. This is why we say "God of Isaac"—it is through this quality of justice that divinity becomes known in the world.[6] MAKE YOUR NAME GREAT: Thus we say "God of Jacob." The Talmud then asks: "Might we mention them all again in concluding the blessing?" The question means: "Might they really not be united, but entirely separate from one another, love standing without justice and justice without love at all?" God forbid! YOU SHALL BE A BLESSING, Scripture adds. The blessing concludes with you, Abraham, and not with all of them, since the final purpose of justice is to be included in love and also to act for the sake of the world, only contracting and limiting love that it might better be received. The *conclusion*, then, should indicate that all is to be contained in *ḥesed*, that the limiting acts only to bring forth compassion, by which the light of *ḥesed* may be received by God's creatures. The love of God is eternally over those who fear Him.

---

6. People may come to know God only in measured and limited ways, according to their abilities to apprehend Him. It is therefore limitation that is the best teacher.

LEKH LEKHA

Amen Selah. May this be His will. Blessed is the Lord forever. Amen. Amen.

V

AND THE SOULS WHICH THEY HAD MADE IN HARAN.

Onkelos translates this passage as: "The souls which they had brought to the service of Torah."

To understand this matter we must recall that all souls have some attachment to the Torah. One who studies Torah and fulfills its commandments properly, serving God in truth by means of that Torah, raises up such souls. But the fallen souls exist not only in Israel; various holy souls have been scattered among the nations as well. Abraham our Father fulfilled the entire Torah. This has been taught on "because Abraham . . . kept my charge, my commandments, my statutes and my laws" (Gen. 26:5), indicating that he observed even the laws of food preparation for the festivals.[1] Thus he raised up those souls among the nations that were related to Torah and drew them to their source. Because he attached himself to the root of those souls in Torah, they too were raised up along with the soul of Abraham himself. That is why they sought to be converted and joined to Abraham, so that he would point out a path for them. This is the meaning of "brought to the service of Torah": He returned those lost souls to their own root.

We must understand, however, why it was that God commanded Abraham to GET YOURSELF OUT OF YOUR LAND . . . and I WILL MAKE YOU A GREAT NATION. Nothing is impossible for the Creator. Could He not have made him a great nation right there in his own country?

God conducts the world by means of seven qualities. These are the seven-day cycle of the world, sometimes known as the cosmic days or the days of the construct.[2] They begin with *ḥesed*, of which Scripture says: "The world is built by *ḥesed*" (Ps. 89:3). Just as the

---

1. The rabbis' point is that Abraham observed even the finest details of the law, including matters nowhere mentioned in Scripture but added only in later times.
2. The seven lower *sefirot*. See Introduction.

113

world is conducted by means of these seven "days," so must the individual servant of God, the microcosm in whom these are implanted in the form of love, fear, glory, and the rest, conduct his own life as well. Every person is given a choice, and he may turn these qualities any way he likes. Even though they flow from the highest place, as love is rooted in the world of supreme *ḥesed*, they may be used for good or for ill. In the state in which man receives them each contains a mixture of good and evil. Thus they are called the "fallen qualities."

This is what all our worship is about: to purify these qualities within us from their own evil and to raise them up to God by using them in the act of His service. This comes about by means of proper seeing: When a bad form of love or fear comes to a person, he must look into it and tremblingly say in his heart: "This love is fallen from the World of Love, from the love of the Creator, blessed be He. It is my task to raise it up. How then can I do the evil act, causing it to fall still further? And if I find my love-energy aroused by this wicked object, fallen material creature that it is, how much greater should my love be for God and His Torah, through which all being was created; He is the joy of all joys!" Similarly should one deal with all the other qualities as they arise; a person should be entirely too much in awe of God to use the King's own scepter in such a way as to arouse His anger, rebelling against His will as though He does not see. Rather, when some quality wells up in him, even if manifesting itself in a negative or external way, he should take this opportunity as an opening to bind himself to that same attribute as it exists above in God. Then he raises all that is fallen to its root. God has no greater joy than this.

Abraham our father, peace be upon him, held fast to that quality of love until he was called "Abraham My lover" (Isa. 41:8). It is with *ḥesed*, love, that one must begin in the repair of one's personal qualities. God wanted Abraham to go down into the nations of the world where those qualities were in a very fallen state, especially to Egypt, a place steeped in carnality, of which Scripture says: "Their issue is like that of horses" (Ezek. 23:20). Abraham, the master of love, had to go and lower himself to their level in order to uplift the love that had fallen there. In order to raise any person, as we know, you have to lower yourself to his rung. That was why Abraham used to take in guests, share food and drink with them, and afterwards say to them: "It is not *my* food you have been eating" and so forth. It was through their attachment to things of this world, such as eating and drinking, that Abraham was able to bring himself to their level; as he ate and drank with them, he brought them under the wings of the *shekhinah*. Thus we speak of bringing guests *in*, and for this reason the act of hospitality is said to be greater than that of greeting the *shekhinah*.[3] In this way a person binds fallen things to their root, fulfilling heaven's greatest joy. This is why it was after eating that he said: "It is not my food you have been eating." So it was when Abraham wanted to repair *ḥesed*, uplifting the bad forms of love from among those nations in whose midst there dwelt holy souls. Then too he had to lower himself to their level. Of this Scripture says: "There was a famine in the land and Abram went down into Egypt" (Gen. 12:10). This was "a famine not for bread and a thirst not for water, but to hear the word of the Lord" (Amos 8:11). The qualities were very much fallen; Abraham first wanted to raise up his own quality, that of love, which was in a fallen state. Of this Scripture says: "A man who takes his sister— that is *ḥesed*" (Lev. 20:17).[4] The point is that you must set your mind to know that even this love is a fallen fruit of the divine tree, the attribute of *ḥesed* above. As he sought to raise them up Scripture takes care to say: "Abram went *down* into Egypt"—an act of descent and humiliation, lowering himself to their rung so that he be related to them in order to raise them up. The verse goes on to say that Abram went "to dwell there" (*la-GUR sham*). The same term could be translated "to be fearful there" as in "Be frightened (*GURu*) before the sword" (Job 19:29). As one goes down to their level one has to do so with a certain trepidation, maintaining great fear of the Lord so as not to become like them in their failings, making sure that the journey downward is for the sake of rising up again.

This was what the author of the Passover Haggadah meant when he commented on: "He (Jacob) went down to Egypt" (Deut. 26:5), that "he was forced by the Word, teaching that Jacob's intent was not to settle in Egypt, but only to dwell (la-*GUR*) there." The meaning is as we have said above: God intended in the Egyptian exile only that

---

3. He who treats guests as did Abraham brings others to feel the presence of God, an act of greater merit than simply being aware of that presence oneself.

4. *Ḥesed* in this verse is usually translated "abomination"; this is a case in which the original meaning of "love" has been reversed, possibly for euphemistic purposes. The author plays on this reversal of meaning, seeing in the text an indication that even this *ḥesed* is in fact derived from divine love. Abraham in Egypt refers to Sarah as his sister; this apparently is the act of descent to the level of the Egyptians, resulting in the uplifting of their fallen or abused love.

the especially many sparks of holiness found there be raised up and that those qualities be set aright. As long as this had not happened, the Torah could not be received. Torah is the word of God, of which it says: "God spoke all these words" (Exod. 19:25) at Sinai. So Jacob was "forced by the Word" to go down into Egypt, to so effect Israel's redemption that they would come to the level of the divine Word and thus receive the Torah. The true giving of the Torah was the restoration of language. Jacob did not go down to Egypt to "settle" there, to be caught up there along with the others, but rather *la-GUR*, to fear the Lord there so as not to stumble. By being joined with those who dwelt at the very lowest rung he was able to raise up those qualities that were in need of redemption.

It was in this sense that Abraham said to Lot: "For we are brothers" (Gen. 13:8). In fact Lot was his nephew, not his brother. Abraham meant to say that even though Lot was steeped in carnality—as we learn from the incident involving his daughters,[5] since the rabbis say "He who burns with untoward lust will ultimately consume his own flesh"—he saw that this too was a form of fallen love. Its source was the World of Love, Abraham's own quality, in a most holy and divine sense. Even though Lot's love was in such a fallen state, Abraham saw that it came from the same root as his own. He therefore wanted to raise it up, to close the gap between them, and to cleave to Lot as he joined him to his source.

That is why God commanded Abraham to go forth from his land so that He make his name great, to answer our question above. A person has to humble himself, becoming close to those he seeks to raise up, in order that the border of the holy be expanded and the love of God truly spread forth in the world as fallen love is returned to its root. One who does this is the more to be called a lover of God. This is the meaning of I WILL MAKE YOUR NAME GREAT: by your going, by leaving your land and proclaiming God's love even in the fallen rungs, you become "Abraham My lover." By this you will be considered a greater lover than previously.

Now it is our duty to serve God in the way of our holy ancestors. We their children must follow their example, purifying all our thoughts of evil, and even using those very thoughts for the service of God alone. As long as one's inner qualities have not been purified one

---

5. See Gen. 19:30–38. Lot was seduced by his own daughters.

may not yet attain to Torah, which must be given as a gift from above. Each day we recite the blessing "Blessed are You, O Lord, who *gives* the Torah." Our sages have said of Moses that "Moses kept learning the Torah and forgetting it, until it was finally given him as a gift." This is true of every person: Even if we cannot reach the level of Moses, each in his own way must reach the point of receiving Torah as a divine gift. As long as this has not taken place, even one who studies continuously may not be called a master of Torah; he has not yet seen the truth in Torah.

Now I shall tell you a great thing in connection with this matter. It sometimes happens that a person feels himself to be in a fallen state, overtaken by the negative side of his own inner qualities, especially by improper love in the form of sexual desire. This may even happen when the desired sexual act is a permitted one.[6] Such a person should know that heaven desires to uplift him, using his own natural emotions in order to open his heart to the love of God, so that he may receive the Torah as a gift. Before he is raised, however, he must be lowered, just as our father Abraham went down into Egypt, lowering himself in order to uplift others, fearing God there in the place of which it says: "There is no fear of God in this place" (Gen. 20:11). So it is in every person: When he falls to that place of bad love, he must stand where he is and fear the Lord, having the strength in his very arousal to defeat the evil urge, not to do its bidding or to fulfill his lust. He must use that arousal of love itself for the love of God! This may be done even if a person in fact has to fulfill his conjugal duty as stated in the Torah. Even then he may perform only for the sake of his Creator, fulfilling this commandment as he would those of *zizit* or *tefillin*, making no distinction at all between them, and not seeking to satisfy his lust. One who does this is elevated to a very high rung, raising up with him all the love that had fallen there and restoring it to the heights, to the World of Love itself. That which we said of Abraham, whose name was made great because he went down into Egypt, is true of all people and in all times. In this way one merits the giving of the Torah, just as Jacob went to Egypt "forced by the Word," in order that Israel deserve to receive the Torah. This too is in each person and at every time.

So that you understand this thing more fully, you should recall

---

6. I.e., between husband and wife and at the proper time in the menstrual cycle.

that the Torah is called a *berit* or covenant,[7] as in "Were it not for My covenant day and night" (Jer. 33:25). A man's circumcision is also Torah, for Scripture says: "This is the Torah: man" (Num. 19:14). A man must be whole, complete in his two hundred forty-eight limbs and three hundred sixty-five sinews, parallel to the positive and negative commandments of the Torah.[8] The penis, however, is covered by a foreskin, just as the shell covers a fruit. God, blessed be He, has commanded us to circumcise and uncover the glans, bringing the choice object out of hiding and making it visible. As long as this act has not taken place a man may not yet be considered a part of Israel. But in the same way a person must perform a spiritual circumcision, alongside the physical one; the foreskin of the heart must be removed, in order to reveal the holy life that dwells within. This too is essential to anyone who would be called Israel. Let it not be said that "All the nations are uncircumcised, but the house of Israel are uncircumcised of heart" (Jer. 9:25).

It is known that the covenant of Torah is in the heart, as Scripture says: "Write them upon the tablets of your heart" (Prov. 7:3). Just as the Torah contains two ways, the way of good and the way of evil, and one must break through the shells to reveal the inner Torah, that which is called the covenant, so must a person reveal his own inner self, the holiness that dwells within him. Otherwise the power of evil, the foreskin of the heart, will draw him into immorality and improper sorts of love; from this side of the person comes the love of pleasure and wicked pursuits. We must fulfill "You shall circumcise the foreskin of your heart" (Deut. 16:10). The word *et* in this verse may be taken to mean "with," indicating that along with the circumcision of the flesh must go that of the heart. Along with the physical foreskin, that of the heart must also be removed, lest he be called "uncircum-

---

7. The following somewhat complex section of this teaching is based on the various implications of the term *berit*. Meaning "covenant," it refers commonly to the covenant or ceremony of circumcision. It then serves as a euphemism to refer to the male sexual organ itself. For the Kabbalist, the ninth of the ten *sefirot*, the channel through which all the powers are united and flow into *malkhut*, is also called *berit*, a euphemistic reference to the phallus of the *Adam Qadmon* configuration. See Introduction for further detail.

8. The limbs and sinews of the body correspond in number to the commandments of the Torah. This widespread motif is the basis of the Kabbalistic belief closest to "natural law": The fulfillment of the Torah is the fulfillment of the inner self. The human male is created imperfect, however; only with circumcision is the system of correspondences made complete. This notion is based on the exegesis of Gen. 17:1.

cised of heart." All of this comes about by holding fast to the moral qualities as they exist within the self, employing them in the service of God and raising them up from their fallen state in "Egypt" to their root above. None of them should be allowed to step outside the bounds of the holy, but should be directed to God alone.

Of this King David said: "Yours, O Lord, are the greatness, the power, the glory, the victory, and the majesty, indeed all that is in heaven and on earth; Yours, O Lord, is the kingdom and that which is raised up as head over all"[9] (1 Chron. 29:11). All these qualities are for You alone. The seven *sefirot* are all alluded to in this passage. Five of these are actual moral qualities: love, fear, glory, triumph, and thanksgiving. *Hod* may be read as "thanksgiving" because that word (*hodayah*) is equal to *hod YaH* ("the majesty of God"). The final two, *yesod* and *malkhut*, are not to be considered qualities. *Yesod* is referred to as "all" in the verse; "*all* that is in heaven and on earth" is rendered into Aramaic as "holding fast to heaven and earth." This aspect unites all the qualities and binds them to the deed, which is *malkhut*, the kingdom. "Yours, O Lord, is the kingdom": The deed is called "kingdom," for as long as the deed has not been done and the moral qualities have not yet been put into action, there is no true wholeness. Inner qualities and outer deed are bound together by the covenant, by *yesod*; only of this wholeness that has no lack may one say "*malkhut*," kingdom, for nothing is lacking from the house of the king. *Malkhut* represents completion in the deed. All this comes about through the covenant, which is also the *zaddiq*, the one who binds together all the good qualities from heaven to earth and brings them all into the deed. He is the one who "holds fast to heaven and earth." Thus the *Tiqquney Zohar* said on "Let there be a firmament" (Gen. 1:6)—turn the word "firmament" around and you will find the root (*RaQiYa'*= *'iYQ-QaR*) and foundation of the divine chariot. "That which is raised up as head over all" in our verse is then interpreted as follows: "When do You, Lord, have possession of all these qualities? When one comes and raises them all from their fallen state and returns them to You." But so long as the foreskin still surrounds the *berit*, so long as one's moral life has not been purified, it is not possible to achieve any proper state in the presence of the Lord, since one remains uncircumcised

---

9. The early names of five of the *sefirot* are derived from this verse: *gedulah* (=*hesed*); *gevurah* (=*din*); *tif'eret*; *nezah*; *hod*. The remainder of the verse is therefore often also expounded upon in sefirotic terms.

of heart. The Torah too is a covenant, and when one who is spiritually uncircumcised studies it he sees nothing of its inner nature. There too a foreskin, the shells of the Torah, surrounds the *berit*. Study of that sort will not lead one through the covenantal Torah to its fulfillment in the deed, which is *malkhut*.[10]

The Torah is revealed to a person only in accord with his own inner condition. Therefore when a person circumcises himself in the heart, binding himself to all these upper qualities and seeking to realize them in action, letting nothing slip away, then the Torah too is circumcised, its shells are cast aside, and the inner Torah is revealed to him. Such a person has great joy in that Torah; it helps him and guides him in a proper path to the ever greater perfection of his deeds. By means of the *berit*, all the qualities have been unified in the deed; the further one walks along that path the greater the joy in spirit he will feel in performing God's service. He will become a vehicle for the Creator, reaching that point where he will do no deed unless the God who dwells within him directs him to it. Of this state the holy Zohar said: "The horse is second to the rider, not the rider to the horse." Just as the rider uses the bridle and reins to direct the horse wherever he wants to go, so does the Torah, when its *berit* is revealed, lead man in the direction that God, his "rider," desires. The Torah becomes a rein in the rider's hands. Such a person merits to receive the Torah as a divine gift. All this is due to the circumcision of heart, an act that also guards him regarding the covenant of the flesh, seeing that he does not act merely to fulfill his desire, even when the law would permit. By such a covenant the person comes to have all these good qualities present within him.

The opposite is true of one whose heart remains uncircumcised. Then the evil side of each of these qualities comes to reside in the foreskin of his flesh. All of such a person's desires are turned to sexual defilement. He is so sunk in his own lusts that he can hardly function; the only master he can serve is his own desire, no matter what he is doing. Finally he will perform acts that do damage to his bodily covenant, God forbid, and he will sink to the level of a horse, reeking with carnal desire, as Scripture says: "Their issue is like that of horses" (Ezek. 23:20). This has taken place because his "rider" has departed from him; he is no longer a vehicle for the Creator, who used to

---

10. I.e., such study is barren and can produce no fruit in the world of human activity; it cannot lead to the realization of God's kingdom.

guide him by means of that Torah which had never been given him in an inward way. This is why the holy Zohar chose to speak in the metaphor of horse and rider.

For this reason the Talmud tells us that in the days of the early rabbis a young man would go off to the house of study for several years immediately following his marriage. This was in order to break down desire by means of circumcising the heart, setting their moral lives aright and especially uplifting any fallen love through the study of Torah. It is of Torah that Scripture says: "With her love be ravished always" (Prov. 5:15). After these qualities were in proper place they returned home to produce offspring, fulfilling this commandment of their Creator just like any other, filled with love of God and with nothing extraneous.

On the verse "I shall make him a help meet opposite him" (Gen. 2:18), the rabbis commented: "If he merits, she helps; if not, she is opposite him, fighting him." The word *'eZeR*, helpmeet, has the same letters as *ZeRa'*, seed. The "merit" spoken of here refers to triumph: If a person triumphs in his battle against the evil urge, circumcises his heart, and purifies his inner qualities, he then becomes a vehicle for God's presence and his wife is his *'eZeR*, helping him to bring forth true seed, with no admixture of evil, from his circumcised flesh and heart. Such a person acts only to bring forth seed, not to fulfill any desire at all. Such desires come from the evil urge, itself called by the name "uncircumcised," for it derives from the foreskin that hides the covenant. Since this person has already removed his spiritual as well as his fleshy foreskin, the battle with that evil one has already ended for him. "If not," however, if a man has not merited or triumphed over his own evil, most especially over the lust that damages that covenant of the flesh by actual deed, then he will sink ever deeper into those desires. First this will happen when his thoughts during permitted times of intimacy will turn astray, perhaps finally leading him into altogether illicit sexuality. Then indeed she is "opposite him, fighting him."

That is why it was Isaac, the son conceived after Abraham circumcised himself in response to God's command, of whom it was said: "Through Isaac shall your seed be called" (Gen. 21:12). Ishmael, who was born while Abraham was yet uncircumcised, was not to be considered his seed. Even though Abraham observed the entire Torah, indeed even though he had known God since he was three years old, because the foreskin was not removed [his proper seed could not yet emerge]. Abraham did not want to go ahead and perform a circumcision on himself before God commanded it, even though he was already following all the rest of the commandments. The covenant is called "all"; it contains all of the upper qualities within it. It therefore has to be done in a whole manner, and that can be only in response to the divine command. "Greater is he who is commanded and does than he who is not commanded and does." Had Abraham circumcised himself without being so commanded it would have been an unwhole act. And circumcision is an act that could not have been repeated once the command had come.

Every one of Israel has to turn his heart and eyes to this matter of restoring and uplifting the fallen qualities. In whatever area he may experience a personal fall at a given time, be it misplaced love, extraneous fear, or whatever else, he must raise himself up along with that quality, circumcising his heart. Then he will merit to attain all that has been ascribed to the patriarchs. Wherever your eyes or ears turn, when they are so attuned, you will see some divine attribute in a fallen state. Even among the nations and in their deeds this is the case, especially so among the seven nations who inhabited the Land of Israel.[11] Of these nations Israel were commanded: "You shall leave no soul alive" (Deut. 20:16). There the divine qualities were in their most utterly fallen condition, each of the nations embodying one of them. Of Amalek we are told, for example, that "Amalek dwells in the Negev-land" (Num. 13:29). "Negev" refers to the south, and it is known that the attribute of love is that of the southerly direction.[12] In Amalek was concentrated love in its most completely fallen form. Thus we learn that Abraham would "go back and forth to the Negev" (Gen. 12:9): All of his journeys in God's service were to restore love to the love of His great name and to make Him beloved of His creatures. Therefore was he called "Abraham My lover": this attribute was so much his that it was called by his name. And so it was with each of these seven nations: The divine qualities were so very fallen in them that Israel was commanded to leave no soul of them alive. Had this commandment been fulfilled as it was intended, they would have uplifted all those qualities from their broken state, just as God in His wisdom had wanted. Then all the good and salvation that have been

---

11. The Canaanite tribes who had defiled the land before the Israelite conquest.
12. The four central *sefirot* of the lower seven are related by Kabbalists to the four directions: *hesed* = south; *din* = north; *tif'eret* = east; *malkhut* = west.

promised for messianic times (speedily and in our day!) would have come about immediately. But by not keeping the command properly, by leaving something of the seven nations alive, they caused still a greater fall: The foreskin of their heart had not been removed. Finally this brought them to defile the covenant, as Scripture mentions in "they jingled with their feet"[13] (Isa. 3:16) and elsewhere. It was these ill qualities within them that led them ultimately to defile the covenant.

It is in this sense that Scripture says, quoting the spies who went into the Land of Israel, "All the people we saw there were men of *quality*" (Num. 13:32). They saw the *qualities* of divinity fallen in them. But the spies spoke ill and said that "even the master of the house (i.e., God) could not get his vessels out of there." The divine qualities are called "vessels"; in a fallen state they are the "broken vessels." The spies were deniers of God, saying that even He could not raise up these qualities from their fallen state.

Therefore Caleb the son of Jephunneh said: "We shall surely go up and inherit it" (Num. 13:30). We too, with the help of God, can raise up these diminished qualities. God rules everywhere, even among the "shells," and He can turn them according to His will. Thus Scripture says: "Be *silent*, all flesh, before the Lord" (Zach. 2:17) as well as "Caleb *silenced* the people." Through this attribute of silencing, that of "Be silent, all flesh," God helps us to raise up those qualities that have fallen. This task has been placed in our hands. Once the first effort comes from us, He has the power and authority to see that His will is done, that all those qualities are uplifted. May God strengthen our hearts for His service, bless His name. Amen Selah unto eternity. May this be His will. Blessed is the Lord forever. Amen. Amen.

VI

THE LORD SAID TO ABRAM: GET YOURSELF ... ABRAM WENT AS THE LORD HAD SPOKEN TO HIM, AND LOT WENT WITH HIM.

We must understand why the text first refers to "saying" and then changes itself to refer to "speech." Why did Scripture not continue as

---

13. Interpreted as euphemism.

it had begun: "Abram went as the Lord had *said* to him"?

The fact is that Abraham was a "chariot" for the Creator, blessed be He. The verb *'aMaR*, "say," sometimes refers to thought, as in "Say in your hearts" (Ps. 4:5). "Speech" (*DiBBuR*), however, is the tenth rung [= *malkhut*, and necessarily verbal]. For Abraham there was no need that the thought of God be revealed and take on the form of speech; he grasped in God's thought itself the desire that he go forth. He would have gone and fulfilled God's will anyway. But God wanted this further revelation, that of *malkhut*, the kingdom of David and the fourth leg of the chariot, to come forth in speech.[1] It was only then that Lot went with him, and the House of David comes from the family of Lot. David said: "I have come with a scroll which is prescribed for me" (Ps. 40:8). It says of Lot: "Thy two daughters who are *found* here" (Gen. 19:15) and of David: "I have *found* My servant David and anointed him with My holy oil" (Ps. 89:21).[2] That is why messiah, Son of David, will only come unawares; his source was one of unawareness, as in "He (Lot) was not aware as she lay down or as she rose up" (Gen. 19:33, 35). But had the command to Abraham not come forth into speech Lot would not have been able to go with him. Therefore Scripture says: "The Lord *said* to Abram": He would have gone merely in response to the thought of God. But "Abram went as the Lord had *spoken*"—so that Lot would go with him.[3]

---

1. Abraham, who represents *ḥesed*, a higher sefirotic rung, had no need for speech, the lowest rung, in order to apprehend the thought of God (*ḥokhmah* or *binah*). The process of divine self-revelation has its own inner dynamic, however, and had to be played out to the end, to its revelation in speech. The one who truly knows God's will from within may feel no need of the word, but the word must emerge nonetheless. The three patriarchs are the three legs of the *merkavah*, representing *ḥesed*, *din*, and *tif'eret*. David, the embodiment of *malkhut* (= kingdom), is the partially hidden fourth.

2. David was a descendant of Ruth the Moabitess; Lot's two daughters founded the nations of Amon and Moab. The point here is that David's coming of that seed was predicted (scroll = Torah) from the times of Lot.

3. The homily, recorded only in very abbreviated form, seems to mean the following: the true *zaddiq*, bound to the will of God, could live in accord with that will even without revelation in the word. This truth is often embodied in Abraham, who fulfilled the Torah before it was given. In order for there to be reward and redemption, however (messiah, David), there must be a revealed command (speech, Lot) so that man may be rewarded for obeying it.

VII

GET YOURSELF OUT.

Says RaSHI: "For your own benefit, for your own good."

The Psalmist says: "Are you too mute to speak righteousness?" (Ps. 58:2) and our rabbis comment: "What should a person do in this world? He should make himself as though mute. Might this even include words of Torah? No, for Scripture says: 'Speak righteousness.' "[1]

"O Lord, You open my lips and my mouth shall declare your praise" (Ps. 51:17). The Creator's glory fills the whole earth; there is no place devoid of Him. But His glory takes the form of garb; God is "garbed" in all things. This aspect of divinity is called *shekhinah*, "indwelling," since it dwells in everything. It is referred to by the name *'adonay* and is called the World of Speech, since "the heavens were made by the *word* of God" (Ps. 33:6). It was through the Torah or Word that God created the world; all creatures came about through the twenty-two letters [of the Hebrew alphabet] that make up the World of Speech. The *Sefer Yezirah* tells us that these were then fixed in the human mouth. This is the meaning of "O Lord, You open my lips."[2]

This is why the rabbis said that malicious speech or gossip is the equivalent of idolatry: he who speaks in such a way does not believe that his speech is the divine World of Speech, the presence of *'adonay*. These are the ones "who have said: 'Our tongue will we make mighty; our lips are with us. Who is lord over us?' " (Ps. 12:5). This is the meaning of "He should make himself as though mute"—the self should be silenced. One should speak only in such a way that one knows it is the World of Speech within, *'adonay*, that is speaking. They then asked whether this might be true even of words of Torah. Might it be that one should not study until one can feel this faith? But they answered: "Speak righteousness"—Torah study is a good deed even when not in its ideal state.

Similarly the rabbis said: "He who speaks in an idle manner

---

1. One should be silent, except for words of Torah.
2. It is God Himself Who is responsible for the miracle of human speech; thus it is really He who opens the lips as man speaks to Him in prayer.

125

transgresses a commandment," for Scripture says: "You shall speak of them [words of Torah]" (Deut. 6:7) and not of idle matters. But how is it possible to do this, never to speak except for words of Torah? The text should really be interpreted thus: "Your speech shall be in them"—*whatever* you are speaking about you should believe that your speech is of Torah. Speech itself is, after all, the World of Speech, the twenty-two letters of the Torah. A person should thus not mind speaking of matters that concern the conduct of this world, for God created this world through Torah and by Torah He guides it. All the worlds are run in accord with those twenty-two letters of the World of Speech. One has only to maintain faith in this. The one who speaks in a manner that does not help to keep the universe running—this is the one who engages in idle talk.[3]

The rabbis also tell us: "May all your deeds be in the name of heaven." The aspect of divinity we have been discussing, called *shekhinah* and dwelling in the world, is referred to as the "name" of God. The transcendent aspect, YHWH, is sometimes called "heaven," because of its brightness. This is "in the *name* of *heaven*"—to unify these two aspects. So Abram is to go "for your own benefit, for your own good"—how could God ask him to be concerned with such selfish things? Surely he would do the will of God without that! God was rather teaching him how to serve Him: even when you do something for yourself, for your own profit or good, in that too you should be going toward God. *All* your deeds should be in the name of heaven.

VIII

In the Talmudic tractate *Soṭah:* Rava taught: "Because Abraham said: 'I will not take a thread or a shoe-strap'[1] (Gen. 14:23), his offspring were rewarded with two commandments, the thread of the *zizit* [ritual fringes on a garment] and the straps of *tefillin* [phylacteries, attached with leather straps]. Surely *tefillin* are a reward, as Scripture says: 'All the nations of the earth shall see that the name of the Lord is

---

3. We see here how our author's interpretive skill has completely transformed an earlier tradition. The rabbis' rather stern ascetic pronouncement, that all speech other than words of Torah should best be avoided, is here reread to mean that *all* of a person's speech, regarding any matter, may be uplifted and seen as Torah.

1. From the king of Sodom, after helping him in battle. Abraham chose not to be indebted to the heathens.

called upon you and they shall fear you' (Deut. 28:10). Rabbi Eliezer the Great taught that this refers to the *tefillin* on the forehead. But what may be said of the *zizit*-thread [to indicate that it is a reward]? That which Rabbi Meir taught: 'Why is blue given this distinction[2] from among all other colors? Because blue is like the sea, the sea is like the sky, and the sky is like the Throne of Glory. Thus Scripture says: "They saw the God of Israel, and under His feet was the like of a paved work of sapphire stone, as bright as the very heaven" (Exod. 24:9) and "Like the appearance of sapphire stone was the image of the Throne" (Ezek. 1:26).' "

To understand this we must begin with the verse "The heavens are My Throne and earth My footstool" (Isa. 66:1). Any place where God is present may be considered His throne or chariot. Surely this applies to the upper hosts of heaven, since even "the whole *earth* is filled with His glory." The heavens, being spiritual, are not separated from Him[3] and have desire only in the spiritual realm. God's intent in creating man, however, was that he too be a throne for the dwelling of holiness. It would bring Him greater joy that even in the lower world, where His essence cannot be conceived, divinity should nonetheless be revealed. This is why Israel were given the Torah: so that they should attain the rung of the patriarchs, who were a vehicle for God. We their children are to follow in their footsteps, drawing the light of *eyn sof* itself into us, making ourselves into thrones for the blessed God as He dwells in our hearts through our unceasing attachment to Him.

Should it happen, God forbid, that some sin cause a person to be cut off from his root in the Life of Life ("For there is no man in the earth so righteous that he does good and never sins" [Eccles. 7:20], true and wholehearted penitence will still allow him to return to that root. He may yet again be a throne for God, cleaving to Him and drawing that endless light into his heart. But compared to the heavens above, which remain His throne constantly, our rung even at its best may only be considered that of footstool. RaSHI interpreted this to be a "small seat," meaning that we are in *qatnut*, the lesser state.

This is the meaning of "Return, O Israel, to the Lord your God" (Hos. 14:2). By means of this return you will merit that the Lord become *your* God. God will concentrate His divinity so as to dwell in

---

2. *Zizit* originally contained a thread of blue. Cf. Num. 15:38.
3. As is matter.

your heart, and you will become his lower throne or "footstool." This too is a form of intense attachment to God. This is the meaning of "Great is the return, for it reaches unto the divine throne." If a person is cut off from his own root, the return to God is so great that it allows him once again to become God's throne.

Now it is known that the commandment of *zizit* is sometimes considered as precious as all the other commandments put together, since it constantly reminds one of God. When you look at the fringes at the four corners you are reminded of the One whose glory fills all the earth. Scripture also says: "You shall see it and remember all the commandments of the Lord" (Num. 15:39). This is an assurance: it is within the power of the *zizit* to remind a person that there is an infinite Creator and that "the whole earth is filled with His glory," that in all the four directions there is no place devoid of Him. All this is because *zizit* are explicitly called "a reminder" in the Torah. He who merits will understand how this is true in an inward way. Through this commandment a person may be reminded of God and come to return to Him, being a throne for His glory. *Zizit* is related to the word for "peering" (*meziz*) as in "He peers through the lattice" (Cant. 2:9): it is a matter of looking. It is this act of looking that brings one to repent, to restore the infinite light upon one. This was the case with the one called "Nathan of the *zuzita*," for he was grabbed by the *zizit* of his head and brought to repentance. It was *seeing* that gave him the hold to reach repentance. It was the same with that one who sent four hundred coins to the prostitute but repented when he saw his *zizit*. Finally, they said, the beds she had once set out for him in a forbidden way she set out for him permissibly.[4] We know that any illicit love a person feels has to be brought back to the good, that one must begin to love God with that very arousal one had felt improperly. Thus evil becomes a throne for the good. This is the meaning of the "beds" or "couches" in this story: By that very love in which evil had dwelt he was able to turn to God and become a seat for His presence; the forbidden couches now became permitted ones. All this because of *zizit*.

We know, however, that a person must proceed slowly, step after step. It is not right to seek to raise everything up all at once. Thus Scripture says: "You shall not go up by steps upon My altar" (Exod.

---

4. I.e., she became his wife. This well-known Midrashic tale is often quoted to show the moral power of the commandments.

20:23).[5] The steps have to be gradual ones, like proceeding to like, but no two stages identical. First, looking at the *ẓiẓit*, one reaches the state of "sea," as in "the sea of wisdom." You bring your own mind into that great sea; from there you can ascend to "sky" and thence to "the throne of glory." This is the meaning of "It is not in heaven . . . but very close to you; it is within your mouth and heart to do it" (Deut. 30:14). This means that anyone can reach these levels of "sea" and "sky," for they are close. This is only true, of course, if it is "within your mouth and heart"—your study and prayer must be with heart and mouth united, not divided against one another. Thought and word must be joined. Understand this.

Thus we see that the commandment of *ẓiẓit* was indeed a great gift to Israel. Without it they would not reach repentance, which comes about through an act of looking.

Sources: *Lekh Lekha*

I

He and I cannot dwell	Sotah 5a
Know where you come from	Avot 3:1

II

Abraham is the soul	Zohar 1:80b
The greater a person is	Sukkah 52a

IV

The Midrash notes	Tanhuma Lekh Lekha 4
Here (in Haran) you will not merit	RaSHI to Gen. 12:1
It first occurred in His thought	Pesikta Rabbati 167a
The holy Zohar says	Zohar 1:4a (Tanhuma Bereshit 2)
A person is obligated to recite	Berakhot 54a
Suffering purges a person's sins	Yoma 86a
A single hour of peace	Avot 4:17
Honi the Circle-Maker	Ta'anit 23a
Might we mention them all	Pesahim 117b

---

5. The verse may also be read: "You shall not go up in ascents," meaning here that it is wrong to ascend too hastily.

THE LIGHT OF THE EYES

V
The act of hospitality is greater	Shabbat 127a
He who burns with untoward lust	Bereshit Rabbah 51:9
Kept learning the Torah and forgetting	Nedarim 38a
All that is in heaven and earth	Zohar 1:31a
Thus the Tiqquney Zohar says	Tiq. 157b
The horse is second to the rider	Tiqquney Zohar 134a
For this reason the Talmud tells us	Ketubot 62b
If he merits, she helps	Yebamot 63a
Abraham observed the whole Torah	Yoma 28b
Since he was three years old	Nedarim 32a
Greater is he who is commanded	Baba Qama 38a
Even the master of the house	Sotah 35a

VI
The House of David comes	Bereshit Rabbah 50:10

VII
What should a person do	Hullin 89a
Malicious speech or gossip	Arakhin 15b
He who speaks in an idle manner	Yoma 19b
May all your deeds be	Avot 2:12

VIII
Rava taught: Because Abraham said	Sotah 17a
Great is the return	Yoma 86a
Nathan of Zuzita	Shabbat 56b

WA-YERA
Genesis 18:1–22:24

INTRODUCTION. The section *wa-yera* continues with the portrayal of Abraham as the ideal Jew or as a representation of all his descendants. The opening teaching sees Abraham as Everyman, using the fact that his name does not appear in the reading's opening verse as an indicator to that effect. Every one of Israel, as he sits at the "opening" of his inner "tent," that in him which is open to repentance, meets Abraham, Isaac, and Jacob—the three men/angels—who will lead him to the good.

In much of Jewish mystical literature there is a flirtation with a desire to transform the patriarchs into divine or angelic beings. At very least they are the ideal manifestations of divinity as it exists in human form. The rabbinic Abraham, "for whose sake the world was created," and who already in early sources tends close to divinity, is now the human embodiment of God's love, but also a dwelling place on earth for divine wisdom, the original creative force from which all else is derived. The second teaching in our section follows that Kabbalistic literary tradition; Abraham here is clearly the symbolic manifestation of *ḥokhmah* in the world.

An important aspect of Abraham's spiritual attainments, according to a great many of the later Jewish teachers, was his observance of the commandments even before they were given. The Talmudic sources insist that he knew—and presumably had discovered on his own—all of rabbinic legislation in addition to the written Torah itself. In this there undoubtedly lay a polemical opposition to the Pauline Abraham, the man of faith without the law. Jewish spiritual literature frequently sought to comment in one way or another on the

131

nature of Abraham's relation to the commandments. Our second teaching here depicts him as *hokhmah*, learning the whole Torah as a single point before it devolved into words and letters. The fourth teaching, however, shows another aspect of Abraham: the one who fulfilled the *mizwot* in an ideal way. A close reading of this teaching will present one of the richest portrayals available of the life of the commandments as a spiritual path.

The sixth homily in *Wa-Yera* turns aside a bit from the portrayal of Abraham and deals with the issues of sin and repentance. It was of the very essence of Hasidic teaching to believe that *teshuvah*, the return to God, is always possible, and that there is no one in whom the light of God is so dim that it cannot be rekindled. This is the essential task of the *zaddiq*, here depicted as uplifter of souls and helper in repentance, showing especially by example how the divine presence can be found in all that is. This *zaddiq* is also represented in the Abraham who, as we discover elsewhere in our section, sits at the very gate of Hell, waiting with infinite patience to redeem his children.

I

THE LORD APPEARED TO HIM AT THE TERE-BINTHS OF MAMRE, AS HE SAT NEAR THE TENT-OPENING IN THE HEAT OF THE DAY. HE RAISED UP HIS EYES AND SAW: BEHOLD THERE WERE THREE MEN ... HE RAN FROM THE TENT-OPEN-ING TO GREET THEM, AND HE BOWED TO THE EARTH.

The holy Zohar asks who these three were, and answers that they were Abraham himself, Isaac, and Jacob.

The holy Torah, being eternal, must apply to each person and to every time. The truth is that the Creator, blessed be He, is to be found within every Jew, even the most wicked or the greatest sinner. This is witnessed by the thoughts of repenting that come to the sinner each day. This is God Himself appearing to that person. When he follows those thoughts, lifting up his mind, he then begins to think: "When will my deeds reach those of my ancestors!" It is our ancestors, the patriarchs, who are the chariot of God. Of this chariot the author of the *Tiqqunim* said: "Horse is second to rider, not rider to horse." The horse has to go wherever the rider leads him, whether to a river or even to some unpleasant place. It is the will of the rider that guides him. A person who has become a chariot for God's great name goes only where God wants; he does the bidding only of God, not of the will for evil.

This is the meaning of THE LORD APPEARED TO HIM and not "to Abraham": God appears to every one of Israel. AT THE TEREBINTHS OF MAMRE: the word *elon* (terebinth) may also mean "strength" (*'elon/'alam*), and the word Mamre may be related to "rebel" (*mamreh*). Even in the strength of one's rebellion against God, even in the most wicked person, God appears. Thoughts of penitence come to him. HE SAT NEAR THE TENT-OPENING: an opening is given to the one who seeks repentance. THE HEAT OF THE DAY: In the flame of his desire to return. HE RAISED UP HIS EYES: He directed his mind upward. BEHOLD THERE WERE THREE MEN: Abraham, Isaac, and Jacob. He then sees the rung of his forefathers, that they were a chariot for the great name of God. When he sees this HE runs TO GREET THEM saying, "When will my deeds equal theirs!" He too longs to become a chariot for God, going only where His will takes him. FROM THE TENT-OPENING: he gets to all this from that opening which was made for him. Then HE BOWED TO THE EARTH: bowing is an act of drawing forth; he draws something forth into his earthliness. Understand this.

II

"Abraham our Father fulfilled the entire Torah before it was given."

Torah comes from divine *ḥokhmah* and *ḥokhmah* is called a point. In *ḥokhmah* the entire Torah is contained or garbed in a single point. That is why such Torah is "hidden from the eyes of all living and even from the birds of heaven" (Job 28:21), for it is all within a single point. Therefore Scripture says "saying," as in "God spoke all these words saying" (Exod. 19:25). The rabbis taught that He said the entire Torah in a single word; He "said" the entire Torah as it is in that single point of *ḥokmah*, the *yod* of His name YHWH.

But who can grasp the Torah as it is there, all in a single word? That was why Israel said to Moses: "You speak to us and we shall listen" (Exod. 20:16). Let this Torah come down further into *da'at*, represented by Moses. Therefore "Moses spoke and God answered him with a voice"[1] (Exod. 19:19): It now descended further, to the level where it was vocalized, a rung represented by the *vav* of God's name. Torah goes from *ḥokhmah* to *binah* and thence into voice; only then can Israel apprehend it.

Abraham our father, however, was a chariot for that upper level, for the point that is *yod* of the name. He grasped it as it exists in a single point. It is for this reason that Scripture says THE LORD APPEARED TO HIM, without mentioning Abraham's name. As a chariot for *ḥokhmah*, Abraham was "hidden from the eyes of all living." He had reached so hidden and transcendent a state that he could not be called by name. Scripture points to this in "These are the generations of heaven and earth as they were created" (Gen. 2:4), in which *Be-HiBaR'aM* may also be read *Be-'aBRaHaM*: he was the very existence of the world, serving as a lower vehicle for *ḥokhmah* above. "You have made them all in wisdom" (Ps. 104:24). "The Lord by wisdom has established the earth" (Prov. 3:19). Wisdom (= *ḥokhmah*) is the life of all the worlds. The preceding words in the Genesis passage, *Toledot Ha-shamayim Veha-areẓ* ("the generations of heaven and earth") may be read as an acronym for *tohu*, chaos. Before Abraham came along the world was one of chaos and confusion; the generation of the flood, of Babel, and the rest. When the rabbis said: "The world exists for six thousand years, two thousand of chaos, two thousand of Torah, and two thousand of messianic times," RaSHI commented "the two thousand of Torah begin with Abraham."

We are told that Abraham had a daughter whose name was *ba-kol* ("in all"). The law is that a daughter inherits a tenth of her father's property. This world in which we live is the tenth, that of *malkhut*, the letter *heh* of God's name. The same *Be-HiBaR'aM* is also read *Be-Heh BeRa'aM*, meaning that this world was created through the letter *heh*. "The Lord by wisdom has established the earth" then indicates that the father brought forth the daugher; *ḥokhmah* is the father in whom all creatures originate. Abraham was a vehicle for that aspect

---

1. The Kabbalistic background of this paragraph is as follows: Torah begins in *ḥokhmah*, where it is a single point, in no way differentiated from the being/nonbeing that is God. This Torah cannot be attained by mortals; it presents itself only as mystery. In order to reach this world, the Torah must pass through *da'at*, Moses, who also represents a synthesis of *ḥokhmah* with *binah*, understanding. Moses then draws Torah further into *tif'eret*, the rung below his own, which is that of voice. Only as it passes through Moses does the Torah receive its voice; only as such can Israel attain to it.

of divinity; therefore it is said that he had a daughter named "in all."
In all things did he serve the Lord![2]

III

It is difficult to understand how Abraham permitted himself to establish a covenant with Mamre the Canaanite. If Abraham was observing the whole Torah, why did he not follow "You shall make no
covenant with them" (Deut. 7:2)? Yet Scripture says of Mamre and
the others: "They were Abraham's covenant-partners" (Gen. 14:13).

The point is that Abraham saw that his descendants would never
be able to inherit the land as God had promised unless they entered
the covenant of circumcision. This is proven by its converse: When
they abandoned that covenant they were exiled from the Holy Land.[1]
Abraham had to circumcise himself and accept this form of covenant.
This is the meaning of "They were Abraham's covenant-partners":
They caused Abraham to accept this covenant, for he saw that without it his offspring would not be able to inherit their land. Thus too
RaSHI says on AT THE TEREBINTHS OF MAMRE that Mamre
counseled Abraham to perform the circumcision. Could it be that
Abraham, who fulfilled the entire Torah, had to ask Mamre to advise
him on such a matter? The answer here is the same: His encounter
with Mamre convinced him to circumcise himself, so that his descendants might inherit their land.

IV

In the Tractate *Shabbat:* "Rabbi Judah said in the name of Rav: 'The
welcoming of guests is greater than greeting the *shekhinah,'* for Scrip-

---

2. *Hokhmah*, the first *sefirah* by Hasidic count, is referred to as the "primal father";
this aspect of divinity is father to the lower rungs, to *tif'eret* as "son" and *malkhut* as
"daughter." It is they who in turn beget those souls that come into the lower world.
Abraham, father of all Israel, was the embodiment of *hokhmah* (through *hesed*) in the
lower world. As such, he and his daughter were parallel to *hokhmah* and *shekhinah*
above. Note how the final line, however, mitigates the radicalism of such a teaching,
and gives it instead a devotional focus.

1. The reference is apparently to the hiding of circumcision in Hellenistic times,
to which the author means to attribute the destruction of the second Temple and the
later dispersion.

ture says 'PASS NOT AWAY, I PRAY YOU, FROM YOUR SERVANT' (Gen. 18:3). Said Rabbi Eleazar: 'Note that the ways of God are not those of man. Among people, a lesser person could not say to a greater one "Wait until I come to you," but Abraham was able to say that to God.' "

We must understand this verse that says PASS NOT AWAY. How could this be said with regard to the presence of God, since the whole earth is filled with His glory and there is no place devoid of Him? How then could one possibly say PASS NOT AWAY, as though to assume that afterwards that place would not contain his glory? This is simply impossible. We must also understand how Rav's claim that making guests welcome is greater than greeting the *shekhinah* can be proven from this passage. Might we not say that in the performing of that commandment one also evokes the presence of the *shekhinah?* Commandment, after all, is called *mizwah* because it joins together (*mizwah/zawta*) the part of God that dwells within the person with the infinite God beyond. It may be, then, that the *mizwah* is not really greater than greeting the *shekhinah*, but rather that it too contains the *shekhinah*, and in fulfilling it one has both [commandment and presence]. We also have to understand Rabbi Eleazar's point here, that the lesser does not ask the greater one to wait, and yet Abraham did so.[1] Could we not say that there too, in the greeting of guests, there was a receiving of the *shekhinah?* This is especially so since the righteous are called "the face of the *shekhinah*" in the Zohar, as His presence dwells in them. When Abraham received the guests, that is, the angels who appeared to him in human form, surely that in itself was an act of greeting the *shekhinah*.

The truth is, however, that the real fulfilling of *any* commandment lies in the greeting of the *shekhinah*, in becoming attached to God or joined together. Thus the rabbis said: "The reward of a *mizwah* is a *mizwah*," meaning that the commandment is rewarded by the nearness to God that the one who performs it feels, the joy of spirit that lies within the deed. This indeed is a "greeting of the *shekhinah*,"

---

1. The awkwardness of persons in the text of Gen. 18:1–3 leads the rabbis to so interpret it that Abraham is speaking with God when they are interrupted by the three angelic visitors. Abraham asks God, who is paying him a sick call as he recuperates from circumcision, to wait for him until the guests have been properly welcomed.

and without it the commandment is empty and lifeless, the body-shell of a *mizwah* without any soul. Only when it is done with the longing of the divine part within to be connected to its root, along with the divine part of all the rest of Israel, can it be called a *mizwah*. In all service of God, whether in speech or in deed, both body and soul are needed to give it life. That is why the wicked are called dead within their own lifetime: their deeds are without life.

This is what really happened to our father Abraham. He was engaged in discourse with God ("greeting the *shekhinah*"), as we learn from the verse THE LORD APPEARED TO HIM. When he saw the guests coming, he asked of God that there too, while he was to be engaged in welcoming the guests, PASS NOT AWAY, I PRAY YOU, FROM YOUR SERVANT. There too may I remain attached to You, so that this not be an empty *mizwah*. Be with me so that I may perform the *mizwah* in such a state that it too be a "greeting of the *shekhinah*."

Now Rav's point that the welcoming of guests is greater than greeting the *shekhinah* is proved by Abraham's action. Were this not the case, Abraham would hardly have left off a conversation with God to go do something of less certain value. This is especially true since "they appeared to him as Arab nomads"; they did not have a divine appearance. The *mizwah* itself was very great even if it were not a "greeting of the *shekhinah*." Abraham decided to fulfill this commandment with absolute wholeness. Therefore he said: DO NOT PASS AWAY, I PRAY YOU, FROM YOUR SERVANT.

Now we also understand the point being made by Rabbi Eleazar. Indeed among people the lesser person cannot ask the greater to wait for him while he attends to some other matter. The greater one will not be present in that other place; if he is here he cannot be there! But of God it is said: "The whole earth is filled with His glory!" He asks that God not depart from him; "there too may I not be cut off from my attachment to You." He could say this only because wherever one goes he does not go away from God. He is there as He is here; Abraham only asked that he not be cut off from Him.[2] Understand this.

---

2. Even though God is everywhere, man may often *feel* himself to be cut off from God's presence. This seems to be the subject of Abraham's request.

V

THE LORD APPEARED TO HIM ... IN THE HEAT OF THE DAY.

The rabbis say that Abraham our Father is seated at the entrance to Hell, in order to save the wicked. He recognizes the Jews when he sees their circumcision—except for those who have illicit relations with non-Jewish women. Their foreskins are pulled back over them and Abraham cannot discover who they are.

All that our father Abraham did was for the sake of drawing near the wicked; his desire was to bring them too under the wings of the *shekhinah*, to raise up fallen souls from among the nations. We have explained this already, in connection with the verse "the souls they had made in Haran" (Gen. 12:5), translated by Onkelos as "the souls they had brought to the service of Torah." He did this through his own involvement with the Torah of God; by this means were the fallen souls among the nations drawn to him to be converted and uplifted. He then brought them into his covenant of circumcision, a covenant that is best guarded, as we have already learned, by the one who circumcises his heart as well as his flesh.

Abraham has not changed his ways; as he did then, so he does even now. He sits at the gate of Hell, raising up those souls that have fallen away from their root and plummeted downward. As long as they have at least kept the covenant and not brought the *'orlah*[1] over them, they can still be saved by him. He does this to fulfill his Creator's will, for God Himself takes great joy in seeing these holy souls raised up.

This is the meaning of THE LORD APPEARED TO HIM: God appeared even in THE TEREBINTHS OF MAMRE. The word *'elon* may refer to the wicked, as in *'aloney ha-bashan* (literally "the oaks of Bashan"; Isa. 2:13). *Mamre* indicates that they *rebel* against the glory of God. There too God appeared to him. He saw that even there one could find something of divinity, doing God's will by uplifting them from their fall. Thus HE SAT NEAR THE TENT-OPENING IN THE HEAT OF THE DAY. This refers to Hell, of which it has been said: "Behold a *day* comes that burns like an oven" (Mal. 3:19).

---

1. Literally "foreskin" as above, but also having the meaning here of "evil forces," parallel in usage to *qelipah*, "shell."

RaSHI said of Mamre that it was he who counseled Abraham concerning circumcision. This too may be interpreted in our way: Mamre refers to rebellion; in the sinner's very rebellion against God Abraham saw a way to serve Him, doing God's bidding by raising him up. He saw this because he was sitting NEAR THE TENT-ENTRANCE, at the gate of Hell. This was the "counsel": it was the rebellion of the wicked against God that gave Abraham the idea of serving Him there too, bringing great joy to God as His will is done.[2] All of this is "concerning circumcision," here better to be read as "because of circumcision." Abraham uplifted those who had maintained the covenant and not covered themselves with 'orlah, since "the whole earth is filled with His glory," even the lowest realms. Whatever a person sees in the world can lead him to cleave to God, even the rebellion of the wicked. . . . But none of this can happen in one who has so disfigured his circumcision that no sign of holiness can any longer be found in him.

Learn from this how a person should turn his eyes and his heart to do the will of his Creator, even in the lowest matters. Thus will we merit both this world and the next. Amen Selah unto eternity. May this be His will.

VI

THE LORD APPEARED TO HIM.

It is known that the word "Torah" means "teaching," and that it is so called because it teaches one the path. We must then find a way, in each story of the Torah and in every word, to take some counsel for our path in God's service. Of course we can never fully understand the Torah's secrets before messiah comes (speedily and in our day!); only of that time it has been said, "Earth will be filled with the knowledge of the Lord" (Isa. 11:9). Nevertheless, we may still interpret it in a multiplicity of ways.[1] Indeed we are obliged to seek out those hints in the Torah that might help us in the life of service.

---

2. The point is that the *zaddiq* must follow Abraham's example, associating with the wicked and seeking to raise them up, rather than isolating himself from them.

1. Literally "according to *PaRDeS*," the classic fourfold interpretation of Scripture.

THE LIGHT OF THE EYES

Now since the world was created "in the beginning," which has been interpreted to mean both "for the sake of Torah" and "for the sake of Israel," it is clear that Torah and Israel were made never to be separated from one another; Israel is ever to cling to the Torah. And if any single person of Israel cuts himself off from the Torah, it is up to the righteous in his generation to bring him back. It is they who "bring the precious out of the vile" (Jer. 15:19), the vile being the forces of evil in which the one who follows his own desires gets caught; he becomes "vile and gluttonous" (Deut. 21:20).

Of the *zaddiq* who succeeds in drawing the wicked near again Scripture says: "If you bring the precious out of the vile, you shall be as My mouth" (Jer. 15:19). This means that just as I created heaven and earth by the word of My mouth ("By the word of the Lord were the heavens made"—Ps. 33:6), so will you by the words of your mouth bring forth a new heaven and a new earth. Of this Scripture says: "As the new heavens and the new earth which I make shall remain before me" (Isa. 66:22). The Zohar notes that this verse does not say "which I have made" but rather "which I make," showing that God is forever making them, in the present. Now even though the *zaddiq* makes them, God says "I make." The *zaddiq* does his work together with God; they become one, as it were, to the point where God may be considered the Maker. All this happens when the *zaddiq* brings forth some new Torah "from the vile." . . .

In order to understand how this operates, we begin with a series of verses from Scripture:

> Go my children, listen to me; I will teach you the fear of the
> Lord.
> Who is the man who desires life, loving days and seeing
> good?
> Guard your tongue from evil and your lips from speaking
> guile.
> Turn from evil and do good; seek peace and pursue it. (Ps.
> 34:12–15)

Why does this sequence begin with "Go"? Why not "Listen to me, my children" or the like? And similarly may various other questions be raised.

The Talmud teaches that "if one betroths a woman on the condition that he be a righteous person and he turns out to be wicked—that woman is nevertheless betrothed." This is so, the Talmud adds "because he may have had a thought of repentance." This would make it appear that as soon as a person has such a thought he is called "righteous." But that seems impossible, for we know that there is no sinner in the world who does not have such thoughts every day. The Talmud itself elsewhere teaches that "every day a voice goes forth from Mount Horeb, saying 'Return, O backsliding children!'" This voice gives rise to thoughts of penitence, for "even if he does not see, his 'star' sees."[2] The soul hears the sound of the voice and begins to contemplate repentance, even among the wicked. This is well known to the rabbis. Do they then mean to tell us that there are no wicked in the world?

The truth is, however, that for the wicked such thoughts alone do not suffice. If a person takes a candle into a place of especially heavy darkness, like a room beneath the ground, the candle will go out as soon as he enters. This is because the darkness is so very thick and concentrated there. So is the wicked one sunk deeply into his *qelipot*, dwelling in darkness for a very long time; his darkness too has become very heavy. The inner bits of holiness have fled him, because "man and snake cannot live in a single cage." The thought of repentance departs as quickly as it comes, and nothing is done about it. "The candle of the wicked flickers" (Prov. 13:9). Such a one has to break through that darkness by means of fasting and mortifications in order to attain repentance.

In this sense the Talmud taught: "Three books are opened on the New Year. The wholly righteous are immediately inscribed and sealed for life; the wholly wicked are immediately inscribed and sealed for death. Those in the middle hang in the balance until the Day of Atonement." How can the righteous be inscribed "immediately"? It is as we have said above—for them a thought of repentance suffices, since they walk in God's way and serve Him always. Even if such a person has done an evil thing, he is so surrounded by holiness that as soon as he stumbles the light of desire for repentance will put him back on the course. He has not fallen into deep darkness as has the wicked; it is of him that the Talmud speaks [in the matter of the betrothal]. The phrase "he turns out to be wicked" then means "if some bit of evil is found in him." The book into which the righteous

---

2. "Star" (*mazal*) here refers to unconscious processes within the self.

are inscribed on the New Year is the book of those righteous ones for whom a penitential thought will suffice. Those written immediately "for death" refers to those who cannot be inscribed for life "immediately"—for whom the thought alone does not suffice, but who must first purify their flesh.

But who can bring the wicked to a desire for such purification? Scripture says of this, "All your children shall be taught of the Lord" (Isa. 54:13); God teaches every person how to return to Him. God has so humbled Himself, even down into the lowest rung, that it truly may be said, "His kingdom rules over all" (Ps. 103:19). His kingdom flows forth everywhere, even into the *qelipot*. "You shall be unto Me a kingdom of priests" (Exod. 19:6) means that Israel are to proclaim His kingship wherever they are; on whatever level he finds himself, there should a Jew attach himself to God. Even if he falls into the very *qelipot*, even there the *zaddiq* should hold fast to his path. "The righteous one falls seven times and arises" (Prov. 24:16). And King Solomon also said: "There is a vanity that happens upon the earth: there are righteous men who get that which is in accord with the deeds of the wicked, and so are there wicked who receive as should the righteous" (Eccles. 8:14).

The *zaddiq* who falls into a place of darkness is like the emissary of the king who has gone forth to conquer a distant land so that it too will be called by his king's name. When that *zaddiq* falls, surely he must hold fast to his way and arouse in himself the attachment to God. When he does so, all the wicked who have fallen into that same place will rise up with him, especially so if they are of the same soul-root as the *zaddiq*. As he raises himself up, he holds tightly on to them as well. He is able to hold them because he and they are related through the *mizwot* that the wicked have performed. "Even the emptiest among you are as filled with *mizwot* as is the pomegranate with seeds!" Even if the *mizwot* have been done emptily, they are still "your temples are like a pomegranate split open" (Cant. 4:3—*RaQaH*, "temple"/*ReyQ*, "empty").[3] Because they are *mizwot* the *zaddiq* stands in relation to them, so that even when he falls to the very depths, he

---

3. The image of the open pomegranate, well known in Midrashic sources, is one of richness and fullness. Even the sinners of Israel are as lush and full with *mizwot* as the pomegranate is with seeds.

may bring the kingdom of God there with him.[4] This may happen only when the wicked do not oppose the *zaddiq* and continue to believe in his righteousness. They then become "the wicked who receive as should the righteous." This happens because of the *zaddiq's* fall.

Due to our many sins, however, "sin crouches at the entrance" (Gen. 4:7); right at that entrance to the body which should be the place where holiness comes in (the holiness of "I shall dwell within them"—Exod. 25:8)—at that very place, the mouth, a person may also become defiled. Lies, slander, tale-bearing, gossip, all prevent holiness from entering the one who speaks them. In the end he winds up speaking ill also "of God and of His anointed" (Ps. 2:2), saying all kinds of slanderous things about the *zaddiq*. As a person is, so does he see others. The *zaddiq*, in whom there shines the light of God, sees no evil; true goodness so dwells within him that wherever he turns he sees only good. The wicked one too sees only his own quality, and there is no *zaddiq* in whom some drop of it cannot be found. "There is no man so righteous on earth that he does good and sins not" (Eccles. 7:20). Sin indicates a lack in the person; the wicked one sees it and begins saying this and that about it, finally including lies as well. Such a one cannot be raised up by that *zaddiq*, since he has kept himself so very far away. This also lessens the sinner's chance of separating himself from transgression when the opportunity again comes his way.

The Talmud tells of a prayer that said: "May the fear of heaven be upon you like the fear of flesh and blood." The Ba'al Shem Tov interpreted the prayer in this way. When a person sins he says, "I hope no one sees me!" A person who wants to sin will hide himself in hidden chambers, to the point where he begins to imagine that people are watching him and he becomes frightened. Now we know that "there is no place devoid of Him" and the life of the Creator is everywhere. "His kingdom rules everywhere," even among the evil forces. Without His presence nothing would exist at all; even in sin itself there is, as it were, the life-flow of the Creator. The wicked one denies that life and casts it away. Understand this. The fear that comes

---

4. The passage is obscure, perhaps intentionally so, on the matter of who it is that falls and who brings the kingdom of God. The mention of the *mizwot* performed by the wicked serves to prevent the conclusion that it might be the *zaddiq's* own fall or sin that brings him into relation with the wicked.

on him as he sins really is the fear of heaven, so reduced as to come down to his place in order to arouse him to leave evil behind and not to sin. This is the life that dwells within the transgression. The wicked one takes that holy spark and draws it down into the place of evil; he finds in it no help in leaving his sin. This is because the covenant of the mouth and the covenant of the flesh are tied to one another. He who has violated the covenant of language will also sin with regard to the flesh. Those sinners who speak ill of the *zaddiqim* and so defile their mouths will surely wind up violating the other covenant as well.

This is also the meaning of "He looks in through the windows; he peers between the lattices" (Cant. 2:9). The subline fear so reduces itself in order to awaken the sinner that he actually thinks there is someone peering in the windows or between the cracks and looking at him! This makes him fall into terrible inner darkness; darkness becomes so heavy and concentrated within him that there is no chance for the holy light to penetrate it.

Thus it is said, "He who guards his mouth and tongue keeps himself from trouble" (Prov. 21:23). "From trouble" (*Mi-ZaRot*) here can also be read as "strait" (*MeYZaR*), referring to that narrowed concentration of inner darkness which results from such sin. Or it can be as we first translated it, for such troubles can destroy one, as in "You have consumed us by means of our iniquities" (Isa. 64:6).

The sages taught: "Great is repentance, for it makes even willfull sins become as though merits." Now we are able to understand this. There is, as we have said, good in everything, even in sin. It was only the one who had defiled the covenant of speech who did not want to see this good. When he repents, however, setting aright that which had been wrong in him, the good he had formerly pushed aside is able to come forth. Whole regret for his former deeds reestablishes that good; sin is then separated from it and falls away. The main thing is to keep these two covenants, that of the mouth and that of the flesh, as Scripture says: "If not my covenant with day and night" (Jer. 33:25). He who keeps this dual covenant is called *zaddiq*.

Now we understand "Go my children, listen to me": "Go" means that wherever you go, even if you turn away from me and want to sin, "I will teach you the fear of the Lord." That fear will reduce itself and be with you, as we have said. Or else it may come to you through that *zaddiq* who enters the place of *qelipot*, as in "Who is the man who desires life, loving days and seeing good." He is the one who sees the good in every place, separating both himself and that

144

good from the evil there. How does one do this? "Guard your tongue from evil" in the first place. But even if you did not do so, and found yourself violating the covenant and therefore unable to see any good for a while, you may still "turn from evil and do good." "Do" here means that you actively restore that good as you turn from your sin and acknowledge your regret. Then you may "seek peace and pursue it." Our rabbis said: "Seek peace here and pursue it elsewhere." "Peace" (*shalom*) here may also mean "wholeness"; it is now the wholeness of God that you are to pursue, seeking that His kingdom spread forth over all being, even over the place of sin. Make Him King even there. Destroy no longer, but raise up that good to its source above.

And so THE LORD APPEARED TO HIM IN THE TERE-BINTHS OF MAMRE: The Zohar teaches that Abraham is the soul. God appears to the soul even in the strength of rebellion, as we have taught earlier. But then why is the person to whom He appears not transformed at once? Because *HE* WAS SEATED AT THE TENT-ENTRANCE: this refers to the evil urge, who seats himself at the mouth, the entrance to our bodies, defiling our speech and not allowing the holiness of God to enter. AT THE HEAT OF THE DAY: He gets his victim hot and excited to sin. The main thing is therefore to guard one's mouth and tongue. For one who does, it will go well in this world and the next.

VII

In the Talmudic tractate *Baba Mezi'a:* "Rabbi Yose asked why the three consonants *'YV* of *'elav* in the verse 'And they said *to him:* "Where is Sarah your wife!" ' (Gen. 18:9) are marked by special dots in the text. He answered: The Torah here teaches proper manners, that a person should ask after his hostess." RaSHI in commenting on this passage in the Bible is still more explicit, saying that you should ask the host about his wife or the hostess about her husband, since this verse indicates that they also asked Sarah where Abraham was (*'YV* = *'ayo,* "where is he?"). But Scripture in its plain meaning does not seem to indicate this at all.

The truth is that they only asked Abraham where Sarah was, as Scripture says. Their intent was that by seeing Sarah they would have revealed to them the rung of Abraham. A man represents the

145

hidden world, as is known,[1] while a woman represents the revealed world. The entire quality of man, whether for good or evil, is visible in his wife, his parallel "revealed world." All of her husband's deeds flow into her and are revealed through her to the one who has the sight of the mind's eye. He can see in her that man's rung and all of his deeds.

Now it is known that the angels do not attain a rung as high as that of the great *zaddiqim*. The rabbis have said that "the righteous are greater than the ministering angels and their place is more inward than that of the angels." This means that they are on a higher rung. Therefore the angels could not apprehend the quality of Abraham except by seeing Sarah. In this way they could come to know Abraham, "the hidden world." This is what was meant by "they also asked Sarah where Abraham was"—their reason for asking after Sarah was that through her they might come to know him.

Blessed is the Lord forever. Amen. Amen.

Sources: *Wa-Yera*

I
The holy Zohar asks   Zohar 1:98a

II
Abraham our Father fulfilled   Yoma 28b
The entire Torah in a single word   Mekilta Yitro 4
Be-HiBaR'aM/Be-aBRaHaM   Tanhuma Bere-
                                            shit 2

Six thousand years   Sanhedrin 97a
Abraham had a daughter   cf. Baba Batra 16b

IV
The welcoming of guests   Shabbat 127a
The reward of a *mizwah* is a *mizwah* Avot 4
The wicked are called "dead"   Berakhot 18b
They appeared as Arab nomads   Sifre 'eqev 38

---

1. In Kabbalah, man is represented by *tif'eret*, higher and more hidden than the feminine *malkhut*.

WA-YERA

V
Abraham seated at the entrance to hell   'Eruvin 19a
RaSHI said of Mamre   RaSHI to Gen.
                                              18:1

VI
The new heavens   Zohar 1:5a
Every day a voice goes forth   cf. Avot 6:2; Jer.
                                              3:14
Three books on the New Year   Rosh Hashanah
                                              16b
May the fear of heaven be upon you   Berakhot 28b
Great is repentance   Yoma 86b
Abraham is the soul   Zohar 1:80b

VII
Rabbi Yose asked   Baba Mezia 87a
The righteous are greater   Sanhedrin 93a

ḤAYYEY SARAH
Genesis 23:1–25:18

INTRODUCTION. The reading opens with the death of Sarah, here interpreted immediately to represent the body, which must undergo a spiritual death in the life of Abraham, the soul.

Direct allegorical interpretation is rather unusual for the Hasidic preachers; usually they preferred the unique combination of Kabbalistic symbolism and fanciful homiletics that so characterizes most pages of this work. Here the author draws on an allegorical tradition that dates back to very early times: Abraham and Sarah as body and soul. Immediately, however, he turns it to a moralizing purpose that is typically Hasidic: Humility of spirit allows room for the presence of God in the self, bringing about the symbolic "death" of the body so that the soul might have true control over the mature human being. These same interpretations are then used in a much longer homily, one that combines them with some other by now familiar motifs of Creation through the Torah and the presence of God in all things. Especially noteworthy in this second homily is our author's negative attitude and at best grudging concession to medicine as practiced by the physician. The Hasidic masters served as folk healers, using elements of prayer, amulet, and herbal medicine to effect cures. They were wary of more "scientific" approaches to healing, both because they claimed to heal the body without reference to the ills of the soul (and does not illness come as punishment for sin?) and also because in many cases they represented the first signs of secularization or assimilation in the closed world of East European Jewry.

The second and larger part of this portion (beginning with number III) contains a series of homilies on Genesis 24:1, "Abraham was

old and had attained his days, and the Lord blessed Abraham in all."
This verse has a long history of esoteric interpretation among the rabbis, going back to a cryptic statement to the effect that "in all" was in
fact the name of a daughter born to Abraham in his old age. Beginning with the twelfth-century *Bahir*, mystical authors have sought in
this daughter some reference to the *shekhinah* or to divine wisdom.

Our author's interpretation of this verse takes us to yet another
realm of Kabbalistic lore. Certain portions of the *Zohar*, following on
an ancient tradition known as *shi'ur qomah*, ascribe to God a bodylike
form, and go to great lengths in detailed description of this manlike
figure. In this representation, which many Kabbalists took great
pains to insist was not literally intended, the "head" was taken to represent the highest divine realm, *arikh anpin* or the long-suffering and
endlessly merciful aspect of God. These mercies come down to the
lower world through the "beard" of this divine figure; it was because
of this association of the beard with the flow of mercy that Kabbalists
and *ḥasidim* were careful not to trim their beards, keeping them full as
a this-worldly symbol of the flow of divine compassion from above.
Because the words *ZaQeN* ("old") and *ZaQaN* ("beard") are identical
in their Hebrew consonants, and because the elder and the beard are
often thought of together with one another, comments on Genesis
24:1 will often refer to this tradition.

Discussion of God the merciful and long-suffering inevitably
calls to mind the thirteen attributes of divine mercy, listed in Exodus
34:6–7, taken by the rabbis to be the Bible's most essential revelation
of God's character. Since the earliest times their recitation has formed
the core of all liturgies of penitence in Judaism. These qualities are
now associated with the "beard" of God, so that they become "the
thirteen attributes of the beard" in the standard Kabbalistic formulation. In the final teaching of our section, these are in turn associated
with another thirteen as well, the thirteen hermeneutical rules by
which the Torah is to be interpreted. This association too has a long
history, and represents the mystics' attempt at spiritualization of even
the seemingly most prosaic of sources.

*   *   *

THE LIGHT OF THE EYES

I

THE LIFE OF SARAH WAS A HUNDRED YEARS AND SEVEN AND TWENTY.

It is known from the *Midrash ha-Ne'elam* that the body is called Sarah. It is so designated for its relation to the word *serarah*, rule, since it is in the nature of corporeal things to rule over others. The soul is there called "Abraham."

The rabbis have taught: "He who seeks to live must cause himself to die." It is in the nature of a person, from his very birth, to be drawn by passing vanities, through which he seeks to aggrandize and glorify himself. He who wants to draw the true life of God into him, that of which it is said: "I dwell with the low and humble of spirit" (Isa. 57:15), must first put to death his natural self, which has been with him since birth. He must become humble of spirit in his own eyes. The Talmud commented on "What does the Lord God ask of you" (Deut. 10:12): "read not *mah* (what) but rather *me'ah* (hundred)." Moses taught the people to hold fast to his own rung, that of "We are what" (Exod. 16:7). For this the Torah praises him, calling him the most humble of men. But even within humility there are various gradations, some of which are quite far from truth. This will be understood by anyone who has looked into the matter. Some people certainly appear to be humble, and yet God's promise is not fulfilled in them; they have not truly achieved humility. This is what is meant by *mah* and *me'ah*. *Mah* ("what") represents humility, but it must be of that sort that has the *aleph* added to it, as does the word *me'ah*. *Aleph* stands for the One; humility must have room to contain the One.[1]

Thus THE LIFE OF SARAH WAS. When is Sarah, the body, truly alive? A HUNDRED (*me'ah*): when it serves humbly in such a way that the *aleph* enters it. AND TWENTY: before the heavenly court one who is not yet twenty years old is not liable for punishment. A person does not reach full consciousness until he attains twenty years. Then, when that person serves God in truth, he also uplifts the years of his youth. This happens through that *mah* of humility. Thus Scripture says: "The measure of my days, what (*mah*) is it" (Ps. 39:5). Even his period of childhood, a time when he was surely

---

1. The last few lines are paraphrased for the sake of clarity.

fully engrossed in a lower state, may be raised up and redeemed by one who walks in the ways of God after he is twenty years of age. This is what King Solomon meant when he said: "Rejoice, O young man, in your youth ... but know that for all these things God will bring you into judgment" (Eccles. 11:9). When you reach the age of knowing, then you must set about making amends.

AND SEVEN AND TWENTY, THESE WERE THE YEARS OF THE LIFE OF SARAH. RaSHI comments: And all of them were equal in goodness. When a person reaches that level of *me'ah*, humility containing the presence of God, then even the years of childhood, the time of the seven-year-old, and of youth, the twenty, are uplifted. SARAH DIED: The physical self of the body must be put to death. IN KIRJATH ARBA: literally "the city of the four." This refers to the four-letter name of God, YHWH, praised be He. THAT IS HEBRON: "Hebron" is from *HBR*, to join together. Formerly the letters of God's name were separated, but now they have been drawn close. And then ABRAHAM CAME: The soul comes forth, for now it is strengthened and can lead the body, which it could not do previously. TO MOURN SARAH AND TO WEEP FOR HER. Once a person reaches maturity, he is mournful and regretful of his former deeds; he weeps over the folly of his youth until that too is raised up. Then he will fare well in this world and the world to come.

II

THE LIFE OF SARAH WAS ...

We begin with a teaching of the rabbis: "If a person has a headache, he should study Torah, for Scripture says of Torah's words: They are a chaplet of grace upon your head (Prov. 1:9). If his throat ails him, he should study Torah, for the verse continues: And a chain about your neck ... If his entire body is in pain, he should study Torah, for it says: Healing to all his body (Prov. 4:22)." In order to understand this we must first recall that "In the image of God He created man" (Gen. 9:6). RaSHI comments on this: "In the form that had been prepared for him, the very image and likeness of his Creator." But the Creator has no depictable form—He is endless and beyond conception! Creation, however, was for the sake of Torah and Israel, as the rabbis have explained around the word *bereshit*.[1] The word *elohim*, the designation for God in that same first verse of Genesis, refers to a contraction. Since God is endless, the creation of the world had to involve a contraction of the light, so that He might enter the lower worlds. God remains infinite and the worlds cannot contain Him, but since He desired their creation He so contracted Himself, as it were, that they could bear to contain Him. It is in this aspect that He is called *elohim*. The real nature of this *zimzum*, however, involves the Torah, since it was into the letters of the Torah that God contracted Himself. It was then through the letters that the world was created: Thus are God and Torah one. The Torah is His very self, through which He created the world. That Torah contains two hundred forty-eight positive commandments and three hundred sixty-five prohibitions; these are called the *shi'ur qomah*[2] of the Creator. The Torah is a complete form, and man has been created through Torah and in its own likeness, with two hundred forty-eight limbs, three hundred sixty-five sinews, each limb corresponding to its own commandment in the Torah. Understand this matter, of which we have spoken several times.

Creation took place in this way so that man might draw forth the flow of perfect life from the Torah, which served as artisan for man's creation.[3] When he fulfills the Torah with all its commandments, both positive and negative, letting not a single one slip away, life flows from each commandment into its parallel limb or sinew in him. Even though we cannot fulfill all of the commandments in deed, we certainly can do so in word. Thus have the rabbis said: "Whoever studies the teachings concerning the burnt-offering, it is as though he had offered it." The same is true of all the other commandments; as long as the person himself is prepared to fulfill them and it is not he who holds back the deed, then the spoken word concerning that *miz-*

---

1. See above, bereshit 5.
2. Literally "measured form"; the supposed huge bodily likeness of God, based on an ancient tradition of mystical speculations related to the depictions of God in the allegorical understanding of the Song of Songs.
3. This discussion is based on the opening homily of *Bereshit Rabbah*, a play on the various meanings of *amon/oman*. From the context below it is clear that our author understands the role of Torah as that of artisan or creator rather than that of passive plan or blueprint. This is possible only because he has already identified Torah completely with God; thus is the classic "demiurge" problem of this passage here avoided.

wah is itself taken as a deed. All of the above is true in reverse as well: If one causes a certain commandment to be lacking from the "bodily" form of the Creator, the sinner will suffer a corresponding lack of the life-flow into that very limb of his own; both soul and body will be damaged, and he will suffer illness in that limb, Heaven forfend. If such a person has no awareness, he will call in a doctor to heal him. The truth is, however, that he ought better to return to his Maker, the Torah. A person knows instinctively how to examine his deeds and seek out the nature of his sins. He is like a vessel, carefully fashioned by some wise craftsman. If anything happens to that vessel, it must be brought back to its original maker; no one else will know what is wrong with it. The same is true here: you must go back to the one who formed you in order to regain the light of Torah, containing the infinite light of *Eyn Sof* contracted within it. Then you will need no physical doctor, and healing may reach you in just a moment. You will be whole in all sorts of ways: in body, in possessions, and in family. All the ill that had happened was only for the sake of this restoration. Therefore the rabbis said of the one who turns away from Torah: "The crooked cannot be set aright" (Eccles. 1:16). This too is the meaning of "You shall be whole with the Lord your God" (Deut. 18:13)—when are you whole? When you hold fast to the Lord and to His Torah. Then is He your God (*elohim*), as He has contracted Himself into the Torah. Then may you be whole in all ways, in body and in soul.

Of this the rabbis said: " 'He shall surely be healed' (Exod. 21:19)—from here is derived the authority of the physician to heal." Might you have thought that one is not to practice healing? Yes, in truth a person should do as we have said, and not seek healing for the body alone. But since he lacks awareness and has thus placed his faith in such healings, and God has no desire that this person die, therefore has the physician been authorized as a healer. The truth remains, however, that of the Scripture: "If you will truly hearken . . . all the illness which I placed in Egypt I shall not place upon you, for I am the Lord your healer" (Exod. 15:26). The rabbis commented: "I shall not place it upon you. But if I should do so, then I am also 'the Lord your healer.' " This matter has been discussed by the MaHaRSHA, who was concerned that the Torah never mentions the question of undeserved illness. He claimed, however, that such cases too are really a part of "I shall *not* place," since God is ever present and both Torah and repentance preceded the Creation itself.[4] Even if I do cause illness, it is as though I had not, since the healing preceded the world into existence. This is also the reason why, in specific cases as well, God always creates the healing before He inflicts the blow.

It is known that the Torah is composed of twenty-seven letters. Twenty-two of these represent complete mercy, while the five doubled letters[5] stand for divine rigor; it is from these that the forces of judgment arise. One who cleaves to *Eyn Sof* by means of the Torah includes these five letters within the twenty-two merciful ones. The Torah cancels out one of the two forms, and those judging forces are uplifted. Now no one can reach this rung of attachment to God and His Torah except through humility; only then "do I dwell with the lowly and humble of spirit" (Isa. 57:15). Then the heart may become a dwelling-place for God, and nothing will be lacking in that palace of the King; such a person will be whole in every way. We have taught something similar on the verse "What does the Lord God ask of you?" (Deut. 10:12). This level of "what," another name for humility, asks of you that you fear the Lord. When you have no humility you have no such fear, for it is humility that brings about the fear of God. When a person is not humble, "He and I cannot dwell in a single enclosure." Then he will have no fear of God, since God is not present to him. When God dwells within a person, however, then His fear falls upon him; the great King both stands before him and dwells within him! For this reason that word *mah* ("what") is interpreted to read *me'ah* ("hundred"): the aleph is added, because it is through humility that the One comes to dwell with a person.[6]

Now this is THE LIFE OF SARAH WAS A HUNDRED YEARS. Sarah represents the body, as the Zohar has taught. When does the body have true life? When it is *me'ah:* When it is so humble that the One is joined to it. AND SEVEN AND TWENTY: When all the twenty-seven are "equal for goodness," when the five doubled letters are counted within the twenty-two. YEARS: These are the rungs, for each letter is a separate rung, and then all of them are of

---

4. Our author is paraphrasing the comment of Rabbi Samuel Edels (1555–1631), who claimed that since the power of healing is present in God even before illness occurs, the temporary presence of illness in the righteous is no violation of the Torah's assurance.

5. *Mem, Nun, Zade, Peh, Kaph*, the letters having a separate form when occuring at the end of a word.

6. See the preceding homily.

equal goodness. All of this comes about because SARAH DIED, bodily desires must be put to death, IN KIRJATH ARBA, where the four (*arba'*) letters of God's name are joined together, THAT IS HEBRON, which means "joining." Afterwards it says ABRAHAM CAME, for then does one gain a soul TO MOURN FOR SARAH, remorseful over the past.[7] Understand this.

Thus Scripture said, "It shall be health to your navel" (Prov. 3:8) (*sarekha/Sarah*). It is known that negative and judging forces exist because of the breaking. Before this world was created, God built other worlds and broke them apart. The intent of this was that there exist paths of both good and evil; had there been no breakage, there would be no evil. God wanted there to be a choice between good and evil; that is why the breaking took place. It is known, however, that this happened only from the "navel" downward. This is why that heretic said: "His upper half is called Ormuzd, while His lower half is Ahriman."[8] His intent was to indicate a separation, God forbid. The true way is rather to bring together good and evil, so that all may be good. This is the meaning of "health to your navel"—the uplifting of those forces. Thus Scripture further says, "I was His nursling" (Prov. 8:30), read by the rabbis as "His artisan" (*amon/oman*). The verb of that verse may also indicate future: "I shall be" or "I am ever" His artisan. It is always this way: Torah is the artisan, repairing all the damage done in this world.

We have explained something similar in connection with that story of Rabbi Eleazar ben Simeon, who once saw a particularly ugly man coming toward him. (The ugliness here referred to was that of his soul, which he had seriously defiled, since he was a great sinner.) The rabbi castigated him for his ugliness, to which he replied: "Go to the artisan who made me!"[9] The point is that the wicked should not

---

7. Humility leads to the presence of God within the self, including a new awareness that had previously been lacking. The newly aware soul will then feel remorse for its earlier way of living.

8. The author has here combined a notion of sixteenth-century Kabbalah with a Talmudic reference—perhaps fourth century—to Persian dualism, unwittingly indicating a parallel between them. Lurianic Kabbalah claims that the breaking of the vessels took place only in the lower half of the sefirotic configuration. When depicted in the *shi'ur qomah* form, it may be said that only those *sefirot* from the navel downward were broken. The heretic (in the Talmud text he is called a "magus") reads this as dualism, contrary to the proper devotional intent of the Kabbalist, who seeks to reunify the broken universe.

9. The original Talmudic story refers to physical ugliness, and the rabbi is told to address his complaint to the ugly man's Maker.

be brought to the public eye, but rather back to their Maker—in repentance. Here too we learn to hold fast to Torah. See also what we have said about this elsewhere.

The rule that all of this teaches is as follows: *There is nothing besides Him; He is the core of every thing.* When a person believes this with perfect faith he will need no other help; everything else will be set aright of its own accord. Of greatest importance [for this healing] is the prayer of the needy one, the prayer most acceptable to God. Our sages tell us that the prayer of the sick person is better received than the prayers of others for him. This is true despite the Talmud's tale of Rabbi Yohanan ... [who was able to cure others by holding their hands but could not cure himself]. The Talmud there adds that "a prisoner cannot release himself from his place of bondage." The intent there however is that the words "Give me your hand" and "He gave him his hand" contain acronyms, each of which forms one of the seventy-two names of God.[10] It was by means of this name that Moses brought up the casket of Joseph, as is known.[11] This name is particularly useful for raising things up. If, however, "the righteous are greater in their deaths than in their lifetimes," why did Joseph not come forth on his own? It is because this kind of immediate result through the use of a holy name can only be brought about by another. That is why the Talmudic story pointed to this name; it was by means of this name that Rabbi Yohanan had the sick man rise up from his illness. It is to this situation that "a prisoner cannot release himself ..." applies: The name may only be manipulated by the help of others. God, as it were, concentrates Himself in that name, so that the sick one be raised up. All this happens through the *zaddiq* who is tied to Him; he becomes one with Him, as it were. Thus have we interpreted the [Talmudic passage in which God asks:] "Who rules over Me? The *zaddiq*." It is because the *zaddiq* is so fully bound to God that he may reach the Hidden World, that place where there are no negative forces but only simple mercies. He brings up the negative judg-

---

10. The seventy-two names, or more properly the seventy-two letter name, refers to an ancient esoteric reading of Exodus 14:19–21, in which the first letter of each word is counted thrice, reading first forward, then backward, then again forward. Each of these letters in turn implies an entire name. The resulting seventy-two letters and the verses connected with them were widely used in both mystical and magical ways.

11. One of the miracles of the Exodus, according to the rabbis, was the discovery of Joseph's casket, which had been sunk deeply into the Nile. Moses had to find it in order to fulfill the promise made to Joseph in Genesis 50:25.

ments with him and "sweetens" them in their source. This is the meaning of "I decree but the *zaddiq* nullifies it": The "I" of God refers only to the lower Revealed World. It is only there that the decree and judgment exist. God in the hidden world is called "He"; He nullifies the decrees,[12] as has been said. Understand this.

III

ABRAHAM WAS OLD. (Gen. 24:1)

Our sages said: Until Abraham there was no old age. When people could not distinguish between him and Isaac, Abraham himself came forth and prayed for old age.

This passage has already been explained to show that what Abraham was calling for here were the thirteen attributes, the qualities of the "beard."[1] But now we too shall speak of it, for we have something new to add. It is known that the world was created so that God be known, in order that His attributes be revealed. Were it not for Creation, over what could He be called "merciful and gracious, long-suffering and full of compassion"? That was why He needed to create the world: so that He have an object for His mercies.

The same is true of all the rest of the divine qualities; they could not exist without some arousal from below. Of this Scripture says: "No plant of the field was yet in the earth, and there was no man to till the soil" (Gen. 2:5). RaSHI comments: There was as yet no human who could appreciate the benefits of rainfall. When Adam came along and realized that the rains were needed by the world, he prayed for them and they came forth.[2] Nothing is possible without some arousal

---

12. What we have here is a daring mystical transformation, through the figure of the *zaddiq*, of an ancient magical tradition. The *zaddiq* can effect healing because he is one with God; bound at once to heaven and earth, he can bring healing from above to the one for whom he prays. The God to whom he is attached, however, is that of the Hidden World (*HaBaD*), in which there is not yet any negativity. The *zaddiq* nullifies the decree because he has attained to greater heights than the aspect of God out of which the decree emerged. Mystic and sorcerer are here quite indistinguishable as the *zaddiq* himself comes to be identified with the "He" of God.

1. See introduction to this section.

2. Note the subtle shift from "object" of divine compassion to that of "arouser" of the divine qualities. The Kabbalist is not content to remain the passive recipient of divine love, but seeks an active role in bringing it into the world.

from below. When we walk in His path, being merciful and compassionate as He is, we draw forth His desire to rule the world according to these same qualities.

For this reason the world remained in a state of chaos until the time of Abraham. The generations of the flood, of Babel, and of Sodom offered Him no one to whom He might reveal His attributes. They did not deserve them, for they offered no "arousal from below." The world remained in a state of chaos, as is known. Therefore Scripture speaks of "the generations of heaven and earth" (Gen. 2:4), the first letters of which form an acronym for *tohu*, "chaos." These words are followed in the text by *be-HiBaRe'M*, "when they were created," the literal equivalent of *be-'aBRaHaM*. When Abraham came into the world and walked in God's ways, offering loving-kindness to all His creatures, then was a desire aroused in God to conduct His world according to the thirteen attributes. Of this the sages said: "You shall walk in His ways" (Deut. 28:6)—just as He is merciful and compassionate, so shall you be, and so forth.[3]

All this is well and good with regard to all the latter attributes. But what shall be said of the first, for the attributes say: "A *God* merciful and compassionate." How can one "walk in His ways" in this attribute of *'El*, "God"?[4] The answer is that this attribute contains within it all the others. With whatever attribute God conducts the world, be it mercy or rigor or any other quality, we recognize His divinity in it. We must not say: "The world just goes on; it is only an accident." This is the first attribute: God, the recognition that all is His blessed divinity.

This is the meaning of "people could not distinguish between Abraham and Isaac." God conducts the world in both ways: with the Love of Abraham and the Fear of Isaac. People were not capable of realizing that both were the same God. This was the case until Abraham taught them, as our sages recall: "After [Abraham's guests] ate and drank, he would say to them: 'Praise the One of whose food you

---

3. Our author is claiming that the Talmudic rabbis intended *imitatio Dei* as he does, that by acting in a Godlike manner one calls forth the parallel quality from above. It is not clear that this is the intent of the Talmudic passages.

4. Man can be merciful and compassionate, but surely man cannot be God.

have eaten. Do you think it is of mine you have eaten? It is rather of God's, the One who spoke and created the world.' " Understand this.

IV

AND THE LORD BLESSED ABRAHAM IN ALL. (Gen. 24:1)

The Midrash asks by what merit Abraham was so fully blessed, and responds "for tithing." And of the tithe Scripture has said: "I will surely open the floodgates of the sky for you and pour down boundless blessing" (Mal. 3:10).

There are various channels through which divine blessing flows, from source to successive recipient, until it reaches the human world below. When people on earth conduct themselves improperly they cause those channels to be stopped up. Through such conduct a person brings himself to the place of judgment; the forces of judgment stand in accusation and do not permit God's bounty to flow into that person. This is called the closing of the channels. The act of tithing has the power to neutralize these judging forces, sweetening them in order that they too may agree to the flow of blessing.

To understand why this is so we must recall that "as a person measures out, so is it measured out to him." If one here below acts in accord with a certain quality, that same quality is aroused above. If a person acts mercifully in this world, mercy is called forth from above; it is in that way that the forces of judgment are transformed. The opposite, God forbid, happens in the same way. Thus by giving the tithe, which is a form of charity, divine mercy is aroused at the same time from above. So must a person, through all these qualities, approach the good and liken himself to his Creator. "Just as He is merciful, so you be merciful."

Now of Abraham it is written ABRAHAM WAS OLD AND HAD ATTAINED HIS DAYS. The verse seems to be repetitious. "Old," however, refers to those thirteen qualities of the elder or the "beard." He fulfilled all thirteen qualities of those upper "days," using every one of them to draw himself nearer to that ultimate divine good in which there is no judgment at all. This is why it is asked how Abraham merited such fullness of blessing; the merit here represents a triumph over those forces of judgment . . . since surely "there is no man in the earth who is so righteous as to do good and not sin" (Eccles. 7:20). But Abraham was blessed by God along with His retinue.[1] This means that the forces of judgment agreed to Abraham's blessing. But would there not have been some negative force holding back on the blessing? No, by merit of the tithing, for Scripture has said: "Abraham gave him a tithe from all" (Gen. 14:20).[2] By this he so uplifted the forces of judgment that they too agreed that his blessing be complete.

V

ABRAHAM WAS OLD AND HAD ATTAINED HIS DAYS, AND THE LORD BLESSED ABRAHAM IN ALL.

The following difference of opinion is recorded in the Talmud: One says this means that Abraham had a daughter whose name was *ba-kol* ("in all"), while the other says that he had no daughter. RaSHI brings still another opinion, to the effect that *ba-kol* is numerically equivalent to the word *ben* ("son").

To understand the meaning of this debate we must first recall the verse "Your name shall no longer be called Abram; your name shall be Abraham, for I declare you the father of many nations" (Gen. 17:5). On this the rabbis say: "I now add the letter *heh* to your name. Abram could not father children, but Abraham shall."

All the worlds were created through the letters of the Torah, as Scripture tells: "I was His artisan" (Prov. 8:30). This means that God concentrated His presence in the letters, reducing the intensity of light in accord with that which the worlds would be able to bear. This flow of divine life began with the letter *aleph*, the Torah of the

---

1. Lit.: "and His court"; the rabbis depict God as a judge, surrounded by the angelic personnel of His courtroom. Should not the accusing angel then have held out against Abraham's blessing? But, based on an exegetical principle derived elsewhere, Scripture seems to indicate that this blessing was also given by all of the divine court. This could happen only because Abraham's goodness in giving the tithe was sufficient to cancel those judgments that surely stood against him.

2. The homily plays on the relationship between *ba-kol* ("in all") of our verse and *mi-kol* ("from all") in 14:20.

highest emanated world. The light in this world was too bright for the lower worlds to receive, however, for this was the brightness of God Himself.[1] God therefore went on further, reducing His light along with the *aleph* into the letter *bet*, the letter with which the Torah opens. *Bet* [bayit = "house"] means concentration, as is known, for this was the letter through which He first so reduced His light that it could be received by the worlds. Afterwards He went on to reduce it still further, taking *aleph* and *bet* along into *gimel*. And so the process went, from letter along to letter. The closer one is to *aleph*, the brighter the light, the higher and more refined the spiritual sensitivity. Finally the chain of letters reaches down to *taw*, the lowest of the rungs and the point of final choice between good and evil. *Taw* [indicating the future tense] can mean "you shall live" or "you shall die." The conduct of all the world, from *taw* up until *bet*, has been placed in the hands of Israel. They are to bring all the rungs back up to *aleph*, to God, the single one and the cosmic *aleph*, uniting everything with Him. In this way they bring forth divine life and bounty, into all the worlds and on all His creatures.

This is the secret of that speech [the sacred tongue, Hebrew] that has been given to Israel; the twenty-two letters of the Torah are firmly fixed in the mouth of every one of them. The word for "speech" (*DiBBuR*) may also refer to "conduct" or "leading"; Israel are to lead all the worlds and unite them to the one. Just as all of them were created by the divine word, so are they to be conducted by sacred speech. One who attains the rung of sacred speech, whose talk is pure and holy,[2] can bring divine blessing and life into all the worlds. This aspect of Israel's life is called *bat*, "daughter," for it encompasses the letters from *bet* to *tav*, into which God has concentrated Himself in all the worlds. The task has now been given to Israel.

Abraham our Father so served God with love that he came to be called "Abraham My Lover" (Isa. 41:8). God gave over to him the con-

---

1. The World of Emanation, the highest of the Kabbalistic universes, is in no way separate from God. Note that our author is about to retell the Lurianic tale of *zimzum* or the reduction of divine light without any reference to "breakage" or to cosmic cataclysm. The Gnostic myth has been tamed in Hasidism.

2. Sacred speech then has a moral component; what is proposed is not simply a magical usage of the Hebrew language. When one realizes that in fact the author and his generation virtually *never* spoke in Hebrew, but rather in "profane" Yiddish, it becomes clear that "holy speech" here in large part uses Hebrew as a metaphor for purity of speech.

duct of all the worlds, placing within him this speech, centered in the five openings of the mouth.[3] This is the meaning of God's adding the *heh* [= five] to Abraham's name; it was through this that he became "father of many nations," father and leader of the great host of the world's peoples, by means of these five openings of the mouth. Now this is ABRAHAM WAS OLD AND HAD ATTAINED HIS DAYS, AND THE LORD BLESSED ABRAHAM IN ALL: By attainment of the upper "days," which are the highest qualities, he merited to have speech given to him for the conduct of the worlds. This was his *bat* [written *bet taw*]: all the worlds created by the concentration of divinity from the letter *bet* down to the letter *taw*.

There are, however, three things that bring a person's sin to the fore, and one of them is concentration in prayer. This refers to the person who thinks of himself during prayer that he has reached some high rung of attainment. You should rather ever be moving from rung to rung, at all times adding to your humility as well. That is why Moses our teacher, who was on a higher rung than all of Israel, is referred to as "more humble than any person on the face of the earth" (Num. 12:13). This is why one of the Talmudic masters says that Abraham did not have a daughter. Of course there can ultimately be no difference between the sages; this one means to say that Abraham considered himself as one who had no *bat*, as one who had not yet attained such a rung, as he says of himself: "I am dust and ashes" (Gen. 18:27). It was because of this that he in fact merited to have that *bat*. As for the view quoted by RaSHI, that *ba-kol* numerically hints rather at a *ben*, a son, it may be similarly explained. *Ben* is related to the word for building, *BiNyan*. Scripture tells us of Lamech, the father of Noah, that "he fathered a son" (*ben;* Gen. 5:28). RaSHI himself there asks why the word *ben* is in this case added,[4] and he responds that it was "from him that the world was built up." Here too *ba-kol* refers to *ben* because the world is built up and led forward by Abraham, through the *heh* that has been added to him, the five parts of speech. This is *ba-kol*, "in all": His leadership is to be in all the worlds.

---

3. "The five openings of the mouth" refers to an early Hebrew tradition of linguistic categorization ("dentals", "labials", etc.). This system is first presented in *Sefer Yezirah*, and has very frequently been given one or another esoteric interpretation.

4. In all the previous "begats" the text merely says: "Jared begat Enoch"; "Methusaleh begat Lamech," etc., while here the text first says "a son" and then adds that he was called Noah.

That was why Abram did not father children; until he had reached the point at which speech was given to him, he could not yet be a father. Abraham did father children, for those openings of the mouth by which he conducted all the worlds had now been given him. Surely through that word he could draw forth offspring for himself as well.[5] Blessed is the Lord forever. Amen. Amen.

VI

ABRAHAM WAS OLD AND HAD ATTAINED HIS DAYS.

In the Midrash: "Rabbi Judah bar Ilai opened with the verse: 'Bless the Lord, O my soul; O Lord my God You are very great; You are clothed in glory and majesty' (Ps. 104:1). You were made majestic and glorified at Sinai when Israel said: 'We shall do and we shall listen.' Another interpretation: You glorified Abraham with the glory of old age, as Scripture says: ABRAHAM WAS OLD AND HAD AT-TAINED HIS DAYS."

To understand this we must recall that until Abraham there was no old age. It was he who prayed and brought it forth.

We know that there are thirteen attributes of God, sometimes called the thirteen qualities of the beard (or "the elder"). These are "The Lord! The Lord! God merciful and compassionate . . ." (Exod. 34:6). They are the glory and majesty of God, just as (though different in a thousand, even in infinite, ways!) in a human man the beard is considered the glory of his face. In a spiritual sense that is utterly to be distinguished from the corporeal parallel, these thirteen attributes of God's "beard" are His glory and greatness, by means of which He conducts the affairs of His worlds and creatures. Man is a microcosm, embodying in his physical form the likeness of that spiritual form above. The image of these upper qualities has been stamped into the Jewish person as they have come down, link after link in the chain, from above. By this likeness he is able to glorify and make great the

---

5. The surprising final line makes it clear that Abraham's former sterility was a condition of the spirit. When he perfected himself as a lover of God, he was given a gift of verbal potency, the word that contained within it some of the divine power of creation through the word. Such potency cannot be separated from the potency needed to create in the bodily/genital realm as well.

name of God, by holding fast to the good that is in each of these qualities.

The fact is that each of these attributes, by the time it reaches the form it is to take in man, contains a mixture of good and evil. This must exist for the sake of free choice; "this parallel to that has God made" (Eccles. 7:14). As there is good in each of these qualities, so does each of them have an evil aspect, the *qelipah* form of this quality, as it is to be seen in idolators, containing no good at all. The Israelite has to cleave to the positive side of each attribute, through them cleaving to God Himself. This is the essence of our worship, as the rabbis have said concerning the verse "Cleave to Him" (Deut. 10:20)—"Is it possible to cleave to God? Is He not a consuming fire?" And they respond: "Cleave rather to His attributes. Just as He is merciful, so you be merciful," and so forth. These qualities should become firmly fixed in you; apply them always, until your entire conduct is in accord with the attributes of God.

[With regard to these attributes] the rabbis have said: "When Israel perform them before Me in this order, I shall forgive them."[1] The intent is not only that the thirteen principles be read, but that they actually be acted out in one's life. When a person holds fast to the good in these qualities, and defeats that evil which is there by virtue of human nature, he merits to have wisdom flow into him from above. He has, in fact, become attached to His Creator through living with those divine qualities.[2] The meaning of it is this: The Torah is interpreted according to thirteen principles; these are the same as the thirteen qualities of which we have spoken, for they are the very root of Torah. Once a person holds fast to these ways in his life, bringing such qualities forth from within his own self (for these qualities are to be seen in a person by his deeds: his compassion for others, his patience, his acts of kindness) into the world of deed, he has fulfilled the purpose for which they were brought down into the corporeal world of man. Then he deserves to receive from above the light of those same qualities as they are in their spiritual form, where they are identical with the thirteen principles by which the Torah is interpreted. All are one; they too are "The Lord! The Lord! God merciful . . ."

---

1. The Talmud refers to the *recitation* of the attributes in a prayer for forgiveness; the author takes "perform" (*'oseh*) in literal sense.

2. And it is therefore natural that God's wisdom flow into him, for he is no longer separated from God.

This is why the rabbis say on "You shall give glory to the old" (Lev. 19:32): "This refers to the one who has acquired wisdom"[3] It is the one who has acquired these divine qualities, bringing them into actual deed for the sake of heaven, and thus holding fast to his Creator—he is the one who is the true "elder," having acquired wisdom. In this way the light of the thirteen exegetical principles shines down on him from Wisdom above, and since Torah comes from *hokhmah* and God and Torah are one, [such a person] truly cleaves to God. . . . This is why God commanded that such an elder be glorified. Once he has acquired this degree of wisdom, he is in fact one with God, by means of these divine qualities, God's glory. Scripture adds: "And you shall fear the Lord" (Lev. 19:32)—this refers to the divinity concentrated in that person. For by those qualities and their performance it is God Himself, as it were, who is united with that person.

Now it is known that the human form, removed and corporealized as it may be, still contains the two hundred forty-eight limbs and the three hundred sixty-five sinews, parallel to the spiritual form above. The spiritual light becomes coarser as it descends through rung after rung, until in this world it appears in most coarse corporeal garb. It is still rooted in the divine light, however, and that is why in the human form man has a beard, the glory of his face. Therefore the holy books tell us not to pull out even a single hair of the beard, and the Torah itself commands us not to cut the beard's edges (Lev. 19:27). This is all because the beard points to those thirteen utterly spiritual qualities of the "beard" above. By the spreading forth of the divine qualities, garb after garb, rung after rung, they have come to be in this physical garb, as represented in the beard of the human body. The beards that idolators have, however, represent "this parallel to that," the negation of each of these qualities, the very opposite of their holiness. The divine chariot too has its parallel among the *qelipot.*

This, then, is the meaning of "O Lord my God, You are very great." Through these divine qualities that are God's "glory and majesty," the thirteen qualities of the "beard," "You are clothed," God is so garbed that He is finally impressed into the corporeal human body. Into man's soul are stamped those spiritual qualities by which he can cleave to God; it is in this way that "You are very great," Your name is exalted and glorified throughout the world. The Psalm goes on to

---

3. *ZaQeN* is taken as an acronym for *Zeh she-QaNah hokhmah.*

say: "You spread forth light like a garment," meaning that He clothes the sublime light. Understand this.

At Sinai Israel said: "We shall do and we shall listen." They said it this way as we have taught: No one can receive wisdom from above, or Torah, until he has first acquired those thirteen attributes by which Torah is to be interpreted, and these are the very same qualities as those of "The Lord! The Lord!" and the rest. These must be acquired by each for himself, and only by the deed performed in absolute truth. Afterwards one may attain to the light of spiritual wisdom, which comes from these same thirteen attributes above. For this reason Israel said "We shall do" and then "We shall listen." . . . That is why God answered, when Israel said this, "Who revealed to My children this secret that the ministering angels use?" For Scripture says: "Bless the Lord O His angels . . . who perform His word to hear the sound of His word" (Ps. 103:20). Now in truth the angels too receive from one another; this is their form of deed. They too act according to the divine qualities as they are garbed in them, according to their rung. They are loving and compassionate in receiving from one another, and so are all the other qualities found in them on their level, which is a lowly rung in comparison with that which is still higher. In this way they merit "to hear the sound of His word," coming to them from the thirteen spiritual qualities above them; this is their "hearing," as distinct from that which they have "done" first by way of preparation.[4] So it is with man: First he acts out the attributes in deed; afterwards he may be attuned to hear from the higher mind and wisdom. This is the receiving of the Torah, both collectively and individually, in the present, always, in each and every one.

This is why the Midrash began its comment on ABRAHAM WAS OLD: HE HAD ATTAINED TO HIS DAYS by quoting "Bless the Lord, O my soul . . . You are clothed in glory and majesty," saying that "You were glorified at Sinai when Israel said: 'We shall do and we shall listen.' " In truth it is all one: "You are clothed in glory and majesty" refers to the "clothing" of the divine glory, that is the glorious supernal "beard" with its thirteen attributes, in the deeds of humans through the imprinting of these attributes within them. It is by means of this that they attain to the giving of the Torah with its

---

4. To paraphrase: The angels too have a realm of "action"; this comes to the fore in their relationship with one another. The daily liturgy reads: "All of them receive the kingdom of heaven from one another, and they lovingly grant one another leave to sanctify their Creator."

thirteen qualities from the light above. This is why Israel said "We shall do" before "we shall listen": They wanted first to acquire those qualities in deed, and only then could they expect to hear the sound of the divine word . . . and this is also why the verse ABRAHAM WAS OLD: HE HAD ATTAINED HIS DAYS is used in this context: these qualities, in their positive form, are referred to as "days"; their negations are called "nights" or "darkness." The qualities are days because of their brilliance above.[5]

Now Abraham our Father was the first among the faithful. He referred to the Lord as "God of Heaven" (Gen. 24:7) and not of earth, because he said: "Previously He was only the God of heaven; the people of this world did not recognize Him. Only because I have gotten people to call on Him is He now the God of earth." His divinity was not made known in the world until Abraham; there was no one to draw forth the light of those qualities from above by embodying them in his deeds and thus to cleave to Him. The qualities were present only in their negative or broken state, and because there was no one to fulfill them on the level of deed, there could be no hearing of wisdom with its thirteen qualities of the "beard" from above. . . . This is the meaning of "Until Abraham there was no old age[6] in the physical form as well, since nothing was drawn forth from above to be thus embodied. Abraham prayed [literally "sought mercy"], that is, he performed these deeds of mercy, compassion, and all the rest, and then there was "old age." Then there was a flowing forth from the thirteen qualities of the "beard" above that became clothed in the corporeal as well, until "old age" appeared in this world too. . . .

This too is the meaning of AND THE LORD BLESSED ABRAHAM IN ALL. By coming into those upper "days," the thirteen attributes of the "beard," and drawing forth their light on him from above, Abraham was able to be blessed by "AND the Lord"—by the Lord and His entire court. Since he had brought forth that light which is also the secret essence of Torah, even the judging forces were sweetened and agreed to his blessing. He had defeated the evil

---

5. Both "days" and "qualities" (*yamim; middot*) are frequent Kabbalistic terms for the *sefirot*. Our author has labored hard *not* to portray either Abraham or Sinai in terms of journey through the sefirotic world; he is interested rather in transformations that take place while man remains in *this* world. Here, however, the earlier sefirotic locus of his sources peers through; ATTAINED HIS DAYS has frequently been interpreted in terms of voyage through the upper rungs.

6. Old age (*ZiQeNah*) = beard (Aram. *DiQeNa*). It is not clear at this point whether the author thinks of pre-Abraham humans as ageless or beardless.

that lies within those qualities for the sake of the good, as in "Turn from evil and do good" (Ps. 34:15). . . . Thus we have explained above: He who restores these qualities below merits to have the light of wisdom shine down on him from above. This means that he will know and understand even that of Torah which he has not learned from books; the light that shines down on him is that of *interpretation*, of the thirteen principles of exegesis. Such a one will teach well and act well, even in areas where he has not studied. The Mind above speaks through him.

This will help us to explain a statement of Rabbi Simeon: "Wherever the letters are mostly undotted, you interpret the letters; wherever most of the letters are dotted, you interpret the dots."[7] Divine wisdom, *hokhmah*, is represented by the letter *yod* of God's name, itself no more than a dot. So high and lofty is *hokhmah* that we can never fully grasp it; it is divinity itself. The *yod* has no fully drawn out form as do the other letters, but it is from the *yod* that all the letters come. No matter what letter it is that you want to write, you have to begin it with a point; only from there can the form of the letter emerge. So it is that from *hokhmah* above all the letters and all the qualities are drawn forth. When you begin to form a letter, beginning from that first point, the letter that you intend to write does not yet have any form that can be grasped. So in *hokhmah*, which is called *yod*, there is nothing yet that can be grasped. Only as the lower qualities spread forth from it can it be perceived that they in fact emerged from *hokhmah*.[8]

This is the meaning of "Wherever most of the letters are dotted"—the dot refers to *hokhmah* above, that shines down on a person. Where this shining is more than the letters, is beyond what he has learned in books, "you interpret the dots"—you interpret the Torah according to this dot of light from *hokhmah* above, even in matters that you have not learned from books.[9] All this comes about by prop-

---

7. The principle refers to a certain small number of words in Scripture that are traditionally written with dots over them (as distinct from vowel pointings), e.g., Gen. 18:9 (in connection with which the principle is stated) and 33:4. The dots indeed do indicate an ancient exegetical tradition.

8. Here the homily is more conventionally Kabbalistic: the *middot* are now the lower *sefirot* that emerge from their hidden sources in *hokhmah*. This section is not evenly joined to the earlier parts of this teaching.

9. The intellectual tradition is set aside in favor of the charismatic; the true teacher is the one who has the word of God in him as received from above. This charism, it is quickly added, may only be the result of righteous and compassionate living.

er living out of the qualities, by which one merits the thirteen qualities of Torah from above. But "where the letters are mostly undotted, you interpret the letters"—this person's Torah is mostly just what he learned in the books; he has just the slightest bit of that light of wisdom. "You interpret the letters"—all he has to teach is that which he has learned from the books; since he has not yet perfected the qualities in his life, he has not yet received the light that shines from their counterparts above.

May God grant that we be among those who do perfect those qualities, and may He cause the light of His sublime wisdom to shine down upon us.

Amen Selah unto eternity. Blessed is the Lord forever. Amen. Amen.

Sources: *Hayyey Sarah*

I

The body is called Sarah	Zohar 1:102a
He who seeks to live	Tamid 32a
The Talmud commented	Tanhuma Qorah 32

II

If a person has a headache	'Eruvin 54a
Whoever studies the teachings	Menahot 110a
The one who turns away from the Torah	Hagigah 9a
The authority of the physician	Baba Qama 85a
I shall not place	Sanhedrin 101a
That heretic said	Sanhedrin 39a
His artisan	Bereshit Rabbah 1:1
A particularly ugly man	Ta'anit 20b
Rabbi Yohanan	Berakhot 5b
The casket of Joseph	Zohar 2:46a
Who rules over Me?	Mo'ed Qatan 16b

III

There was no old age	Sanhedrin 107b
Walk in His ways	Sotah 14a
Abraham taught them	Bereshit Rabbah 54:6

THE LIGHT OF THE EYES

IV
The Midrash asks   Tanḥuma Ḥayyey Sarah 4
As a person measures out   Sotah 8b
Just as He is merciful   Sotah 4a
Along with His retinue   cf. Bereshit Rabbah 51:2

V
The following difference of opinion   Baba Batra 16b
Add the letter *heh*   Pesikta de-Rav Kahana 191a
Concentration in prayer   Berakhot 55a

VI
In the Midrash   Tanḥuma Ḥayyey Sarah 3
There was no old age   Sanhedrin 7b
When Israel perform   Rosh Hashanah 17b
The old who has acquired wisdom   Qiddushin 32b
Even a single hair   Shulhan 'Arukh   ha-Ari,
                                                  qevi'ut ha-torah 12

Who revealed to My children?   Shabbat 88a
Previously He was only God of heaven   Sifre Devarum 313
Wherever the letters are undotted   Bereshit Rabbah 48:15

TOLEDOT
Genesis 25:19–28:9

INTRODUCTION. Though the Biblical text of this section is concerned primarily with the tale of Jacob and Esau, we find that our homilist has not yet finished with Abraham and Isaac, and they remain central throughout the discussion here. This is partially a result of the attachment to opening lines; the section opens with "These are the generations of Isaac, son of Abraham." But it is also because Isaac, the most mysterious of the patriarchs, has not yet received his due.

Little of Isaac's character, or even of the events of his life, is directly revealed in Scripture. We see him as a youth on Mount Moriah and hardly meet him again until he is old and blind at the final blessing of his sons. Later interpreters, and particularly the Kabbalists, sought to compensate for this lack. Isaac, they claimed, represented the darker side of God, the force of divine judgment and rigorous demand, in contrast to his father Abraham, the symbol of mercy and compassion. Building on a much older rabbinic idea of God's having an Aspect of Mercy and an Aspect of Justice that sometimes seemed to contend with one another, the mystics constructed a dialectical theology around these two poles of the "Abraham" side of God, representing limitless love and compassion, and the "Isaac" side as its antithesis. They noted that the demonic (personified in Esau) was in fact a perversion of divine justice that emerged when rigor and demand were not tempered with compassion. They also saw, however, as does any parent, that the firmness of Isaac in fact embodied the greatest in divine compassion. These two forces were to be synthesized in Jacob, called "the choicest among the patriarchs," after the demonic forces were expunged through the birth and separation of Esau.

171

THE LIGHT OF THE EYES

Our section opens with a short teaching on the paradigmatic power of the patriarchs; it is they who show us the path that leads to the uplifting and transformation of evil, the central task of religious life. The greatest enemy, our preacher claims, is resignation, the sense that an evil or undesirable quality is a person's lot and that it cannot be changed. The belief in the possibility of change, growth, and ultimate transformation is essential to the Hasidic view of life.

This is followed by a long teaching on *zimzum*, here depicted as the containment of God's love. In order for love (Abraham) to act effectively in the world, it is in need of that restraint that will allow it to be properly channeled. This is brought about by Isaac, representing fear or awe in the inner life of the one who seeks God. Fear of heaven and awe before the majesty of God build the house in which love is to dwell; without them its energies cannot be properly preserved or communicated. All this is taught in the context of the tale of Sarah's laughter when she is told that she is to bear a child. No mocking is seen in her laughter here—it is rather a laugh or smile of pious joy and anticipation. Her questioning is read not as question but rather as marvel at the incredible wonders of God and the miracle that is about to take place in her loins.

The fifth teaching in this section is perhaps one of the clearest statements of the author's religious values in all of *The Light of the Eyes.* He comments on the wells dug by Isaac, long seen among the mystics as turnings to the inner wellsprings for the waters of Torah and the presence of God. He opens with a kind of ecstatic recital of the presence of God in all things. Soon he turns, however, to ask what is to be done in those moments and places where such feelings of awareness seem distant from the person. This is his real concern; when ecstasy is present, its own power will uplift and there is little that need be said. It is rather the uplifting of those burdens that keep us from feeling the presence that is his central task. Once again he speak of transformation, uplifting, and "sweetening" of both sin and feelings of guilt or judgment that keep the person from a life of intimacy with God. Again in the final teaching of the section he returns to this motif, here discussed in the context of Jacob's blessing and employing a particularly striking symbol of the wine that Jacob offers to his father in the moment when he seeks that blessing.

If Hasidism is to be depicted authentically, it must be understood within the context of oppression and persecution within which Polish and Ukrainian Jewry lived some two hundred years ago. Everything in contemporary experience—and of course there were exceptions—tended to confirm an old prejudice of the Kabbalists that did not accept the full humanity of the gentile world. Israel represented the forces of good in God's world, and there was no role left for the gentile, given the tendency of the Kabbalah toward a radical dualism, than that of agent for evil. This view of humanity forms the basis for the sixth teaching in this section, and it is against this background that it must be understood. The author struggles with the presence of light among the nations, as witnessed by the righteous proselytes who emerge from time to time and are joined to the community of Israel. He sees the task of Israel as one of seeking out such "fallen" sparks of light and of returning them to their source. He cannot, however, be expected to go beyond his times to see this light having a legitimate and independent existence *within* the gentile world; the best he can do is seek to redeem the light and then watch the nations fall, illusory as the demonic forces themselves will ultimately prove to be, as their source of life is lifted out of them.

*   *   *

I

AND THESE ARE THE GENERATIONS OF ISAAC, SON OF ABRAHAM. ABRAHAM BEGOT ISAAC.

RaSHI comments that the "generations" are Jacob and Esau, about whom this section is to speak. On ABRAHAM BEGOT ISAAC he says: "Because the cynics of that generation had said that Sarah was pregnant by Abimelech."

The Rabbis have a well-known principle: Wherever the text begins with the word "these (*eleh*), it seeks to begin a new matter, setting aside that which came before. Where it says: "And these" (*we-eleh*) it adds to that which has come before. Now how is that applicable to this section? The immediately preceding verses are about the generations of Ishmael. One would surely then expect to find here, "These are the generations of Isaac," setting them off from what had come before. We also seek to understand how this applies to every person, since both books and sages tell us that the entire Torah is bound to apply to all persons and to all times.

THE LIGHT OF THE EYES

It is known that "the patriarchs are the chariot." Since the son is just like a limb of his father, we too are considered as "feet" of the divine chariot; Scripture does speak of Israel as "six hundred thousand on *foot*" (Exod. 12:37). It is the father who "gives to his son beauty, wisdom, and strength." Our inheritance as God's servants and chosen ones from our holy forefathers is as follows. The Torah says: "You shall love the Lord your God" (Deut. 6:5). But how is it possible to love God, since we cannot even conceive Him? Abraham our Father gave us the quality of love as an inheritance, in order that we might be able to love God. Scripture also says: "You shall fear the Lord your God" (Deut. 6:13); this too seems to be impossible, but Isaac our Father left to us the quality of fear. The same is true of "Know the Lord your God and serve Him" (1 Chron. 28:9); this our father Jacob left to us, for it is known from the Kabbalah that Jacob represents knowledge (*da'at*). In this way we can, if we so desire, know the Lord.

The rabbis tell us that when God was about to give the Torah He went around to the children of Ishmael and asked them if they would receive it. They asked Him what was written in it, and when He mentioned "You shall not commit adultery" they said "We do not want it." He then went to the children of Esau, who asked a similar question. When He said: "You shall not murder" they too refused it.[1] This shows that there existed in Ishmael a fallen love, manifest in the form of incest. The secret of the "breaking" is well known, and we have explained it elsewhere at length: God created worlds and destroyed them, [some remaining portion of the destroyed world becoming the source of evil,] in order that there be free choice, reward and punishment. This is why the previous section of the Torah concludes, in speaking about Ishmael, "He fell upon all his brothers" (Gen. 25:18)—this refers to that fallen love.[2] This is not the lot of

---

1. The story is a part of the old rabbinic apologetic for the chosen people concept. The point is that other nations could have become God's chosen ones, but only Israel was willing to accept Him without condition. The details refer to the fact that the Arabs (Ishmael) did not observe the same marriage taboos as did the Jews and that the Romans (Esau; later the Christians) were seen as murderers without conscience. The tale exists in several versions.

2. See note 1. He reads the verse as attributing to the Ishmaelites misplaced sexuality in the context of familial love.

God's people, His portion Israel, for we have that knowledge of "Know the Lord your God and serve Him." We have to raise up our love to the Love above, as we have said elsewhere. This the Ba'al Shem Tov (his soul is among the hidden treasures of heaven!) said on the verse "If a man takes his sister, that is *ḥesed*" (Lev. 20:17): This refers to fallen love, and it has to be uplifted.[3] The same can be applied to all the qualities.

This is the secret of the *waw* in *we-eleh*, the AND that precedes the GENERATIONS OF ISAAC; the *waw* refers to that knowledge by which one lifts up those fallen qualities. Then indeed he "adds to that which has come before"—he has broadened the realm of the holy, bringing forth the holy sparks from the shells and raising them up. The wicked and the foolish say that they can do nothing about it; "What can I do? God has given me this bad love." These are in fact the "cynics of the generation" who said: "By *Avi Melekh* ("my Father the King") Sarah is pregnant. The body is Sarah, as the *Midrash ha-Ne'elam* tells us. They say that this evil love has come into the body from God Himself, like a fetus into the full belly. "What can we do?" But what did God answer [to quell the claims of the cynics]? He formed the features of Isaac's face to exactly resemble those of Abraham. In the moment when that bad love comes to you, you should be taken aback and tremble greatly before the Lord, as though you had received a slap in the face; then you begin to resemble Abraham.[4] Then you begin to make this love resemble the Love above, saying, "Is this not fallen from that higher Love, the quality of Abraham?"

The Jacob and Esau "about whom this section is to speak" exist in every person, for each contains a mixture of good and evil. The good is called Jacob and the evil Esau; RaSHI's intent in calling atten-

---

3. The word *ḥesed* in that context is usually translated "abomination." The Ba'al Shem refers to this usage in making his homiletic point. This interpretation is rather frequently quoted in the name of the Ba'al Shem Tov. It must have been one of his most daring and memorable aphorisms, and it goes to the very core of Hasidism's message as he taught it: *Everything*, even that which we most despise or fear, is a gift of God that can be uplifted.

4. This paraphrase seems to capture best the somewhat obscure intent of this line. He seems to be reading *qelaster* ("features") as *ki-li-setar* ("like slapping"); this is what gives one the sudden tremble that is essential to the transformation.

tion to them there is that the good must be separated from the evil in order to be uplifted. Understand this.

II

AND THESE ARE THE GENERATIONS OF ISAAC, SON OF ABRAHAM.

In the Midrash: "Rejoice greatly, O father of the righteous" (Prov. 23:24). When Isaac was born, joy was awakened in the world; heaven and earth and all the constellations rejoiced, as the prophet says: "Were it not for My covenant, day and night, I would not have set the bounds of heaven and earth" (Jer. 33:25). "Covenant" here refers to Isaac, as Scripture says: "I shall fulfill My covenant with Isaac" (Gen. 17:21).

To understand this Midrash, we must first go back to the verses of *Wa-Yera:* "Sarah laughed within herself, saying: 'Now that I am withered, am I to have pleasure—with my lord so old?' Then the Lord said to Abraham: 'Why did Sarah laugh . . . ? Is anything too wonderous for the Lord?' . . . Sarah denied it, saying: 'I did not laugh,' for she was frightened. He replied, 'But you did laugh' " (Gen. 18:12–15).

How can these verses be understood? They are seemingly very surprising—did Sarah not believe the announcement that she was to bear a child? What was this laughter? Sarah our Mother was a prophetess, one possessing the Holy Spirit. On the verse "All that Sarah your wife tells you, listen to her" (Gen. 21:12), the rabbis have said: "Listen to the Holy Spirit within her." From this they learned that Abraham was second to Sarah in the matter of prophecy. How then could she not have believed God's own announcement and assurances? And then her denial—was she denying it before God? We also have to understand what the rabbis said about this passage: They said that God changed the words of His report to Abraham for the sake of domestic peace. Though she had said "My lord is old," God reported her words as "I am old." But what was the conflict that required such peacemaking? Suppose Abraham had heard her speak the truth and say of him that he was old?

The secret of the matter is as follows. We have already said elsewhere on the verse "On the day when the Lord God made earth and

176

heaven" (Gen. 2:4) that God's first intent was to create the world through justice alone. When He saw that such a world could not survive, He brought forth the attribute of mercy and joined it to that of justice. The conclusion we have drawn there makes it clear that things had to be just this way: It had to first enter His mind to create with justice alone, and then mercy had to be added. The building of the world took place by means of love, as Scripture says: "The world is built by love" (Ps. 89:3). But people would not have been able to receive God's great love without something that would bring about *zimzum*, the reduction of love's intensity to the level where people could bear it. That was why the world was created in such a way, by the joining together of justice and mercy; justice brought about the reduction of mercy, so that it would not come forth in a strength beyond human power to absorb it. Otherwise the world would not have been built at all; were it not for *zimzum*, the intensity of divine love would have caused the world to pass out of existence. Thus the joining of justice to love was itself an act of love; it too made for the existence of the world, for without it love's act too could not have become real.... This is the sweetening of judgment and its inclusion within love, for the very sake of the world's existence. This reflected no change in the divine will; in fact it had to be this way. That is why *be-HiBaR'aM* (Gen. 2:4) contains the letters of Abraham, but in improper order. It shows just this: that the Creation was by a joining of direct light and refracted light. Abraham, with the letters properly written, represents the direct light; the jumbling of the letters represents the refracting. God said "Enough!" to His world; He limited the directly flowing love that it not flow endlessly.

Just as Creation took place through the joining of love and justice, so do all of God's actions in the world. Before some act of love is to come about, great or small, even in the life of an individual, there first has to be a *zimzum*, in order that the love might be properly received.

The same is true in the life of a person who wants to come close to God and to walk in His ways. He who wishes to model the qualities of His Creator must have something in himself that reduces and contains the love. To help you understand this, we might reflect on the fact that the Torah begins with the letter *bet*. *Bet* represents a *bayit*, or house, made to contain that which is within it. Now the Torah is a "Torah of love" (Prov. 31:26), but it too needs an aspect of containment, so that it may be received. This aspect that contains the

Torah of love is fear, as in "his fear of sin should precede his wisdom."[1] The fear so contains the Torah of love that the Torah will be able to bring you to deed, to bear fruit in action. Without fear to contain that love, the love itself would not be able to do its work, which is to lead to action and bring you close to God. . . . Thus can God's intent be fulfilled, that we "observe it and do it" (Gen. 2:15).

This is the spirit in which our sages said: "Too bad for the one who has no house and makes a doorway." Fear of God is the house, the containing power that reduces the Torah of love sufficiently that it can be brought into fruitful deed in the active realm.[2] Indeed too bad for that person: Since he has no house for containment, as he walks thought the gateway of Torah he walks into a place without limits; Torah itself then cannot act on him in accord with God's intent, that of leading him to "observe it and do it." He cannot observe or guard it, since his Torah is without limit. . . .

That is why the Torah begins with the letter *bet:* before your wisdom, before Torah, you must have a house, one made of the fear of God. Then "Whoever's fear of sin precedes his wisdom, that wisdom will survive"—it will attain fulfillment. Where "the fear of sin does not precede wisdom, that wisdom will not survive"—Torah's love then spreads forth without any bounds, and so fully overwhelms any possibility of action that there winds up being no fulfillment.[3]

When a person first has a house, a *bet* that is an opening into the Torah, he can fulfill the commandment of welcoming guests; he can show them the way to walk, and feed them of the fruits of the Torah-tree as he has reached them. Through the Torah that he apprehends, he may bring other people to the way of God, each in accord with his own needs and abilities in the world of deed. All this comes about because he has that fear, the house that can reach out to them and contain for them the Torah's love in such a way that they can receive it. . . . This could not happen if he had no house. Where could he bring his guests? Having nothing to contain those words of Torah that come out of his mouth, he would not be able to sufficiently re-

---

1. The phrase from *Avot* is used to show that although God's Torah is a teaching of love, it is only the God-fearing person who is prepared to receive it. The comingling of love and fear of God in the human sphere is the earthly parallel to the joining of justice and mercy that is needed to sustain the world.

2. The author has in mind the manifestation of divine love through the life of *halakhah,* with all its very measured and limited actions.

3. The author has now read the passage in *Avot* as a piece of religious psychology: The unlimited love of the ecstatic does not lead him to the life of moral deed.

duce the Torah of love so that others could accept it. Rather than being brought to deed, they would be negated from being—and this would accomplish nothing at all.[4] The one who has a house can bring his guests into it and make them into servants of Torah, as Scripture says of "the souls that they had made in Haran" (Gen. 12:5): "made" is translated by Onkelos as "made servants of Torah." This came about by means of the house, by means of *zimzum*.

This then is "I shall fulfill My covenant with Isaac"—Torah, which is the covenant, can be fulfilled only through Isaac, the fear of God and the *zimzum*. . . . This too is the meaning of the binding of Isaac by Abraham. Abraham our Father brought the love from above down on his generation. Scripture speaks of him as "Abraham My lover" (Isa. 41:8): by his hand love came into the world. That love was so intense, however, that it permitted no action.[5] Then *gevurah* or "the fear of Isaac" also had to be brought into the world, so that the deeds of love that Abraham had already started could continue. The fear of Isaac reduced and contained the love so that it might be received. But then the two—love and fear—had to be comingled. That was why Abraham was commanded to perform the *Akedah*, an act of binding; by arousing that cruelty within his own self, that fearsome aspect, for the sake of his love of God, the quality of Isaac came to be subsumed within that of Abraham.

The wicked try to pull the forces of *gevurah* away from those of love; they cause both themselves and the world to fall into the hands of those truly demonic forces that branch out of that [left] *gevurah*-fear side, the fallen powers of judgment that come from there. The righteous, by uplifting themselves along with those negative forces and bringing them back to their source, subsume them into the love, and then those very forces in fact become helpful. It is those *gevurah* forces, the fear of Isaac, that contain the love so that we can receive it. This comes about both through study of Torah and in all of ordinary living.

When our Father Abraham came into the world, the two thou-

---

4. It seems likely that there is a polemical intent in this passage. There was much variety of opinion in the Maggid's school about the value of ecstasy in itself and its relationship to the life of religious action.

5. The text is repeatedly vague on this point. Does the intense power of unrestrained love *destroy* the recipient (i.e., lead to mental imbalance or even death); does it *incapacitate* him in ecstasy so that he cannot act; or does it metaphysically threaten to destroy the lower world, the realm of action, altogether? All of these are possibilities—indeed they are elsewhere too not distinguished—in this and cognate writings.

sand years of Torah began.[6] Until then had been the two thousand of chaos. Scripture attests to this by "These are the generation of heaven and earth" (Gen. 2:4), forming an acronym of *tohu*, chaos, immediately followed by *be-HiBaR'aM*, the reference to Abraham.[7] Generation, the very opposite of chaos, came about through Abraham. It was only from Abraham on, in contrast to the prior times, that there could be true birth, true generation. Those who lived before his time remained in chaos because of their improper deeds, because they separated Isaac's fear from its inclusion within love, thus drawing themselves over to the truly demonic forces of judgment, and blocking out love or any of the other qualities by which the Creator leads His world.[8] ... All this came about because Abraham was a man of love, and he had begun to raise up those fallen forces, helping them to take their part in the revelation of God's true qualities. By his quality of love alone, however, Abraham remained ineffectual, for the love he had was without *zimzum*. Things could not truly be set aright until the birth of Isaac, until fear was revealed in the world, by which love could be contained. Only then could the world prosper, could the negative powers be uplifted, and could the two thousand years of Torah come to be.... Thus was Torah, which started in the days of Abraham, properly opened with a *bet*, a house in which it could be contained. And so Scripture is, in fact: *b*ereshit *b*ara ("In the Beginning God created ...").... Today, too, the Torah of every person has to begin with a *bet;* even in the present, our fear must precede our wisdom in order that our wisdom might be sustained.

Now we are ready to explain the Scriptures:

"Sarah laughed within herself"—this was a true laugh of joy, for she had received the good news in faith. She knew there was nothing that could hold back God's power to save; she was only astonished at the magnitude of the miracle. Because the preceding generations had lived so badly, those evil forces that had fallen from the world of fear, cut off from love, made it seem unlikely that true birth, coming from "extending kindness" in the thirteen attributes, might take place. Such birth would indicate the presence of God's will (*NoZeR/Ra-*

---

6. Following a Talmudic statement: "The world exists for six thousand years; two thousand of chaos, two thousand of Torah, and two thousand of the messiah." The statement has been frequently quoted, and given varied interpretations.

7. See above, *Lekh Lekha*, 4.

8. Here follows a summarizations of *Hayyey Sarah* VI, that on the thirteen qualities of the beard/elder.

ZoN), the "elder." She was tremendously shocked by the force of the miracle that God had wrought, for it just seemed impossible that the divine qualities would be revealed below (as we have learned on "until Abraham there was no old age," etc.). . . . Before she was told of Isaac's birth, Abraham himself was not yet fully an "elder" in this sense; only after Isaac was born and raised does it say: "Abraham was old." This was why Sarah was so surprised at the miracle, the bringing forth of children from those divine potencies above in the midst of so lowly a generation.[9] The human mind simply could not conceive that such might happen; this was the reason for Sarah's laughter.

"With my Lord so old"—this refers not to Abraham, but to God. The text means to say that "Now that I am withered . . ." is not a question, but an account of what had already happened, for our rabbis tell us that at that very moment she began to menstruate.[10] She said: "Now I see the truth of the miracle. But still I am amazed 'with my Lord so old,' that the attributes coming from the 'elder,' the 'beard,' which is God Himself, are present. It is a shock that these could be revealed in my generation." (While we have learned above that Abraham brought forth these same qualities from above, he did not do so until after the birth of Isaac, for only then were love and might joined together as the fear of God was revealed in the world.) . . .

"Then the Lord said to Abraham: 'Why did Sarah laugh, saying: "Can I still give birth, even though I am old?" ' " But why should she have been surprised at this? The answer lies in the word *af* ("even"), which can also mean "anger." In a time when there is such anger in the world, in a generation where anger really rules, how can I give birth from the "elder"?

"I am old"—[Here God is no longer quoting Sarah, but speaking of Himself] saying that this flow comes forth from the "elder," from the thirteen qualities of the "beard" in God.

"Is anything too wondrous for the Lord?"—I shall bring about that birth in her from the realm of the miraculous, that place where

---

9. It is not clear how the generation in which Sarah lived or those preceding had propagated themselves in the author's view. He seems to be making a distinction between "true" birth, birth of the *zaddiq* or the one with a divine soul, and other human birth—but he does not say so directly.

10. They understand *'ednah* in the verse not as "pleasure," but rather as "period," based on the Aramaic *'idan*.

there are no negative forces at all. This is the *aleph*, the Cosmic One, a place of whole and simple mercy with no admixture of judgment. This is the meaning of "Children, life, and sustenance depend not on merit but on *mazal*"; that *mazal* turns out to be none other than the One [beyond where any merit could take one], *'aLePh*, identical in letters with *PeLe'*, "miracle."[11] "Is anything too wondrous for the Lord" refers to that realm of miracle where judging forces do not reach at all.

Once Isaac's birth had been announced, his quality of the fear of God began to appear in the world. Then Abraham's love was set aright, properly contained in a "house" so that it might be effective toward the world's redemption, and then the time of Torah began, opening with the *bet*. Bit by bit were the forces of evil sweetened, until Isaac came along and uplifted them all as he joined himself to Abraham. This is what "God changed for the sake of peace"—when Isaac was born and that pure and miraculous mercy was revealed, He changed those forces by sweetening them with love. All this was indeed "for the sake of peace"—peace is the inclusion of the judging forces within those of love, so that all the good qualities of God may be revealed in the world.

Now as soon as God said "is anything too wondrous," bringing forth the birth from the realm of the miraculous, that "birth" in fact took place, for the word of God is not bound by time and not lacking in active fulfillment. The mercies came forth from that uppermost realm, and the birth of Isaac was already there *in potentia*. The "fear of Isaac" was born into the world; Abraham's love was contained to fit the world's need. Then, even though the physical birth had not yet taken place, the quality of Isaac was established in the world so that the two thousand years of Torah, already started by Abraham, might begin in full. Now the *bet*, the "house" of the fear of God, could come forth.

Now Sarah is no longer surprised by the miracle ... and her faith is much strengthened. (Of course she had faith beforehand as well, but there are countless levels within faith.) In that moment, in fact, when the word of God announcing the birth of Isaac was spoken, the fear of God was brought forth and all the good in the world

---

11. The greatest miracles in human life come from such deeply hidden realms within the Godhead that we cannot say they are given in response to merit. God the universal *aleph* is Himself the miracle; these gifts come from Him alone.

was made stronger. This was Sarah's denial—she denied all other gods but Him alone. While she had been a very righteous woman even prior to all this, the appearance of Isaac's fear made her faith greater, causing her to deny other gods on a level higher than that which she had done before. Faith has no measure. Understand this. "Whoever denies idolatry is as one who has accepted the entire Torah." ... This came about "for she was frightened"—the Torah provides the reason for her denial; she was able to further deny idolatry because she was "frightened," namely because that fear which was to appear with the birth of Isaac had already come upon her. ... By then she was no longer surprised that God's qualities were to be revealed, and she began to say: " 'I did [do] not laugh.' Now that God has already said: 'Is anything too wondrous,' I am not laughing; it is no longer laughable. ..." He replied: "But you did laugh" previously; then you did not yet have this increased faith and this higher rejection of idolatory, for the mercies of God had not yet come forth from the world of the miraculous, and the birth of Isaac was not yet known.[12] Understand this.

This is why the Midrash refers "Rejoice greatly, O father of the righteous" particularly to the birth of Isaac. Now that the fear of God had come forth into the world, Abraham's own quality could be properly meted out; this is an occasion for great joy. It was Abraham's own love that rejoiced, for only now was it so established that it could do its work toward redemption; the fear of Isaac was now present to so house it as to help it to contribute to the world's well-being. "Heaven and earth" rejoiced, all that were created through the Torah and are ruled by it always. None of them was in proper condition so long as Isaac had not been born and fear had not come forth to provide proper containment for the love. The world, which lives by Torah, was simply not conducted in a whole manner before Abraham; that was still the period of chaos. There was not yet a Torah of love that could rule the world, for there was not yet a measure that could distribute that love so that the world could bear it. Therefore the Midrash concludes: "Were it not for My covenant day and night"— this is the Torah, God's covenant—"I would not have set the bounds of heaven and earth"—the very existence of heaven and earth comes about through the covenant of Torah, which ever gives them life as it

---

12. Despite Sarah's "conversion," it is good that she remain aware of her formerly unenlightened state.

rules them. And heaven and earth could never have received this love from Torah had the *zimẓum* brought about by fear not taken place. . . .

Now this is the meaning of AND THESE ARE THE GENER-ATIONS OF ISAAC, SON OF ABRAHAM. When Scripture said: "These are the generations of heaven and earth as they were created," it hinted at "chaos" and at the birth process that began with Abraham. But all of this required the quality of Isaac as well, as we have explained . . . so THESE ARE THE GENERATIONS; now there is generation, birth, in contrast to the chaos that had come before. This happens through ISAAC, SON OF ABRAHAM, the one who contains the Torah's love so that there may be true birth. This is not to say that Isaac's quality itself is the source of birth, without the love. Scripture makes sure we understand this by adding ABRAHAM BE-GOT ISAAC. Along with (*et*) Isaac, as the Isaac-forces of *gevurah* were included within those of love, so that they too became love—since this inclusion is what permits the world to be—in that way could there be birth . . . as the two became one and were joined for common purpose.

Blessed is the Lord forever. Amen. Amen.

III

JACOB WAS A PERFECT MAN, ONE WHO DWELT IN TENTS. (Gen. 25:27)

The matter of the "garbing" of the Torah is well known. The power of the Creator is to be found in all things; through all things one should seek to be drawn near to him, no matter how earthly or corporeal the thing might appear. We have stressed this a number of times. This was the way of Jacob; Esau, however, sought out luxury itself. For this reason Scripture says: "I love Jacob, but Esau I despise" (Mal. 1:2–3). It is that which is *with* (*et*) Esau that I despise, the dedication to luxury. . . . This is JACOB WAS A PERFECT MAN, a whole person, becaue he DWELT IN TENTS, because of the garbing and the hiding: Hidden within every thing he saw the clear light, and was able to raise it up and join it to its source. In this sense he lacked for nothing, for he made everything into the service of God. Surely there can be no greater wholeness than that of restoring everything to its root. This too is the meaning of "He smelled his garments" (Gen. 27:27)—serving God through the ways in which He is garbed in all things also brings Him pleasure. Through this he was blessed. This also is "like the smell of a field blessed by the Lord," on which RaSHI says "a field of apples."[1] This one unifies all things and brings them to the field above. One has to go step by step in this matter. Start things out here and you will be helped from above. This is why Scripture says: "May He give" (Gen. 27:28), waits a while, and then says it again (28:4).

Blessed is the Lord forever. Amen. Amen.

IV

BECAUSE ABRAHAM LISTENED TO MY VOICE AND KEPT MY TRUST. (Gen. 26:5)

The Midrash here records a controversy between Rabbi Simeon [ben Yohai] and Rabbi Levi. One says that it was Abraham's innards, his two kidneys that flowed with wisdom, that enabled him to keep the trust, while the other says that he studied Torah on his own.[1]

It is known that "This is the Torah: man" (Num. 19:14), [i.e., that Torah has a human form]. Torah comes from divine wisdom, the World of Thought. It has a fully laid-out form, consisting of two hundred forty-eight positive commandments and three hundred sixty-five prohibitions. Since man is derived from Torah as his spiritual source, he too has two hundred forty-eight limbs and three hundred sixty-five sinews, even in his physical form.

Before an artisan sets out to create any particular thing, he draws a precise image of it in his mind, just as it is going to be. Only afterwards does he set about executing that image. So it was with man: First Scripture says: "The Lord God formed man" (Gen. 2:7) and

---

1. The author reads the subject of "He smelled his garments" to be God rather than Isaac: in Jacob's approach to him, God sensed an awareness of the garbing of His own presence in all things. This presence is here identified with *shekhinah*, frequently referred to in Kabbalistic writings as the "field of holy apples."

1. The question is whether Abraham was a recipient of divine revelation from within the self, or whether it was by rational and intellectual process that he kept God's trust. The trust is taken by both to mean the Torah, as will presently be made clear.

afterwards "He made him."[2] The term "formed" here refers to an image (*YaẒaR/ẒiYYuR*); first came that form as it exists in the spiritual universe, the World of Thought, and afterwards God brought it forth in deed as the physical body.

A person must take care that he not deny both thought and deed by transgressing the Torah. Torah is the image in which God first conceived the world in His mind; "the final deed was in thought from the first." This is the image of God in which man was created: the Torah, concentrated from the world of divine thought so that it might be dressed in garments. We have shown elsewhere how the Torah is comparable to the form of the human being, like him being made of both matter and form. This is in order that man might be able to hold fast to it.

This also is the meaning of RaSHI's statement that man was created "in the form that was prepared for him, the image of his Creator." The word for "Creator" here is *yoẓero*, again to be interpreted as we have above. RaSHI means to say that man came forth below just as God had depicted him in His mind.

Since all things that exist in the world contain the Torah as the power of their Creator within them, we must treat them in consonance with the divine intent. Only in this way will we be kept from denying both the intent of God and the fact of His creation. In our own physical form we can come to understand the most sublime spiritual matters; "in my own flesh I see God" (Job 19:26)! Yes, for a person who is not cut off from the source indeed is one with God. One must take care, however, not to use this realization for any personal gain. When we do so, we cut ourselves off.[3] The point is rather to kill off selfhood, for "Torah does not exist"—is not really alive and one with the source—"except in the one who kills himself. . . ."[4] He has to kill his own self and act only for the goal of pleasing God.

---

2. The latter phrase as quoted does not exist in the Biblical text. The author seems to have in mind Gen. 5:1, which he then would translate "according to the image did God make him." This accords with RaSHI's reading of Gen. 1:27, quoted below.

3. The point seems to be antimagical. Once the perfected person realizes his oneness with the self of God, he faces a grave temptation to try to exert Godlike powers. Hasidism was aware of such powers, indeed at times ascribed something like them to the *zaddiq* (see above, *Ḥayyey Sarah* 2), but was at the same time extremely guarded about them.

4. The Talmudic original adds "for its sake." A counsel of ascetic devotion to a life of study has here been reread as a mystical counsel on the need for ego death in the one who has discovered God within his own self.

"Know Him in all your ways" (Prov. 3:10) then becomes; "Be united with the sublime form; be the image of your Creator!"

Now in the human form, besides those two hundred forty-eight limbs and three hundred sixty-five sinews, there is also hair. What place does it have in that spiritual form that is the Torah? Surely that part of man also comes from above. The hairs are related to those things that the sages have added to the Torah's six hundred thirteen commandments. Various protections have been placed about the Torah to keep the person far from sin. Of these the sages said: "Make a guard about My guarding." Just as it is the function of hair on the human body to keep us from cold, so did His wisdom decree that in the spiritual realm the sages might make such protections as well.

Now we may understand the Midrash in which one of the rabbis said that Abraham's two kidneys flowed with wisdom: He reached that certain rung at which he was able to conceive the entire Torah, even though it had not yet been given. He conceived the Torah as it was in the divine mind before it was given, as we have discussed it in another context. The other sage claimed, rather, that Abraham had learned it "on his own"; he followed "In my flesh I see God," analogizing from his own physical body to the holy spiritual form. Even that which the rabbis were to add to the Torah he understood from his hair, and observed that too, as the sages have noted: "Abraham our Father observed the entire Torah, even to the 'eruv of foods.[5] This is the meaning of GUARDED MY TRUST: even that which was only for the sake of guarding, an ordinance of the rabbis, he observed.

Abraham was able to do all this because he brought to his own self that death of which we have spoken. All his deeds, even all his sight, were only for the sake of heaven. Whatever he did, he did it without selfish intent; he did not see his own self or his own form in things, but rather saw in them that which could bring him to liken himself to the form above. He saw the inwardness that lies hidden in all things, the "tent" of which Scripture speaks when it says "If a man die in a tent" (Num. 19:14). In a tent you only see that which is inside.

---

5. The practice of beginning the preparation of Sabbath food before the start of a festival that falls on the Sabbath eve, thus permitting further food preparation for the Sabbath on the festival. The point is that this is clearly a rabbinic invention, one without the slightest hint in the Biblical text itself. Even this, claim the rabbis, was observed by Abraham. The extreme is used in the context of the rabbinic claim (contra Paul?) that there can be no piety, even for Abraham, outside that of the Torah.

His desire was not for himself, God forbid, but was only to be like unto his Creator and to do His will.

V

THE SERVANTS OF ISAAC, DIGGING IN THE VAL-
LEY, FOUND A WELL OF LIVING WATERS. THE
HERDSMEN OF GERAR QUARRELED WITH
ISAAC'S HERDSMEN, SAYING "THE WATER IS
OURS." HE NAMED THAT WELL 'ESEQ ("CONTEN-
TION") FOR THEY HAD CONTENDED WITH HIM.
AND WHEN THEY DUG ANOTHER WELL, THEY
DISPUTED OVER THAT ONE ALSO, SO HE NAMED
IT SITNAH ("HARASSMENT"). HE MOVED FROM
THERE AND DUG YET ANOTHER WELL, AND
THEY DID NOT QUARREL OVER IT. THIS ONE HE
CALLED REHOVOT ("BREADTH"), SAYING "NOW
THE LORD HAS GRANTED US THE BREADTH TO
INCREASE IN THE LAND." (Gen. 26:19–22)

ON THAT DAY THE SERVANTS OF ISAAC CAME
AND TOLD HIM ABOUT THE WELL THAT THEY
HAD DUG. THEY SAID TO HIM: "WE HAVE FOUND
WATER!" HE CALLED IT SHIVE'AH, AND THAT IS
WHY THE CITY IS CALLED BE'ER SHEBA UNTO
THIS DAY. (Gen. 26:33–34)

The Midrash adds: We do not know if they had found water or not. But when the text says: "We have found water!" it becomes clear that they had succeeded.[1]

We begin to understand this passage with the verse: "They have forsaken Me, the source of living waters, and hewed them out cisterns, broken cisterns, that cannot hold water" (Jer. 2:13). He, the blessed Lord, is the source from which life flows forth into all the living in every way. There is none beside Him! Whoever holds fast to Him cleaves to the very source of life, the one whose waters will nev-

---

1. The point of the Midrash is obscure. It seems to be playing on *wa-yomeru lo* ("They said to him") which could also be read: "They said: We have not . . ."

er prove unfaithful. This is true so long as there is no separation on our part, for if our sins come in to separate us from the fount, life itself will pass out of us. From God's side there is no interruption of the flow; "only your sins separate" (Isa. 59:2). This is true except for the one who intentionally draws his life-flow from the "other side"; he indeed is cut off from his root above. He is called "separator of the one"; [rather than the true living waters] he has only water gathered up in broken cisterns, the broken vessels into which some sparks of life have fallen.

The patriarchs opened up the channels of mind in the world, teaching all who were to come into the world how to dig within themselves a spring of living waters, to cleave to their fount, the root of their lives. Their disciples were called "servants," as in the servants of Isaac mentioned here, for their service of God came about through the patriarchs. After the death of Abraham, however, the wellsprings of wisdom were sealed, sealed by the "Philistines," representing the evil in man that overtook the world. The lowest of the elements, that of earth itself, became the strongest, and the power of spirit and mind was diminished. Then Abraham's son Isaac came along and followed in his father's footsteps. He taught the people of his generation how to dig again into that living fount of waters; he taught them by means of various wonderful and mysterious processes of mind. "Isaac returned and dug the wells of water" (Gen. 26:18). All this came about through faith, which is the prerequisite for all. You must have full faith that the glory of God fills all the world, that there is no place devoid of Him and none beside Him. Then, by means of that faith, you will come to a longing and desire to cleave to God. This state is referred to as *naḥal*, a stream or valley, containing also a reference to the verse *Nafshenu Ḥiqetah La-'adonay*, "our soul waits for the Lord" (Ps. 33:20). In this way you come to your root, the spring at the well of living waters. That is THE SERVANTS OF ISAAC, DIGGING IN A VALLEY (*naḥal*); they were digging in "our soul waits for the Lord." . . .

Now I have to help you to understand the names that were given to the three wells. The patriarchs looked with their mind's eye down through to the end of the generations, seeing each with the troubles that would pass over it. So long as the first Temple stood, there was a great abundance of true knowledge in the world. People knew how to approach and to bind themselves to the living wellsprings much better than they have during the time of the diaspora. Even other nations had some recognition of the truth and would bring offerings. These are referred to in the prayer of King Solomon, who mentions "the stranger who comes" (1 Kings 8:41). And so we find, near to the time of the destruction, that the emperor sent an offering.[2] Even in Temple times, however, there were both good and evil in the world—until, through the sins of Israel, evil was triumphant and the Temple was destroyed. That was the first well, called 'ESEQ, the well of contention.

Afterwards they dug a second well. This refers to the second Temple, built in the time of Ezra. Then too did knowledge and awareness abound, so that they knew how to dig a well again. But they quarreled over this one as well, and they called it SITNAH. This refers to the accusations of Satan that were called forth, for physical power had again triumphed over things of the mind. Finally HE MOVED FROM THERE, the time of this long exile is to pass, and then he DUG YET ANOTHER WELL. This refers to the coming of our righteous messiah (speedily in our time!), when there will be no more incitement by the forces of evil at all, as Scripture says: "I shall remove the spirit of defilement from the land" (Zech. 13:2). The world will be wholly good and its name will be REHOVOT, for then will consciousness be greatly expanded. "Earth will be filled with the knowledge of God" (Isa. 11:9) and all of us will merit to cleave to the endless light. Then will we grasp the true nature of God, and will hold fast to Him forever. Scripture says, following this account: "He rose up from there [and went] to Beersheba" (Gen. 26:23). The *shekhinah* is called Beersheba; they will merit that high rung. Understand this.[3]

At those times when evil holds a person back and does not let him reach the well, he should still hold onto himself and see in his mind's eye that even in his present state he may encounter God's divinity in reduced form. . . . He should look at the obstacle that holds him back and seek to understand the root of its life. In which of God's qualities is it rooted? In love? Power or fear? Thus may he bring it to its root, knowing that through that quality he is being called to come closer, to begin the service of God in thought, word, and deed. All of these qualities are divine, but have fallen from their place in the

---

2. The reference is in fact to the end of second Temple times.

3. This intense cleaving to God leads directly to union and identification with the *shekhinah*, the highest form of mystical attainment.

breaking; now good is to be made of them again. The same is true if obstacles come to you in the form of harsh judgments; their root is in the world of divine power, the quality of Isaac. Understand that these too come from a high and holy place, and have come down, step by step, into the place of broken cisterns. Hold fast to the quality of divine power and fear of the Lord; bring this service forthwith to your Creator. Then will those judgments be raised up to their root and "sweetened"; their root is the quality of Isaac. If your sins have brought such harsh judgments down upon you, be strong and serve with them into their root; when you bring them to that place where there is only God, the judgments will be sweetened and will disappear.

Thus may we understand the following discussion in the Talmud. Abraham our Father [when confronted with the sins of Israel] said: May they be wiped out for the sake of Your holy name. Isaac said: Take half [of the burden of their sins] upon Yourself and I will take half upon me. Isaac, who represents the rigors of divine power, here was the better defender. This is understandable on the basis of what we have said above: The negative judgments are rooted in this side, and it is to their source, divine power, that they must be brought in order to be negated.[4] "Forces of judgment may be sweetened only in their root." After this takes place, the God of Jacob may appear. That aspect, when mentioned in the liturgy, is preceded by a *waw* ("God of Abraham, God of Isaac, *and* God of Jacob"); this is a *waw* of drawing forth, one of inclusion and the drawing together of all the forces toward the right side.[5]

This takes us back to the servants of Isaac, and the question of whether they had found water. It is the judgments that lie upon us that lead us to the water. His servants CAME AND TOLD HIM: The word for "tell" (*wa-yaggidu/NGD*) can also mean "to draw forth"; we do not know if we have found water until we draw the judgments up and bring them to their root, the quality of Isaac. Then indeed we find water, the waters of mercy, for the left side is included

---

4. The point is one of considerable psychological subtlety: Though Abraham represents divine mercy and Isaac divine judgment, it is to Isaac that the sinner's case must ultimately be brought. The blandishments of an Abrahamic appeal for mercy ultimately are too predictable to be potent; it is the area of judgment/rigor that is disturbed, and it is there that healing must be sought.

5. *Tif'eret*, the aspect of Jacob, represents the synthesis of Abraham and Isaac. Having achieved wholeness, it tends toward the mercy side and draws the whole along with it.

in the right, since judgment itself has been used in the service of God. Really there is no obstacle at all once we see that the obstacle is the very center of our service. We have taught this in connection with "Timna was a concubine" (Gen. 36:12). The name Timna means "obstacle" (*tiMNa'/MeNi'ah*); the one who says that he is kept from God by some obstacle is dwelling among the *qelipot*, the forces of Eliphaz son of Esau, who has none of this awareness. This is why the rabbis say that our father Jacob tried to push her away; He was pushing aside the evil, trying to draw out the life that lay trapped within that obstacle, bringing it to its root by using it in the service of God.

This is "Jacob went out from Beersheba" (Gen. 28:10); he left the place of his birth and went someplace that was strange to him. There he encountered forces of judgment and obstacles; these are called Haran in the text. Then "he came upon a certain place"; the verb *paga'* that is used here refers to two things coming close to one another. He drew near to those obstacles, raising them up to their root above.

VI

THE LORD SAID TO HER: TWO NATIONS ARE IN YOUR WOMB, TWO PEOPLES APART WHILE STILL IN YOUR BODY. ONE PEOPLE SHALL BE MIGHTIER THAN THE OTHER, AND THE ELDER SHALL SERVE THE YOUNGER. (Gen. 25:23)

The rabbis read "two nations" (*goyim*) as "two proud ones" (*ge'im*) and said that this referred to Antoninus and Rabbi.[1]

Because of the sin of Adam and the early generations that followed, holy sparks and souls came to be scattered among the nations of the world. It is through those holy sparks that the nations conduct their affairs; their very life is dependent on them. Without this scattering of sparks they would have no sustenance at all, since all of life comes from the Holy. But it is through these holy souls that have fallen from their source and become "garbed" in them that they are sustained. A case that contains a holy book is to be saved along with the

---

1. "Rabbi" taken alone in rabbinic sources refers to Rabbi Judah ha-Nasi, editor of the Mishnah. The Talmud and Midrash record many tales of his friendly debates with Antoninus, a legendary Roman emperor.

book [in case of a fire that breaks out on the Sabbath], even if the case contains coins. The same is true here: For the sake of those holy souls God concentrates His presence to dwell amid the nations, bringing life to these "cases" for the souls within them. He does this even though the evil there is terribly great and coarse; this is what is meant by the exile of the *shekhinah*.

This is how it is that proselytes emerge from among the nations; one who has such a holy soul is led to conversion. And that is why Israel have been scattered among the nations: to draw forth those sparks of light. By seeing the awareness that exists in Israel and by believing in the Torah that they have been given, [the proselyte is drawn near], for "His kingdom rules over all" (Ps. 103:19). When Israel have contact with the nations, through commerce or even through words that they exchange, the Jew who has proper faith should be seeking out those holy sparks and drawing them near; he extends himself out to them and raises them upward to their root. For this one needs to have proper awareness and an honest and whole prayer-life. It is this that messiah is waiting for: that we complete the uplifting of the sparks. When the work is done, life will pass out of [the nations] and they will no longer exist. "I will cause the spirit of uncleanness to pass away from the earth" (Zech. 13:2). The Creator Himself will no longer need to concentrate His presence amid them; His presence had been there only for the sake of those holy sparks. This is the meaning of "In all their distress, He is distressed" (Isa. 63:9). Just as Israel has been in exile for the sake of uplifting those holy fallen souls, so has the Creator needed, for the sake of His own holiness and so that the cast-off soul not be utterly cut off from Him, to reduce Himself, as it were, down to these lowly places, extending life to these "cases" for the holy. As the nations live their lives through each generation, so are Israel able to uplift ever more of them, bit by bit, until the process is brought to an end (speedily in our day. Amen!). If God did not extend this life to them, they would not exist at all, and the redemption would be impossible. Understand this.[2] When the messiah comes, God will it for our times, the redemp-

---

2. The point is one of dubious generosity: The existence of the nations is for the good, since it allows Israel's redemptive work to take place. Evil is reified in the nations, but only in that reification can it become the object of transforming activity. Of course the actual solicitation of proselytes in the author's time would have been impossible, though there is much theoretical interest evinced in it in Hasidism.

tion will be a complete and perfect one in both of these aspects: the redemption of God Himself, as it were, and that of Israel His people.

We find in the Lurianic writings that the verse "Isaac loved Esau because he had a taste for game" (Gen. 25:28) is interpreted as a reference to Rabbi Akiba, who is said to have spoken through the mouth of Esau. This has to be understood in accord with what we have said. Indeed Esau was completely evil, but Isaac saw, in the course of talking with him, the soul of Rabbi Akiba, one of those holy souls in search of life. Now our father Isaac was a vessel for God's presence; surely Esau would not have been able to deceive him, as might appear to be the case from Scripture itself. The matter is rather as we have said. We may now also understand why the two of them, Jacob the most perfect vessel among the patriarchs and Esau the personification of evil, were linked to one another. Why did God not at least bring them into the world through two separate births? It is hard to understand how Esau could have come out of the womb of the righteous Rebekah, let alone the two of them at once from the same source! But God foresaw in His great sight that Jacob's task was to be the uplifting of those holy sparks. In order to lift something up, one has to go down to the place where it lies and grab hold of it. The two of them had to be in the same place at the same time with great intimacy, so that Jacob could raise up that holiness which lay in Esau. Otherwise Esau would remain completely evil, the product of the excesses of judgment in Isaac, as is known.[3] Jacob was to begin the process of uplifting from his very formation onward, by being together in that same womb. This is "his hand was holding onto the heel of Esau" (Gen. 25:26). The heel is connected to walking and going: all the comings and goings of the nations are through the holiness that is garbed in them. Jacob held onto Esau's heel in order to purify it; the same was true in later generations for those who followed in Jacob's footsteps. Among these was Rabbi, who purified and brought to light the soul of Antoninus. Of this Scripture says: "Is not Esau a brother to Jacob? Yet I love Jacob, but Esau I despise" (Mal. 1:2–3). That verse, when examined in context, is somewhat surprising. God has declared His love for Israel, and Israel has responded with the question: "How have You shown us love?" What sort of demonstration of love does

---

3. Esau in Kabbalistic literature represents the demonic universe. The account of his tribes (Gen. 36 etc.) is read as a catalog of the principalities of evil. The demonic is born of Isaac, the left and judging side of God, and is cut off from the tempering power of divine love or mercy. Judgment without love turns out to be demonic.

God offer when He says: "Is not Esau a brother to Jacob?" But this in fact is the clearest evidence God offers of His love for Israel: the placing of the two of them together in the same womb, so that the one might bring out the holy life-force by which the other lives. This was the nature of their brotherhood; there was insufficient life to sustain them both. This was done so that the evil would be isolated as the life was drawn out of it.[4] This is "the time when man rules over man to do him ill" (Eccles. 8:9): As the Worthless Man brings judgments down on the Holy Man, the latter strengthens himself in God's service and uses the sparks that lie in those very judgments for His service. Of this the Zohar says: "Their oppression hastens Israel's deliverance." Israel depend upon this process of purfication. This is "to do him ill"—Israel continue to reduce the amount of life that is hidden in Esau; surely in this God's great love for Israel is seen, through their brother Esau.

Of this Scripture says: "Because Tyre gloated over Jerusalem . . . I shall be filled, now that it is laid in ruins" (Ezek. 26:1–2), to which the rabbis added: "Tyre was fulfilled only by the destruction of Jerusalem." The sating and fulfillment of Tyre [i.e., of the nations] came about only through the destruction, through the fall of holy souls into their midst. May God will that speedily in our own times the purification be completed, the fulfillment of the holy side and the full expansion of the borders of the holy. Then Jerusalem will be settled and Tyre destroyed, for they will no longer have any of the life of holiness amid them.

That was why God commanded that the offering of shekels be made before the decree of Haman came upon the Jews. The rabbis said that it was the fulfillment of this commandment that negated his decree.[5] Haman had weighed out ten thousand pieces of silver for the lives of the Jews (Esther 3:9). But "the utterances of God are pure" (Ps. 18:31) can also be read as "the utterances of God are permutations" (*ZeRuFah/ZeRuFim*) and the secret of these permutations of language has been given to Israel, in order to turn them to the good. Of the *SHeQeL* that they gave, fulfilling the commandment of God, there can be wrought *Le-QaSH* on the other side. *Le-QaSH* is the

---

4. The language of the original is obscure here, but this paraphrase seems to best capture its spirit.

5. The annual offering of the half shekel, used to support the Temple, began with the first of Adar. The rabbis make the point that God foresaw Haman's decree, one that was to take effect on the thirteenth of that month.

"straw" of "The house of Jacob shall be fire . . . and the house of Esau shall be straw; they shall burn and devour it" (Obad. 1:18). By the flame of Jacob's devotion, performing the commandments both in love and in fear, the power of the holy will grow strong. The letters will be so turned as to bode ill for the idolators; in this and every way Israel so turn the permutations as to uplift the holy from the clutches of evil and to broaden its boundaries.

These are the TWO NATIONS . . . IN YOUR WOMB, the two proud ones. Both of them are important, for even though the one is evil, he is a case or container for the holy, for those great and holy souls that are there within him. Thus have the rabbis further said about the taste of game that Esau put in Isaac's mouth, that Esau used to ask his father: "Father, how does one tithe straw and salt?"[6] The "game" in his mouth were those holy souls trapped there with him. Those souls would speak to Isaac while he was conversing with Esau, especially the soul of Rabbi Akiba.

When Rabbi Akiba first married the daughter of Kalba Shavua, the two of them swore that they would not be supported by her father's money. They made themselves beds of straw, and one day Elijah came to them, dressed as a poor man begging for straw. He said that his wife had given birth and that she needed straw to lie on. Rabbi Akiba gave him their straw. It was all this goodness that Isaac saw as he was speaking with Esau; the holy spark that would one day give that gift of straw was there holding conversation with Isaac.

It was in this same way that they said the "two nations" were the two proud ones, Antoninus and Rabbi; Jacob was already purifying the sparks that would be manifest in them in that later generation. Now we understand what the Midrash means when it tells us that in the future the sons of Esau are to come to Israel and say: "We are your brethren." But God will answer them: "Should you nest as high as the eagle, should your eyrie be lodged among the stars, even from there I will pull you down, says the Lord" (Obad. 1:4). Once the purification is completed evil will surely fall of its own accord, as there will be no more life in it. All its holiness drained, it will have no relationship to Jacob at all.[7]

---

6. Esau deviously asked Isaac questions about fine points of the law to convince him of his piety. Gen. 25:28 can literally be read to mean: "for a trap was in his mouth."

7. Only in the end, as messiah's arrival vindicates Israel, will the nations finally seek to claim brotherhood with them. But then it will be too late: Israel will already have completed the brotherly task that they had borne through history, that of seeking

VII

AND MAY GOD GIVE YOU OF THE DEW OF HEAVEN AND OF THE FAT AND OF THE LAND, AND PLENTY OF CORN AND WINE. (Gen. 27:28).

RaSHI interprets the beginning of the blessing with "and" to mean that God will give again and again.

To understand this: The true service of God is in the mind, as Scripture says: "Know the God of your father and serve Him" (1 Chron. 28:9). Such knowing is joy, for the service of God with an expanded consciousness brings forth joy from the World of Joy. It is well known, however, that if joy is constant its pleasure is diminished; it has to suffer some interruption. When a person serves God with a true feeling of spiritual joy, that feeling rises up to the Creator Himself, and He too takes pleasure in the one who serves Him so joyously. Joy is called forth in the root of all, just as it has been present in that particular part of the all; now that part is joined fast to Him. There is no real pleasure without this attachment; now he has aroused that same pleasure in the root itself. But in order that the joy not be constant [and thereby ruined], his former consciousness is taken away from him and a higher or more expanded mind is given him in its place. This is called the second expansion.

That is why *da'at* or mind is the source from which the letter *waw* of the divine name is drawn forth; it is ever being drawn further and expanded. This is why women are light-headed: they do not possess this element of the constant expansion of mind.[1] The mind given them when they are children always remains the same, never growing. This is the meaning of "God will give again and again"; after mind is taken, it will be given again in a still higher form for that second expansion. Truly "the one who comes in search of purity will be helped." Once he begins the process by arousing himself from below,

---

out sparks of light among the nations and raising them up to God. All that remains of the nations in the end will be that which is worthy of destruction.

1. The author is referring here to the Kabbalistic diagram. *Da'at* is the third of the *sefirot* (by the Hasidic count) and stands in the central column of the chart. In this position, it is the direct source out of which *tif'eret*, the masculine principle of divinity, is drawn. As the male principle, he claims, this element is not fully present in women. The view that "women are light-headed" represents a widespread and ancient male prejudice, quoted here from Talmudic sources.

he may be given mind from that World of Joy so that his worship be strengthened.

Now *da'at* is represented by Jacob, and *da'at* stands at the center, representing the righting of balance and the uplifting of judgment forces. When a person serves God with *da'at* and feels this sublime joy of spirit in his worship, the forces of judgment are indeed uplifted.[2] This is AND MAY GOD GIVE YOU: may *Elohim*, the aspect of divine power, also agree; may it be transformed so that it too cause blessing to shine upon you through Jacob, the *waw* of the transforming divine mind. May that greater awareness of God that you began seeking from below now be granted you from above; may He "give again and again." OF THE DEW OF HEAVEN: that sublime joy from the World of Joy; FROM THE FAT OF THE LAND: may this come about because you sought it from "the land," from below. That is why this blessing is spoken by Isaac, who represents the quality of divine rigor and power, so that through *da'at* it might be uplifted.

The Zohar interprets Isaac's charge to Esau concerning the hunt with regard to Rosh Hashanah. It is then that the aspect of Isaac is aroused to judge the world. Satan too "comes among them," from "traveling about the world" (Job 1:6–7). He had been seeking out the sins of everyone in the world, "to hunt game" for the judge, the fearsome Isaac.[3] God here advises Israel to save themselves by means of the *shofar*, the sound of which awakens "the voice of Jacob," the quality of mercy. " 'The voice is the voice of Jacob' (Gen. 27:22)—so long as the voice is that of Jacob, the hands will not be those of Esau." All the forces of judgment are sweetened when the *shofar* sound calls forth the quality of mercy, the "voice of Jacob." This happens because of the return to God evoked by that call of the *shofar*.[4] "Can the *shofar* be sounded in a city and the people not tremble?" (Amos 3:6). Israel are

---

2. The ecstasy of worship in itself has the power to effect change both in the individual and in the cosmic situation. We see here a central idea of the Kabbalah, the notion that human action, and particularly the fulfillment or transgression of the commandments, has cosmic proportions; the idea has, however, been transformed in the Hasidic reading. Here it is no longer the quasi-magical effect of the act, but the limitless expanse of ecstasy, that is the real source of power.

3. Here Esau and Satan have been fully merged in the Zohar's understanding; both represent the accuser, seeking to denounce Israel for its sins on the Day of Judgment.

4. There is nothing mechanistic about the power of the *shofar*-sound; the real power that moves the universe is that of human repentance.

awakened to repentance and the forces of judgment are transformed; the left has been joined to the right and now together, as right, both are employed in every possible form of God's service. As the past is regretted, so are all their sins forgiven and transformed into merits. This brings to God a doubly great joy, as He sees the *qelipot* uplifted and brought into the holy. All this comes about through the sound of the *shofar*, the voice of Jacob, source of divine compassion.

Thus may we understand that Jacob "brought wine to him [Isaac] and he drank" (Gen. 27:25). The Zohar says that he brought near that which had been far away.[5] We also note that the world *lo* ("to him") in this verse has an unusual double sign in the notations for chant. All this is as we have explained it. Jacob and the mercy he aroused by the *shofar*-sound wrought repentance and converted sin into merit. Those sins were the "wine" that had brought wailing to the world ("Wailing"—*YeLaLaH*—numerically = "the wine"—*Ha-YaYiN*). Penitence, now aroused by Jacob ... and his prayers, brought this wine to Him and He drank; the Creator had great joy as that which was far from Him was now brought near. It was the "voice of Jacob" that brought Him the "wine," the now-forgiven sins of Israel, that they might be returned to the holy. . . . God takes greater pleasure in such an offering than He does in the service of those who have always been righteous, as the sages have said: "The righteous cannot attain to that place where the penitents stand." The doubled musical notation on the word "to him" points to this. We know that these notations come from the World of Joy; as God's joy is doubled when Jacob brings Him this wine, so is the musical note a double one for that word. . . . Immediately afterwards Scripture says "and he blessed him"; even the fearsome Isaac agrees that Israel should be blessed on the New Year with the bounty of all that is good. All this because of that "voice of Jacob" bringing Him the wine to drink and giving Him such great joy.[6] This is the secret of *da'at* and of the sweetening of sins.

Blessed is the Lord forever. Amen Selah unto eternity.

---

5. Wine in Kabbalistic symbolism represents the left side, the forces of judgment.

6. A similar idea is expressed in a widespread Hasidic joke that compares the Day of Atonement (Yom Ki-Purim) to Purim. The two are parallel, so it is said, because on Purim Israel are to become so inebriated that they cannot tell the difference between Haman and Mordecai, while on Yom Kippur God becomes so drunk on the merits of Israel that He too cannot tell good from evil and therefore must forgive all sins.

THE LIGHT OF THE EYES

Sources: *Toledot*

I
A well-known principle	Bereshit Rabbah 12:3
The partriarchs are the chariot	Bereshit Rabbah 47:6
He went to the children of Ishmael	Sifre Devarim 343

II
Rejoice greatly	Bereshit Rabbah 63:1
Abraham was second to Sarah	Shemot Rabbah 1:1
God changed the words	Baba Mezi'a 87a
One who has no house	Shabbat 31b
Fear of sin precedes wisdom	Avot 3:9
Two thousand years of Torah	Sanhedrin 97a
No old age	Sanhedrin 107b
She began to menstruate	Baba Mezi'a 87a
Children, life, and sustenance	Mo'ed Qatan 28a
Whoever denies idolatry	Nedarim 25a

IV
It was Abraham's innards	Bereshit Rabbah 95:3
In the form prepared for him	RaSHI to Gen 1:27
Except in the one who kills himself	Berakhot 63b
Make a guard about My guarding	Yebamot 21a
Abraham observed the entire Torah	Yoma 28b

V
We do not know	Bereshit Rabbah 64:9
The emperor sent an offering	Gittin 56b
Abraham our Father said	Shabbat 89b
Jacob tried to push her away	cf. Sanhedrin 99b

VI
Two proud ones	Berakhot 57b
A case that contains a holy book	Mishnah Shabbat 16:1
Tyre was fulfilled	RaSHI to Genesis 25:23
The offering of shekels	Megillah 13b
Esau used to ask	Tanhuma Toledot 8

TOLEDOT

When Rabbi Akiba first married   Nedarim 50a
The sons of Esau are to come   Yalqut Ovadiah 549

VII
Women are light-headed   Shabbat 33b
Who comes in search of purity   Yoma 39a
Isaac's charge to Esau   Zohar 3:99b
He brought near that which had been far Zohar 3:258b
Wine brought wailing   Berakhot 40a
That place where the penitents stand   Berakhot 34b

WA-YEZE
Genesis 28:10–32:3

INTRODUCTION. *Wa-Yeze* is one of the longest and most highly developed sections in the entire *Me'or 'Eynayim*; the author saw rich potential in the spiritual reading of its opening lines, the account of Jacob's dream. Here a number of themes that were central to the concerns of Hasidism found a seemingly natural Biblical mooring. While similar interpretive devices appear in several of the ten homilies that comprise this section, the amazing variety in the *content* of interpretation is especially worthy of note.

The section opens with a discussion of Jacob's departure from Beersheba and his journey to Haran. The sojourn abroad is depicted as the fulfillment of a mission: Jacob leaves Beersheba, the place of Torah, in order to go seek out those bits of Torah that dwell outside the holy place. This is Jacob's essential task, and all that he does while in the house of Laban, including his adventures with both flocks and daughters, is to be read in this light. Thus are justified the questionable deeds of this most complex of the patriarchs, revered by the rabbis as "the choicest" among them. So too, though without direct statement, does the author suggest the essential character of Israel's dispersion among the nations: Living with Laban and keeping the commandments was to be the fate of Jacob's children for many generations. Perhaps there is also an unspoken reference here to the task of his own generation, that of going forth from the new Hasidic Beersheba, Miezrich of the Maggid's court, and spreading the teaching in places where it had not yet been heard.

In a latter part of the same teaching, Rabbi Nahum offers an interesting Hasidic contribution to the ongoing question of revelation and human creativity in the promulgation of Torah. The problem is formulated in terms of the differences of opinion among the sages: If Torah is one, and the result of revelation, how are such differences possible? The answer offered is that all is indeed one in the mind of God, the ultimate source of all Torah. As the teaching flows through the lower sefirotic world, however, differentiation begins to take place. Each configuration in that lower world offers a unique vantage point from which to view the single truth of Torah. Since human souls are distinct in their "roots" above, each of the sages speaks the truth as seen from within the root of his own soul: Truth is one, but perspectives are many.

The second teaching views Jacob's departure and sojourn in terms of the *zaddiq*'s relationship to a particular place. His presence brings holiness and glory to a place, and as he departs he takes this glory with him. Something of that former place remains with the *zaddiq*, however, and he continues to represent its particular holiness. It appears that this homily was offered by Rabbi Nahum on the occasion of his own or another Hasidic leader's move from one location to another. In later times it was indeed true that a *zaddiq* who moved from one town to another might continue to bear the name of the former place as his own (e.g., the Ruzhyner *rebbe* in Sadegora). The text before us seems to indicate that this was the case already in the earliest days of Hasidism.

It is to the fifth teaching in *Wa-Yeze*, however, that we should turn our greatest attention. Here we have a major teaching on *da'at*, and on the place of this faculty in the religious task. Despite its popularity, Hasidism maintains a verbal/intellectual approach to mysticism, and *da'at*, here depicted as the borderline faculty between the highest reaches of speech and the place of purely silent contemplation beyond, is central to its system. The contemplative faculties above, *hokhmah* and *binah*, while existing in undisturbed silence, are also the sources of both life and Torah. All being and all truth flow from them into *da'at*, the faculty of mind, and only there are they given name. This faculty is represented by both Jacob and Moses; Jacob is here depicted as beginning that revelatory process which was to culminate with the giving of the Torah in Moses' day.

Moving in the other direction, *da'at* is also that power (here, as always, both in the human mind and in the cosmos) which receives the gift of devotional effort in love and fear, channeling these religious emotions so that they may rise higher and reach their final goal.

203

THE LIGHT OF THE EYES

To put it in our language, *da'at* is that which refines and so cools the intensity of religious emotion that it may give way to true contemplation. Given the setting of a religious movement of great popular enthusiasm, coupled with the striving of the Maggid and his followers for an ultimate attachment to God that transcended this enthusiasm and ever sought to raise it higher, we can well understand the great emphasis that our author places on the function of *da'at* as such a channel.

The same teaching also contains some significant reflections on the theology of language, a topic treated with some frequency by the early Hasidic authors. Hasidism takes an extreme realist position with regard to language, claiming that it is in fact the Word itself that lies at the very core of being, all reality coming into existence around the Word of God. This is of course a reification of the opening chapter of Genesis and the notion of Creation *through* the Word; here the essential *product* of Creation is also nothing but the Word itself. It is this Word that is to be uplifted and brought to contemplative silence. Since the Word is so central to all of being, however, transformation of language necessarily bears with it the promise of universal renewal.

Wa-Yeze offers a broad spectrum of the varied teachings contained in the works of the Hasidic masters. Rabbi Nahum, like many others, probably spoke both to a close circle of disciples and to a broader audience of the townspeople of Chernobyl and the surrounding areas. While no formal distinction is made in the editing, it seems likely that some of the homilies collected in such a volume as this were directed toward students, while others were of a more public nature. The final two teachings in the section before us are clearly examples of the latter sort. Essentially moralistic in concern, they seek to infuse the real concerns of everyday people with the spirit of the Hasidic revival. The last teaching in particular, dealing with holiness (defined as integrity) in business dealings, is of this sort. Jews in Rabbi Nahum's time were largely small business people or tradesmen; a teaching that showed them how honest business dealings were a higher form of worship even than Torah itself (traces of Hasidic anti-elitism are to be found here) was indeed of great significance to their lives. It was through teachings of this sort, those that integrated the abstruse mystical insights of Miezrich with the everyday lives of Jews in the towns where they preached, that the Maggid's disciples conquered the hearts of East European Jewry for Hasidism.

* * *

I

JACOB LEFT BEER-SHEBA AND SET OUT FOR HA-
RAN. HE CAME UPON A CERTAIN PLACE AND
STOPPED THERE FOR THE NIGHT, FOR THE SUN
HAD SET. TAKING SOME OF THE STONES OF
THAT PLACE, HE PUT THEM UNDER HIS HEAD.
HE HAD A DREAM . . .

EARLY IN THE MORNING, JACOB TOOK THE
STONE THAT HE HAD PUT UNDER HIS HEAD
AND SET IT UP AS A PILLAR AND POURED OIL ON
TOP OF IT. HE NAMED THAT SITE BETHEL, BUT
PREVIOUSLY THE NAME OF THAT CITY HAD
BEEN LUZ. (Gen. 28:10–11, 18–19)

Our rabbis learned from the Scriptures that he had been "hidden
in the house of Eber for fourteen years" and only afterwards went to
Haran. We wonder why it is that they chose to speak of him as "hidden" rather than saying that he studied with Eber[1] or some other expression. We know, however, that Jacob represents *da'at*, religious
mind or awareness. Jacob and Moses are identical in this, except that
one represents it from within, in a more hidden way, while the other
represents it as externalized.[2] Before Jacob went to Laban there had
been as yet no revelation of this mind or of Torah; all was still hidden. Various elements of the Torah lay scattered about in the lower
universe, because no such revelation had yet taken place. In the house
of Laban too there were elements of Torah; these are seen in the Torah's tales of what Jacob did in that household, bringing forth and purifying roots of Torah from their burial deep beneath the fearful
powers of Laban.

Jacob spent twenty years there with Laban working to bring

---

1. Old rabbinic tradition represents Shem and Eber as having maintained schools
for the study of the ancient natural religion that was their legacy from Adam and
Noah.

2. Moses represents Torah revealed; in Jacob's day it is yet hidden.

forth those roots of Torah. That is why the place is called HARAN, referring to the anger (*HaRoN*) of God; here the Torah-roots were so deeply buried as to call the place one of divine anger. Everything Jacob had to do with Laban, involving both his daughters and his sheep, had to do with this single task, as we know from the various esoteric teachings on these passages. His placing of the stripped sticks in the troughs (Gen. 30:38) so that the flock would bear streaked, speckled, and spotted young were all matters of the most profound secrets and sublime mysteries. His marriage to both Leah and Rachel[3] refers to the written and oral Torahs; he foresaw and prepared the way for the revelation of Torah below. All this was hidden until Jacob's time; because he represented *da'at* he could draw forth the revelation of Torah from BEER-SHEBA, for the upper Torah is called by that name.[4]

Thus JACOB LEFT BEER-SHEBA: He left that place of the Torah's hiding, in order to bring it out into the open. He did this by means of the purifications that he performed in HARAN, the place of the evil forces, behind which the Torah had been hidden. All this was to prepare the coming generations, so that they might receive as revelation that which had formerly always been in hiding. Thus did the Ba'al Shem Tov (his soul among the heavenly treasures!) say concerning Laban's pursuit of Jacob. The portion of Torah contained in those verses that tell of his pursuit and of the argument between Jacob and Laban afterwards—those bits of Torah were still there in hiding with Laban: Jacob had not managed to purify them. God caused Laban to run after Jacob, to bring to him that portion of Torah that had not yet been brought forth. When he reached him, Jacob was able through their conversation to attain to this Torah and purify it, so that nothing more remained with Laban. Everything he did with Laban, all that is told in the Scriptures, was for the sake of Torah and God's service, to bring that Torah out from amid the depths beneath which it was buried in Haran and to rejoin it to the Torah above. That is why, when Jacob first came near to Haran, we are told that "he rolled away the stone from the mouth of the well" (Gen. 29:10). He removed the obstacle that blocks the wellspring of living

---

3. Marriage to two sisters is a violation of Lev. 18:18, a matter that gives rise to considerable speculation by the commentators of many generations.

4. Beer-Sheba, supraliterally "the sevenfold well," is a term for the *shekhinah*, who is also called "Torah," especially the oral Torah, in the uppermost world.

waters, the roots of Torah that were hidden there. He revealed the well (*wa-yeGAL/GiLLaH*), bringing it out from amid the stonelike shells that had hidden it. Of this Scripture says: "Remove the heart of stone from your flesh" (Ezek. 36:26). Then the Torah that was there began to be seen.

This was also why Jacob sent messengers ahead to his brother Esau. These messengers were the angels who had been created in the course of his own study and life in the commandments. He sent them to say "I dwelt with Laban" (Gen. 32:5), meaning it as RaSHI understood it, "and I kept the six hundred thirteen commandments" (*GaR-TY/TaRYaG*). All twenty years he had waited there in order to reveal the Torah with all of its commandments: therefore "I have delayed until now." The Torah is called "Now," as Scripture elsewhere says: "*Now* write for yourselves" (Deut. 31:19). The revelation of Torah is *now*. He means to says that he has delayed because the revelation of Torah was taking place. This is why the rabbis first said that he had been "hidden"; the Torah that Jacob was to reveal by his journey to Haran was yet hidden when he stopped at the house of Eber.

This is the meaning of JACOB LEFT BEER-SHEBA: The Zohar says that he took a step outside, that the hidden Torah of Beer-Sheba came out of its hiding through Jacob. He went outward, to Haran, toward the externalization of Torah, for all [he did there] was hidden Torah. This is true of all matters, including the narratives, that are found in the Torah as we now have it. They are of the very essence of Torah, and if a single letter is missing of those narrative sections, a Torah scroll is deemed unfit for use: they are Torah. There is no distinction made in this between the section commanding *ziẓit* or *tefillin* (fringes or phylacteries) and this portion on Jacob's sticks, how he stripped them, and all the rest. Those who have true knowledge realize that Torah is all one. This is the very body of Torah, as will be known to one who has studied the holy books; this is the secret of secrets, out of which the light breaks forth that shines on the lower rungs. All this comes about through Jacob, the choicest among the patriarchs, of whom it is said: "Then shall your light break forth like the dawn" (Isa. 58:8). "Break forth" has the same letters as "Jacob" (*YiBaQa'/Ya'aQoB*), for the light of Torah is ever breaking forth through Jacob, the mind of Torah, who brings it forth to be revealed and casts aside that which hides it.

Now we may understand that he is first depicted TAKING

SOME OF THE STONES OF THE PLACE[5], yet shortly thereafter
it says that JACOB TOOK THE STONE. RaSHI says that the
stones quarreled with one another, each of them saying: "Upon me
may this *zaddiq* rest his head!" We know how mind is poured forth
from the unified source above and comes down into this world of separation; only as it enters this universe is mind divided. This is the
source of the controversies and divisions among the sages in understanding the mind of Torah, [of which it is said]: "Both these and
those are the words of the living God!" Mind comes from this sublime and completely unified source above; it is divided only as it enters into the universe of distinctions, the place where the souls of
Israel originate. So it is that there were twelve stones, for mind is divided according to one's root in the twelve tribes of Israel. The
twelve stones represented the twelve tribes, but in their root they
were one.[6] Each person's opinions follow the root of his soul. That is
why he understands Torah in a particular way. Another, who says
the very opposite, may be acting just as faithfully in accord with the
root of his own soul. In their source, both are the words of the living
God, since all is one. In the flow of *da'at* from *binah* there is no division or conflict at all; only as mind enters the world of separation is it
too separated and does it flow through varied channels. All the sages
really mean the same thing, however, since all of them are drawing
from the same well, from the same mind. Only in this world of separation do their opinions appear to diverge. When the controversy is
uplifted back to its root, to the world of unity, all become one again,
and then "both these and those are the words of the living God."
Now there were twelve stones, each designated by one of the tribes,
as we have said, but in their root all of their differing minds were one.
That is why the stones were "quarreling" with one another. They
were "stones" (or "rocks") as in "There, the shepherd, the Rock of Israel" (Gen. 49:24). Each represented a part of the truth, just as in the
controversies of the sages concerning the oral Torah. Each said:
"Upon me may the *zaddiq* rest his head," upon me may he rely to act
correctly in God's service and in the commandments. Each of them
intends the truth, for all of them draw from that same source in Jacob. Only because our world is a divided one do they appear contra-

---

5. The word *me-aveney* does not necessarily indicate a plural, and modern translations do not render it that way.

6. As the tribes were yet one in Jacob.

dictory and disputed. But when mind is returned to its root in the one they become one stone again, A PILLAR standing firmly in one place, bearing no dispute or conflict at all.

Thus EARLY IN THE MORNING, he rose to the light of dawn, the light of mind while yet in its source. He TOOK THE STONE THAT HE HAD PUT UNDER HIS HEAD, the head and source that flows forth from the world of oneness. AND SET IT UP AS A PILLAR, standing firmly in one place, without conflict. AND POURED OIL ON TOP OF IT: Light, which is compared to oil, flowed down on it from the source above. Here all opinions were equally good, all of them "the words of the living God." HE NAMED THAT SITE BETHEL, the compassion of God[7], for there it is all compassion, with none of that conflict that appears below. BUT PREVIOUSLY THE NAME OF THAT CITY HAD BEEN LUZ, Luz as in *naLoZ* and *meLiZ*, indicating something crooked, because of the great controversy. When it comes to its root it is called *Bet El*, the innermost divine compassion.

All this Jacob did for the sake of the generations to follow, that they might find a well-traveled path up to the Mountain of the Lord. He did this by that step outside, drawing forth from the upper source, from Beer-Sheba, and moving toward revelation. This is the secret meaning of all the wells that the patriarchs dug: they ever sought the waters of Torah in the earth of the lower rungs. So said the Ba'al Shem Tov on the verse "All the wells that his father's servants had dug in the days of Abraham had been sealed up by the Philistines and filled with earth" (Gen. 26:15). Each of the patriarchs brought forth the revelation of Torah out of the earth, from the lower rungs, by working through the particular quality that he represented. Each thus found that well of living waters which would not become covered with earth. After Abraham died, however, his revelation was sealed over; it was the "Philistines," the forces of evil, that were responsible for this. Isaac came and redug them, as it says: "Isaac returned and dug out the wells that had been dug in the days of Abraham his father" (Gen. 26:18). This too refers to a revelation of Torah. Even today Torah lies hidden in those very particular deeds of Abraham and Isaac; they did this all for the sake of later generations. Were it not for the patriarchs there would be no way to understand

---

7. The name *El* in Kabbalistic usage indicates *ḥesed*, the compassionate right hand of God.

or to draw near to God at all. Everything we do in His holy service, even now, is done along with our holy forefathers. This is the meaning of "Abraham yet stands before the Lord" (Gen. 22:18)—in the present, constantly, does Abraham take his place at the right hand of the righteous, to help us by all that he has prepared and revealed. It is he who shows us how to dig wells of living water in the earth. Then came Jacob, the choicest of the patriarchs. The three of them joined together make up the secret of Torah and of mind. It was through Jacob that the revelation came, by way of Haran and through the earth, thus completing the written Torah, Leah, and the oral Torah, Rachel. By his actions in the house of Laban he brought the twelve tribes forth from there, the twelve representing the twelve possible permutations of the YHWH. This is the meaning of Jacob's saying: "Name the wages due from me and I will pay you" (Gen. 30:28)—this refers to the written and oral Torah; the only "wage" Jacob sought was that they be completed. This was his whole intent.

II

JACOB LEFT BEER-SHEBA.

Another interpretation. RaSHI tells us here that "the departure of a *zaddiq* from a place makes an imprint. So long as the *zaddiq* is in a city, he is its glory, its brilliance, its beauty. When the *zaddiq* leaves, the town's glory is diminished."

To understand this we have to remember that the *zaddiq* is called "all," for he holds fast to both heaven and earth. He joins himself to every rung of being in the world, and has a special attachment to the place where he is, so that all there are joined to him in unity. As he rises upward, all of them rise up with him and are included in a sublime holiness, so that the place where the *zaddiq* lives eventually comes to bear a special holy quality. Its relationship to the *zaddiq* gives it a unique glow of beauty. Such a place is "the four ells of the *halakhah*," and we are told that God has nought but these in His world.[1] As the *zaddiq* is ever bound to his Creator, drawn into His sublime light and beauty, he becomes a kind of temple. We have spo-

---

1. Here *halakhah* seems to be read overliterally as "the place where the *zaddiq* walks."

ken of this elsewhere. Therefore when the *zaddiq* leaves a place, its glory does indeed diminish. The holiness and glory that it formerly had was only because of that person's relationship to it. Now that the *zaddiq* has become associated with another place, holiness has indeed passed on with him.

That holiness, now joined back to its root in the *zaddiq* himself, however, accompanies him always, and no matter where he goes, the *zaddiq* will always bear within him the holiness of his former place and the light and glory that he had brought upon it.[2] Wherever he goes he is considered as one who "comes upon" his former place.... The life he had brought to that place is called "the Land of Israel," and Beer-Sheba includes the entire Land. Our father Jacob brought divine life into Beer-Sheba while he was still associated with that place. Afterwards, when he stepped outside it to go to Haran in order to reveal what had to be brought forth there, he still came upon the life of that first place wherever his foot trod. This is the meaning of JACOB LEFT BEER-SHEBA: Even though he left it to step outside, the aspect of Beer-Sheba went along with him to Haran. When the *zaddiq* left the town, its light departed and was joined to the One. This is why HE CAME UPON A CERTAIN PLACE: Wherever he went he kept encountering that same place that had been so special to him before. By means of the light of that first place, now joined to him forever, HE STOPPED FOR THE NIGHT. Even though he was coming to a place of thick darkness, as indicated by HE SET OUT FOR HARAN ... FOR THE SUN HAD SET, he still took SOME OF THE STONES OF THAT PLACE, he took with him the letters forming the name of his previous place. It is in the letters, as is known, that glory and light dwell, for the *zaddiq* rises upward by means of attaching himself to the letters; from the supernal letters holy life-energy flows down upon the *zaddiq* and his place. This is TAKING SOME OF THE STONES of his *former* PLACE, which ever accompanies him, HE PUT THEM UNDER HIS HEAD, for this life drawn from a holy place would allow night to shine like the day. And so HE LAY DOWN; the *Tiqquney Zohar* tells us that "and he lay down" (*wa-yishkav*) can also be read "there are twenty-two" (*we-yesh kaf-bet*); he lay down in that place where the twenty-two letters of the alphabet gave forth their life. That is why the text goes on

---

2. In practice, a Hasidic *zaddiq* who moved from one town to another sometimes continued to be called by the name of his former place.

to say: "I shall give to you the land upon which you are lying." Ra-SHI teaches that God had folded up the entire Land of Israel under him. The truth is, however, that by the life of Beer-Sheba, which *is* the entire Land of Israel, the Land went with him on his way. The entire Holy Land was under him no matter where his feet trod, for "in the first sanctification the Land was declared holy for that time and for the future."[3] This was true for those who left and were to return. The rest is understood.

Blessed is the Lord forever. Amen. Amen.

III

JACOB LEFT BEER-SHEBA . . .

In understanding this we must remember what we have learned both from books and from sages: Everything in the Torah must apply to each person and to every time.

First we must understand the verses JACOB SAW A WELL IN THE FIELD. THREE FLOCKS OF SHEEP WERE LYING THERE BESIDE IT, FOR THE FLOCKS WERE WATERED FROM THAT WELL. THE STONE ON THE MOUTH OF THE WELL WAS LARGE. WHEN ALL THE FLOCKS WERE GATHERED THERE, THE STONE WOULD BE ROLLED FROM THE MOUTH OF THE WELL AND THE SHEEP WATERED. (Gen. 29:2–3)

The sages have taught us that God created the world through the Torah, that He conducts the world through it, and that all life and energy come from the holy Torah. Torah is thus called a well of living waters; it is in this way that the wells dug by the patriarch are to be understood. They brought the well of Torah into this world, even into the corporeal itself. He SAW A WELL IN THE FIELD; this world is called a field, one that needs to be worked, plowed, and planted. Those who study Torah are called "workers in the field." Jacob found the well that the previous patriarchs had dug, all ready for him. The THREE FLOCKS OF SHEEP are Abraham, Isaac, and Ja-

---

3. A Talmudic phrase originally applied to the conquest of Joshua's day and stating the permanence of Israel's claim on its Holy Land, but here homiletically referred to the days of the patriarchs and their wanderings in the Land.

cob; it is through them that the entire world carries on. THE
FLOCKS WERE WATERED FROM THAT WELL: From there
does life flow forth for all the world.

THE STONE ON THE MOUTH OF THE WELL WAS
LARGE: This refers to the evil urge, who does not let us enter into
the well of Torah. He rouses our pride and self-interest; only the one
who repents can merit to enter. Thus the sages said [of the evil urge]:
"Drag him off to the house of study!" By the *house* they referred to
interior study, the act of repentance. Then "if he is a stone, he will
melt away." He is called by seven names, one of them being "stum-
bling-block (literally: "stumbling-*stone*"). Here by means of Torah,
one of these names—*stone*—is wiped away. This is why ALL THE
FLOCKS WERE GATHERED THERE: It was established that we
should say "For the sake of uniting the Holy One, blessed be He, and
His *shekhinah*, in love and in fear . . . in the name of all Israel"[1] so that
each of us be joined to all of Israel and be unified. God dwells with
that oneness, and then "evil cannot abide with You" (Ps. 5:5); the urge
that is called "evil" cannot be there at all. And so THE STONE
WOULD BE ROLLED: A second name of the evil urge, "evil," has
also be destroyed. Understand this.[2]

IV

JACOB LEFT BEER-SHEBA . . . HE HAD A DREAM; A
LADDER WAS SET UPON THE GROUND AND ITS
TOP REACHED TO HEAVEN, AND ANGELS OF
GOD WERE GOING UP AND DOWN ON IT.

The Midrash says that he saw the angels of Babylon and Greece first
ascend and then come down the ladder. When he saw the angel of
Edom go up he said: "God forbid, might he never be coming down?"[1]

---

1. The Kabbalists, beginning in the sixteenth century, ordained that this formula
of intent be recited before performing any of the commandments.
2. The teaching is never tied back to the original verse, and must therefore be considered fragmentary. It must have had something to do again with his placing his head
on "some of the stones of that place."
1. Babylon and Greece represent the nations responsible for two of Israel's early
tribulations; their stars have both ascended and fallen. Edom or Rome represents the
last exile, to conclude only when messiah comes. Jacob cries out: "Might this exile never end?"

God answered: "Fear not, my servant Jacob, for I am with you" (Jer. 46:28). Even if he comes all the way up to Me, I will take him down, as Scripture says [concerning Edom]: "Should you nest as high as the eagle, should your eyrie be lodged among the stars, even from there I will pull you down, declares the Lord" (Obad. 1:4). This is properly interpreted in the Midrash.

To understand all this we must recall that the patriarchs looked with their mind's eye and foresaw all the later generations, with all their troubles and their exiles. They prayed for all of them. Our father Jacob saw that in the course of exile the gates of prayer would be locked shut, as we have learned: "From the time the Temple was destroyed, the gates of prayer are locked."[2] He sought some release for his offspring, some way in which their prayers might after all be heard. God then showed him that ladder SET UPON THE GROUND. The *shekhinah* is called a ladder, for it is "the gateway to the Lord; the righteous may come through it" (Ps. 118:20). It is set on the earth, for even though the *shekhinah* disappeared after the Temple's destruction, ("the *shekhinah* underwent ten journeys") some bit of it remains. It is by means of this that one may go up to God, as in "I am with him in sorrow" (Ps. 91:15). This is the LADDER SET UPON THE GROUND, even though ITS TOP REACHED TO HEAVEN. Some aspect of *shekhinah* still remains here to help us. Whatever strength we have in the course of this exile to ascend to a higher place comes about through the twenty-two letters that are fixed in our mouths. By that longing which the letters arouse in us, we are able to go up the ladder until we reach our proper rung.

Jacob also foresaw that if the decree of [the first] exile had been delayed but two more years, Israel would have been utterly lost. He prayed concerning this, and God brought about the exile two years before its predicted time.[3] "God did a good deed in bringing about the exile two years before its time." This is FOR THE SUN HAD SET: It set not in its proper time, for the destruction of the Temple was like the setting of the sun. Jacob was at that moment on Mount

---

2. The gates of tears, however, remain open.
3. Based on a Talmudic statement (Gittin 88a) that the Babylonian exile took place 850 years after Israel entered the land. Two years later they would have lived there as many years as the numerical value of *we-noshantem* "long established"; Deut. 4:25), and then they would have been "utterly lost" (vs. 26).

Moriah, the site of the Temple.[4] He took this as his chance to effect redemption in that place, just as Abraham did when he "went in pursuit as far as Dan" (Gen. 14:14). We learn that there Abraham grew weak [for he saw that his offspring were to worship idols there— Judg. 18] and he prayed for them. The same was true of his descent into Egypt: There too he was setting the place aright so that his descendants might one day be able to leave. So it was with Jacob, as he passed by that place where the Temple was to stand. He performed whatever acts were required for his children off in the final generations. Thus TAKING SOME OF THE STONES OF THE PLACE, he was already mourning the destruction, seeing that the gates of prayer would then be closed. But by those stones (and the *Sefer Yezirah* refers to the letters as stones, those letters of *we-yesh kaf bet*, "there are twenty-two" in this verse) there would be redemption in that place even after the destruction, for the power of the letters would arouse God's mercy.

This mercy is represented, according to the Kabbalistic study of divine names, by the name YHWH as vocalized with the *holam* sign (ō). This *holam* is represented by Jacob's dream (*holam/halom*); his dream set the *holam* right, and the ladder was set on the ground. This happened by Jacob's own petition. "And behold the Lord stood over him"—this refers to the *holam* that stands above the name.[5]

Jacob saw that the earlier exiles would take place through powers whose stars would rise and fall rather quickly, their strength being rather limited. But when he saw that this final exile would be that caused by Edom, the prince among all those powers (for all were really but aspects of him), he finally became frightened, fearing that Edom would never fall. Then God reassured him with: "Fear not, My servant Jacob." Truly this final exile will last until God decides to redeem for His own sake. Redemption will take place only through Him, as Scripture says: "The Lord will punish the entire host of heaven in heaven and all the kings of earth on earth" (Isa. 24:21).

And so JACOB LEFT BEER-SHEBA, the rung of the *shekhinah*.

---

4. The old rabbinic sources already ignore the connection of the Jacob narrative with Bethel, the shrine of the northern kingdom, and assimilate this site to that of the binding of Isaac and the future Temple, the only "gate of heaven" that they allow.

5. The vowel sign for ō is called *holam*, represented either by the *waw* with a point above it or, as in this case, simply by a supralineal point. The point is that Jacob's prayer brings the mercies of God down on him.

Having the task of raising up all the future generations, he had to go down from his own rung and lower himself to that level where they were to be. He SET OUT FOR HARAN, the place of judgment forces. That is why HE CAME UPON A CERTAIN PLACE, also interpreted to read "he prayed to God," he prayed for them from there. Understand this.

V

JACOB LEFT BEER-SHEBA . . . HE HAD A DREAM . . . AND ANGELS OF GOD WERE GOING UP AND DOWN ON IT.

The Midrash says that Jacob foresaw the four kingdoms of the four exiles, Babylonia, Medea, Greece, and Edom [= Rome]. He saw each of them rise and fall. God said to him: Why do you not come up the ladder? He replied: I am afraid lest I fall like all the others. God answered: Had you had faith in Me and come up, no nation or culture could ever have had power over you or your seed. Now that you have shown this lack of faith, these nations shall enslave your children. And yet despite this, never say that I am deserting them in their exile. "I will make an end of all the nations among which I have banished you, but I will not make an end of you" (Jer. 46:28).

In understanding this, we must first remember that the source of Torah and the fount of wisdom from which we receive the revealed word is in the thought of God Himself; God's *ḥokhmah* and *binah* are the World of Thought. There the Torah exists in a completely hidden way, not revealed at all. In that place there exists neither speech nor language. In order to be revealed as word, the Torah must pass through *da'at*, that which is to bring it from the World of Thought into the World of Speech. *Da'at* includes both love and fear, both compassion and rigor. It is because Moses represents *da'at* that the Torah so frequently says: "The Lord spoke unto Moses saying, 'Speak unto the children of Israel.' "[1] We have shown this elsewhere as well: Moses brings the hidden Torah from the World of Thought to the children of Israel in the form of speech. By means of *da'at*, the revela-

---

1. Moses, as *da'at*, is the channel of revelation that brings language and expression to that which had formerly been beyond speech.

tory power of speech has been joined to the source of secret wisdom. For this reason the Zohar tells us that "any word spoken by a person without fear and love does not fly upward." As we have said, *da'at* contains both love and fear; only through it can the revealed word be joined to its sublime and hidden source, [even] without understanding.[2]

This is why a person who studies Torah or prays with both love and fear can attain proper awareness and create a channel in his mind and speech so that the eternal fount of wisdom may flow into him. The Torah that he speaks has become completely one with its source in *hokhmah* and *binah* above. Study marked by such love and fear truly shows the rung of *da'at*; its words go right up to their very root, and a great act of union takes place. Study without this content, of course, is not the same. Here the words are cut off from their root; there is no one to join the revealed word to its source in the wellsprings above. Not rising and being joined to its source, the verbal Torah that you study cannot receive the flow of fine oil that might otherwise come upon it.

Thus should you understand "Judgment forces are sweetened only in their root": this refers to *binah*, as we have said earlier: "I am *binah* and *gevurah* is mine," says Scripture (Prov. 8:14).[3] The Torah is called *binah* and it claims the judgment forces as its own; they must all be brought back to Torah, out of which they first arose. It is there that they can be transformed. When such forces come on a person, he begins to become more aware, and love and fear enter into his sacred speech. He then takes hold of himself with this renewed awareness, and this *da'at* binds his words to the World of Thought, bringing about that unification. Then are his words uplifted and bound to their root. Since *da'at* is the joining of love and fear, compassion and judgment, the judgment forces that are now surrounded by compassion may rise up to that World of Thought, the place where there is

---

2. He has now reversed the process, showing that *da'at* is crucial to both directions of the flow. In the transmission of Torah from God to man, *da'at* represents conscious mind, the level of understanding to which speech is first appropriate and where speech may enter. As we turn to God in prayer, *da'at* represents our religious awareness or presence of mind; only with this mind, composed first of love and fear, can prayer ascend to God. Even with proper prayer and inwardness, however, true understanding of *hokhmah* and *binah* is beyond human reach.

3. Conventionally translated: "I am understanding and power is mine," but here meaning that *binah*, the second of the *sefirot*, stands at the head of the left column and is thus the ultimate source of judgment, even of the demonic. See above, *bereshit* 2.

no judgment at all. Only down below are compassion and judgment split off from one another; up above there is only the Torah of Compassion . . . simple mercy . . . thus by means of *da'at* does one attain in utter unity to the World of Thought, the place where judgment and compassion are rejoined and transformed.

What has happened is that those forces, formerly in a downward trend, are now uplifted through *da'at* and made holy again; joined to love, they become the proper fear of God. The good in them has been uplifted and the evil falls away. These forces had come from judgment above, and it was only due to human failings that they had been mixed with evil and become forces of persecution.[4] By studying Torah in love and fear one has taken the good out of these forces to rejoin it to Torah. Thus are the judgment forces sweetened: The good is separated out of the evil, and the evil falls by the way. Thus have I heard in the name of the Ba'al Shem Tov concerning the following passage in the Talmud:

Mar 'Ukva sent this question to Rabbi Eleazar: "There are people standing up against me, and I have the power to turn them over to the civil authorities. What shall I do?" He [Rabbi Eleazar] drew lines on paper and wrote to him: " 'I resolved I would watch my step lest I offend by my speech; I would keep my mouth muzzled while the wicked was in my presence' (Ps. 39:2). Even though confronted by the wicked, I should keep my mouth muzzled." He sent back: "But they bother me terribly, and I have no way to punish them." Rabbi Eleazar answered: " 'Be silent and wait (*titHoLeL*) for the Lord' (Ps. 37:7)—Be silent and He will cause them to drop before you like corpses (*HaLaLim*). Go to the House of Study over them morning and evening, and they will be destroyed on their own." The Ba'al Shem Tov interpreted this passage in accord with what we have taught. Rabbi Eleazar offered great advice, saying that if you go to the House of Study morning and evening, bearing them in mind, the judgment forces in those enemies will be sweetened. The fact that a person has enemies below is only the result of some judgment on him from above, mixed with evil impurities and then garbed in the sort of person in this world who would be appropriate to such a role. The best advice in this situation is not to challenge the enemy, but to go daily to the House of Study, into the innermost Torah, to a place of aware-

---

4. Heb.: *li-fe'ol dinim*. See Introduction on the ambiguities of the term *dinim* and the difficulty in translating it.

ness. By studying and praying with love and fear you will arouse true *da'at*. Then you and your words will be raised up to the World of Thought, that place where there is no judgment, no Satan, no enemy, but only pure goodness. Then you, along with those fallen forces that had become enemies, will be drawn into the good.

All this can happen only when you have truly accepted that those fallen powers contain the holy letters; whatever judgment forces come down on you, they contain fallen letters. That is why we speak about and deal with events that happen to us through language. The very letters through which we talk about the event are letters through which, in their fallen state, the event had taken place. In holding fast to the letters of Torah, through love and fear, the person is drawn by the force of those letters to the Torah's source. Then the fallen letters . . . are also returned to their root, to the good. Everything that comes into this world, whether for good or ill, comes about through certain permutations of the letters. By raising up the good that is within the judgments, the evil that had become mixed with good is separated and falls away and everything becomes a part of the good. Then those people who had been enemies are also transformed into friends; without the judgment forces from above, they will do no ill. This is what Rabbi Eleazar meant when he said, "He will cause them to drop before you like corpses"—the evil in those forces will indeed fall; all life taken from it, it will be as a corpse. The good that had been a part of those forces will have been redeemed, reincluded in the good and transformed into the fear of God. . . . Thus Scripture said: "Be silent and wait for the Lord." Bring those letters that had been a part of the evil up to the world of silence, the World of Thought, in which neither speech nor language has come to be. In that place there can be only good, with no pollution by evil at all. This *da'at* is, as we have said, symbolized by our father Jacob.

This then is JACOB LEFT BEER-SHEBA: Jacob, as *da'at*, left the realm of hidden Torah, that source of wisdom which is called the well of living waters or Beer-sheba (for of wisdom Scripture says: "She has hewn out her seven pillars"—Prov. 9:1). *Da'at* draws forth from this spring and brings it out into speech; only in this way is the uplifting and sweetening of the fallen letters made possible. Thus HE WENT TO HARAN: mind has to go forth to that place of divine anger (*HaRoN*) . . . to bring those forces back up to their original well-springs in the World of Thought. HE CAME UPON A CERTAIN PLACE: The Hebrew verb used for "came upon" can also refer to prayer; you begin to pray from the very place to which you have fallen. If your prayer is a mindful one, combining both love and fear with the letters of Torah, the letters of that judgment place will be joined to them as well. [This place had represented] the hiding of God's face, as in "I will keep My countenance hidden" and this is "for there is no God within me" (Deut. 31:18). It is the damage wrought by sin that takes one away from God: But now that the forces of judgment and the fallen letters are raised up by the presence of mind and are joined to the good, he is able to STOP THERE FOR THE NIGHT, as in "He lies between my breasts" (Cant. 1:13—*wa-yaLeN/ yaLiN*). By repairing the damage and uplifting the judgments he indeed can cleave to God. Evil is there only because "there is no God within me"; once the presence of God has been restored, all is goodness and blessing. And so Jacob lay down there, as one who "lies between my breasts." This refers to the dwelling of God in the midst of the people Israel.

FOR THE SUN HAD SET: We learn elsewhere that "the Lord God is the sun and a shield" (Ps. 84:12). His divinity, despite a thousand differences, is like the sun, in that one cannot look into it except through a shield or visor. Thus can the brilliant light of *Eyn Sof* not be perceived except in greatly reduced form. Now the sun has set before its time by a person's fall into the place of judgment; as he is redeemed from there, the brilliant sun begins to shine on him once again.... All this because he took SOME OF THE STONES OF THAT PLACE: He took the letters (which the *Sefer Yezirah* calls stones) from that very place, and he PUT THEM AT HIS HEAD, he raised them up to the source of the letters, the wellspring of Torah, the World of Thought. In this sense *wa-yaḥalom*, he became well again (*ḤaLom/ḤaLiM*—Aram.); he healed the sickness of the judgment forces and brought them back into the good.

Now there was A LADDER SET UPON THE GROUND. Mind is such a ladder, reaching downward to the most revealed of levels, its TOP REACHING TO HEAVEN, to the place of true liberation, the World of Thought.[5] The ANGELS OF GOD, those emissaries of divine judgment, WERE GOING UP AND DOWN ON

---

5. True liberation is found in the boundlessness of the fully contemplative life, set loose from those attachments to corporeal things that necessarily keep one in a world of limitation. The World of Thought, identified with *binah*, is associated with freedom or liberation by a long Kabbalistic tradition in the exegesis of the Jubilee command (Lev. 25:10).

IT. RaSHI says that each would first go up and then descend. This means that by the true application of mind to prayer and study, performing them with the proper combination of love and fear, the very letters that had formed words of judgment against a person are rejoined to the good. Then the evil is separated and falls aside, as we have said. AND BEHOLD THE LORD WAS BESIDE HIM: Here the name used (YHWH) is that which indicates compassion; the transforming of judgments arouses the flow of divine compassion from the source of life. Now we see that HE LAY DOWN IN THAT PLACE should indeed be interpreted as did the mystics, referring to the twenty-two letters of the alphabet.[6] The letters of Creation were there too, but in a fallen state. By cleaving to the Torah with presence of mind, he able to uplift these letters also and to join them to the good.

In the exile of Israel, some of those judging forces from above take on the form of nations that bring us suffering. Were Israel to have full faith in the power of mind, and apply it to Torah study with proper devotion, they would uplift and transform all such judgments into pure good. Each of those nations would then have only one cycle of ascendency, followed by immediate decline, for the good would have been lifted out from it. It is only because our faith is imperfect that the exile lasts so long. Even those who do pray and study, if their minds are not fully attuned and if not accompanied by love and fear, cannot form the ladders needed for the transformation of judgment forces. This can be done only by mind. The true meaning of exile, then, is that mind is in exile because it is not employed properly in the service of God. The lessening of faith brings about a diminishing of mind; faith, the seventh of the upper rungs,[7] is the gateway through which one must enter to get to *da'at* and all the rest. The *Sefer Yezirah* tells us that God chooses to group all in sevens: seven lands, seven seas, and so forth. Now we understand why this is, for any ascent to the higher rungs must begin with the seventh, that is, with faith.

Now we may understand what the Midrash meant in saying that Jacob saw the four kingdoms, the four exiles. He saw the forces of judgment rising and descending, he saw how . . . such forces might be transformed. God's question to Jacob as to why he did not come up

---

6. See above, the second teaching of this section.

7. Faith is often a name for the *shekhinah*, seventh among the seven lower *sefirot*.

the ladder can now be interpreted; He teaches a great truth to Israel. The fact that we, worthy as we may be, are not uplifted and our exile is not ended is because the Jacob (=*da'at*) in us does not rise upward. This in turn is true because we are of little faith; our mind itself remains in a state of exile. That is why the Midrash says: "Had you shown faith in Me"—for all of this depends on faith. "Now that you showed this lack of faith," the Midrash goes on to say, by not serving God with presence of mind, with love and fear, and thus by not uplifting and transforming those forces of judgment, you indeed will be subjected to these four exiles. Nevertheless, God promises, "I will make an end of all the nations . . . but I will not make an end of you." In the end it will have to be that mind and faith spread forth in Israel; all those nations that had oppressed us will vanish from both this world and the next as the good in those judgment forces is sweetened and the evil falls away.

We are told that the nations are given this world, while Israel have the world to come. We should not, however, take this teaching too literally. We have also learned that all the worlds, all creatures great and small, were created for the sake of Israel. Surely they were not created for one from whom this world would entirely be taken away! Understand the matter rather this way: "For by *yod he* has the Lord formed the worlds (Isa. 26:4).[8] The world to come was created by *yod*, while this world was formed by *he*." This *he* that follows the *yod* is the second letter of the divine name, and these two letters are referred to in the Zohar as "two companions who are never separated." They are joined together as one; there exists no separation between them at all. So it is with the two worlds created through them: They too must be one and inseparable. This world is that of matter, the corporeal, while the other is that of form, of the soul. Just as in the case of a human being, so long as body and soul are joined together he lives, but they part company when he dies, so it is with the two worlds. Israel must therefore conduct themselves in this world by the ways of the soul, that which truly belongs to the next, so that the two worlds never be quite separate from one another. By purifying their bodies and avoiding in this world both the bad and the excessive, they are ever able to convert matter into form. They must use only that of this world needed for the soul, that element of the next world that

---

8. Based on Midrashic interpretation. Literally "For in Yah the Lord you have an everlasting rock."

gives them life. If they were indeed to do so entirely, matter and form would be completely one; matter would be so purified that it too could be called form, its corporeal existence only secondary. Then the life-force from above, that life of the world-to-come, would flow through it as well. All this would come about through the unifying force of mind, of that *da'at* SET UPON THE GROUND but whose TOP REACHES HEAVEN. Mind could make it so that this world too could be considered a world of life. People then would not fear to look at the light from above, their corporeal selves being so purified and joined to the soul. . . .

This world, bearing that divine life within it, has been granted to Israel alone, for it is truly the world to come. The excesses and luxuries of this world that have been assigned to the nations are not even a part of that "body" which the other-worldly soul inhabits. These are outside the body, mere lifeless waste and dross. This is referred to as "this world as dead," bearing within it no presence of the holy life. . . . Anyone with intelligence will be able to see clearly that the things of this world as the nations have them are in fact repulsive, being utterly without life.[9] Indeed one can see that it is all lifeless, mere excess and nothing more.

It is only Israel's lack of faith and mind, needed to bind this world to the world of the soul, that causes the world to fall constantly and to remain cut off from life. Then judgment comes to the world, and it is only for the few righteous ones in each generation who serve God with mind and with love and fear that the world is allowed to exist and does not fall utterly. It is they who turn God's justice back to mercy and bind the world to soul again. Thus Scripture says: "When evildoers rise up against me, my ears shall hear" (Ps. 92:12): The evildoers are the result of judgments, and I raise them up to that place where there is no speech but only hearing, the World of Thought.[10] There they are transformed.

In messianic times (speedily and in our day, God willing!) there will be so much mind-awareness in the world that this world and its corporeal self will indeed be purified and matter will be joined to

---

9. The author may be referring either to idolatry or to course materialism. The life of luxury as lived by the royalty and nobility of Eastern Europe was a natural object for the preachers' derision.

10. *Binah* is beyond voice; one may listen to and be instructed by its silence, but there is as yet no word. The purely contemplative may instruct, but only in silence. It is there that "evil" forces are transformed.

form, the two worlds united. Then evil, excess, and dross will all fall to the side, [eventually] to be purified. The nations that hold fast to them will also then fall, as life is removed entirely from that dross. . . . But this world, precious to God and beloved by Him, has in truth been given to Israel, the people He has loved from among all peoples and cultures. All is one: Divinity above, Israel, Torah, the world-to-come, and this world. All bring forth the flow of His Godliness, this world in a more external way, but containing within it that inward self of the world-to-come. These must be joined into a total oneness, such that will allow body to be translated into soul, just as happens within a single human person. This task has been given to Israel, the people close to Him; no others have a part in it until the redeemer comes. Then matter will be so purified that the term "this world" will no longer apply at all; everything will be one and it will be called the world-to-come. Of this Scripture says: "On that day shall the Lord be one and His name one" (Zech. 14:9).

Amen Selah unto eternity. Blessed is the Lord forever. Amen. Amen.

VI

JACOB LEFT BEER-SHEBA AND SET OUT FOR HARAN.

RaSHI comments: "When he reached Haran he decided to go back. The ground leapt forth to meet him; of this it is said: 'He came upon a certain place.' "[1]

A righteous person serves God by means of the life-strength and mental powers that are given him from above. Each one conceives of God according to his own measure, and in each the presence of God is concentrated, if you will, in just that degree. When the person has lived at that rung for some time, however, that presence of God is taken away from him, in order that he might strengthen himself to come to yet a higher rung of spiritual attainment. So long as he remains at that same rung, he is unable to reach beyond it; the very presence of

---

1. The comment is actually that of the Talmud, not RaSHI. See sources. *Wa-yelekh Haranah* is taken to mean that he arrived at Haran. Realizing that he had already passed the site of Bethel, the place sanctified by his forefathers, he set out to return. Then the place leapt out to him, and he found himself there immediately.

that rung within him and the force of habit blind him to seeing anything higher. Such is the nature of habit, to keep one within its path.
When it is taken from him, the *zaddiq* will reach out to hold fast to his
root.[2] Realizing that he has fallen, he will struggle upward. That
greater struggle will arouse further help from above, for we receive
help only insofar as we arouse it from below, as is known. But then
such a person will indeed be able to reach a higher rung.

Even when this presence does depart from him, some holy imprint of it will remain. It is this that allows him to seek renewed
strength; without it he would just remain in that lower state, distanced from the holy. It is this imprint that inspires him to go onward, and it is of the very nature of the holy that it always leaves
some impression even after it has gone. Of this the rabbis said: "The
shekhinah has never departed from the Western Wall."[3]

"The righteous will fall seven times and rise up" (Prov. 24:16).
Each time he falls, this means to say, he rises to a yet higher rung.
This may be true of the *zaddiq*, but is not true of everyone. For those
who are not among the *zaddiqim*, God takes great concern that they
not be utterly lost to Him. He wants to draw them near; because they
were not bound to God, they indeed did fall into the domain of those
forces of judgment. He who cleaves to God is not subject to such
forces; he is attached to the very source of life, the source in which
there is no judgment. The contrary is true, however, of the one who
does not cleave to Him. Then God brings Himself down in reduced
form, right to that very place where the judged one is. In this way he
is drawn near to God, approaching Beer-Sheba, the place of His fear,
the well of living waters. He who cleaves to that place will be sated
(*SHeVa'/SaVe'a*) with all good forever.

And so JACOB LEFT BEER-SHEBA. Jacob, the lower rung (for
his name does mean "heel"), departed from Beer-Sheba and went to
Haran, the place of judgment forces. But "when he reached Haran he
decided to go back." It was the judgments themselves that caused him
to "return," as he saw the presence of God right there with them.
And then "the ground leapt forth to meet him"; this refers to the
"land of the living" (= the *shekhinah*), for we have been taught that

---

2. Periods of insecurity are essential to the spiritual life; only through them does
the seeker continue to strive and not fall prey to self-satisfaction.

3. Though the *shekhinah* did depart with the destruction of the Temple, a sufficient imprint of it is left to make the Wall a holy place.

"more than the calf wants to suck, the cow wants to nurse."[4] The life above longs to dwell within the person, and is held back only by our inability to receive it. Once he "decides to go back," however, he has set about the process of arousal from below, the "feminine waters," and then the "land" may come forth to meet him. Of this the rabbis said: "One who comes to purify himself is given assistance." Once a person has all this set firmly in his heart, the forces of judgment are themselves transformed and they fall away from him, having accomplished what they were set there to do.

Of this they said: "The departure of a *zaddiq* from a place leaves an impression." When a *zaddiq* leaves a certain [inner] place, he still finds an imprint there; in this way he is able to raise himself to a higher rung, as we have said. Therefore a person should have faith that whatever suffering he undergoes or whatever loss he sustains, even in the smallest way, he is being called to draw near to God, to seek out the presence of divinity there, now drawn down to his own level. Take note of what our sages have taught us: "What is the smallest measure of distress that may still be considered suffering? . . . Even if a person puts his hand in his pocket expecting to find three coins, and he pulls out only two. . . ." Even in something so minor as this you should see the presence of God as having reduced itself to come specifically to you. This is God's mercy, so that none be utterly lost to Him. When you think of things in this way, they really turn out to be just this way from above. Of this Scripture says: "In their distress they sought You" (Isa. 26:16) or "God is in your distress" (Job 22:25). "Distress" refers to the forces of judgment.

We also read in Scripture: "Know today and set it upon your heart that the Lord is God in heaven above and on the earth below, there is none else" (Deut. 4:39). Some bit of suffering or distress, even that as slight as we have mentioned, is sure to come on a person every day. This should arouse his presence of mind, and that mind should draw him near to the source of life. Scripture elsewhere teaches: "By His mind were the depths split" (Prov. 3:20), showing that it is awareness of the mind that causes the lower rungs, the depths, to be split open. So "Know today" means that your mind should be so inspired by the events of each day. "Set it upon your heart" means that you should return to God, who is called "The Rock of my heart" (Ps.

---

4. The *shekhinah*, having a maternal concern for her children, leaps forths to meet and help them once they decide to return to her.

73:26). "The Lord (YHWH)," the aspect of mercy, "is God," the forces of judgment. These forces have come on you as an act of divine mercy, so that you not be utterly lost to Him. "In heaven above" now refers to the *zaddiq*, the one from whom divine life needs to be taken away.[5] "Earth below" refers to the others, those who have fallen down into the place of judgment forces. "There is none else"—there is no other counsel; the *zaddiq* receives one form of help from above, the other receives another.[6] All this is as we have taught it.

Blessed is the Lord forever. Amen. Amen.

VII

JACOB LIFTED UP HIS FEET AND WENT TO THE LAND OF THE EASTERNERS. (Gen. 29:1)

RaSHI comments: Once he had been told the good news and promised that God would watch over him, his heart lifted his feet and he walked with ease.

We read elsewhere: "Behold I send you Elijah the Prophet before the coming of God's great and awesome day. He will turn the hearts of parents to their children and the children's hearts to their parents . . ." (Mal. 3:23). Truly before the coming of messiah (speedily in our time!) Elijah will bring the news. The mind will then become broadened, as Scripture says: "Earth will be filled with knowledge (*de'ah/da'at*) of the Lord as the water fills the sea" (Isa. 11:9). But this quality is present in every Jew and at all times as well.

The Talmud tells of the heretic who taught [that the human being was composed of two parts, each fashioned by a distinct deity]: "From midpoint up, Hormiz, and from midpoint down, Ahormiz.[1]" The truth is, in fact, that the powers of evil and corporeality do well in the lower half of the human being. From midpoint up there is no source of evil. Once it is aroused below, however, that same evil can come to dominate the upper portion as well. This is what led the heretic to think that there were two powers in the universe. A human

---

5. So that he struggle harder to reach a higher rung.

6. There is nothing—whether suffering or the feeling of God's absence—that does not in one way or another represent a message from above to return to His presence.

1. Corruptions for the names of the two principles of Zoroastrianism, Ormuzd and Ahriman. Some versions ascribe the claim to a "magus" rather than a "heretic."

being in reality is a single whole, embracing all of his limbs and organs. The task is to unite the two portions, bringing both to so cleave to the good that the corporeal self will have no dominion, not even in the lower portion. One God created them both; we were fashioned in this way only so that there be moral choice. The lower portion of the self, the "feet," are that which one has to be raised up and joined to the higher self.

Suppose some good news comes to a person just as he is having particular difficulty with a passage he is studying. Before his mind quite absorbs that news, there is a moment when the report flashes through his mind like a single point. This moment is called the presence of Elijah, after which "earth" fills up with knowledge, his mind expands and is quickened. At that point it becomes easy for him to unite his whole self, to bring even his lower parts into the good.[2] The bearer of that good news in fact carried a spark of Elijah in him at that moment, for Elijah is the true bearer of all good tidings in the world. This time he chose to garb himself in that particular person.

That which is called "Elijah" has existed since the six days of creation. At one point, as is known, he took on the form of Phineas.[3] Thus it is that whenever there is good news in the world, each of us runs out to tell it; we feel that the presence of Elijah is about, and we long to have it enter our own spirit. Even if we seem not to be conscious of this, our deeper selves know it. If such a person did in fact have full presence of mind when this happened, he could begin to serve God from the rung of Elijah, and thence attain to a very high level indeed. But the person who receives the good news also gets the spark of Elijah into him; his mind is expanded and he too finds it easy to be close to God, even with his "feet." This is called "the coming of God's great day"—for this has brought about the presence of God within him.

Note that "Behold I *send* you Elijah the Prophet" is in the pres-

---

2. The arrival of good news interrupts the heavy or burdened flow of difficult study and allows for a moment of insight, originating in a flash of sudden mental change and then spreading forth to uplift the mind altogether. Such a moment brings moral healing as well; by the very nature of the suddenness with which it overtakes one, it reveals the wholeness of the seemingly fragmented human person.

3. Phineas, according to the Midrash, was Elijah in a prior incarnation. The phrase *behinat Eliyahu* somewhat qualifies an otherwise very strange claim here that Elijah has existed since Creation. Perhaps a natural outgrowth of many other beliefs concerning Elijah, this formulation is generally unknown even in the Kabbalistic sources.

ent tense; this is constantly happening, in each person and at all times. This quality of Elijah is sent to every Jew, "before the coming of God's day," as we have interpreted it. Then he will "turn the hearts of the parents to the children" and so forth. The upper portion of the person is the "parent," as distinct from the lower half, called the "limb," or the child. It is the upper portion that gives birth to that thought which will bring the lower self back to the good as well. Give some thought to this. In this way "He will turn the hearts of parents to their children and the children's hearts to their parents"; a unification of the heart will come about. The heart in the upper portion will turn to its "children," allowing good to flow to the lower portion as well. Then whatever quality was there in the "children," in the "evil" portion, shall come up from below and be joined to the good. Then indeed you will "Know Him in all your ways" (Prov. 3:6), as the "children's hearts" turn back to the "parents."

VIII

A SPRING AMID THE GARDENS, A WELL OF LIVING WATERS, FLOWING DOWN FROM LEBANON (Cant. 4:15).

The Midrash reads: "A SPRING AMID THE GARDENS—Abraham; A WELL OF LIVING WATERS—Isaac; FLOWING DOWN FROM LEBANON—Jacob."

"She opens her mouth in wisdom" (Prov. 31:26); the Torah comes from *ḥokhmah*, "and the teaching of grace is upon her tongue." The *Tiqquney Zohar* takes the word *HeSeD* ("grace") as *ḤaS D*, "He took pity upon the *dalet*." Now *ḥokhmah* in itself is represented by the *yod*, a point that we cannot conceive at all, "hidden from the sight of all the living, even from the birds of heaven" (Job 28:21). God's gift of the Torah to us in revealed form was an act of divine *ḥesed*, grace of loving-kindness. He was gracious toward the lower realms, taking pity on the *dalet*, on that which has nothing at all (*DaLeT/De-LeT lah*) on its own. He did this so that each of us, each in accord with the degree to which we could conceive Him in our own selves, would become aware of His existence. That is why the sublime wisdom reduced itself from utter transcendence into the form that was revealed: so that we might understand something of His existence.

THE LIGHT OF THE EYES

When a person looks into His Torah, seeing God's *ḥokhmah*, and attains a degree of *binah* ("understanding"), these two qualities are joined together in him as "two companions who never part," just as they are above. Then his mind (*da'at*) is expanded, as the flow of divine life comes forth from the source, the WELL OF LIVING WATERS, source of life. It flows DOWN FROM LEBANON, through the thirty-two paths of wisdom and the fifty gates of understanding.[1] Of this Scripture speaks when it says: "A river flows forth from Eden to water the garden (*GaN*—'garden'—= 53, the fifty-three weekly portions of the Torah) and from there it separates" (Gen. 2:10). Then one comes to the world of separation, in which each sees [as only he can]. All this is God's gracious gift. One whose fear of heaven is complete can hold fast to this well of living waters. Rabbi Meir taught us this when he said: "Whoever studies Torah for its own sake becomes a flowing spring and an endless river." By "for its own sake" he meant that study should seek in Torah a real teaching, one that shows him the path of God. In such a person the well of living waters becomes manifest as a never-ceasing spring. He and that wellspring become one, and then he is called "Rehovot" ("broadening"), for his mind has been expanded.

Thus we are to understand the various wells that the patriarchs dug.[2] Abraham, who epitomized divine love, fulfilled the entire Torah; the two thousand years of Torah began with him. Until his time there was only chaos: The generations of Enosh, of the flood, and of Babel all represent this. From Abraham's day the time of Torah started; the first wells were dug into the living waters. He also brought others of God's creatures to the well. Of these Scripture says: "The souls they had made in Haran" (Gen. 12:5). . . . Then Isaac came along and again dug the wells, as Scripture tells us. . . . He brought people to the living waters by his quality of fear. At first there was some demonic accusation against this, for the first well was called Sitnah (= Satan).[3] Afterwards he did it in a more careful way, and then the well was Rehovot, referring to that expansion of mind. Finally Jacob, who

---

1. The consonants of *LeBaNoN* are numerically equivalent to thirty-two (LB) and fifty (N). The thirty-two paths of *ḥokhmah* and the fifty gates of *binah* are both well-known symbols from earlier Kabbalistic literature.

2. See above, Toledot, 5.

3. The use of fear in bringing people to God arouses a demonic potential. Fear of God, stemming from the left side in the world of religious emotion, has a certain value, but must be evoked with the greatest care.

represents *da'at*, came along, and he "drew near and rolled the stone off the mouth of the well" (Gen. 29:10). Evil is like a rock, and the sages tell us that one of the seven names of the evil urge is "stumbling stone." Jacob saw by his holy vision that this stumbling stone was keeping people away from the well of life. By bringing mind to bear he was able to weaken evil and release its hold, thus making it possible for later generations to reach that well. Had he not done this, the Torah could never have been given to Israel; by this deed he became one of the "legs of the chariot" [i.e., supports of the divine world] above.

After this had happened, the "gift" could be given to the needy [i.e., to this needy world, *dalet*]. The Talmud teaches the following mnemonic for the beginning of the alphabet: *Alef, bet: alef binah* ("learn understanding"); *gimel, dalet, gomel dalim* ("He bestows upon the needy"). Now *alef* refers to *hokhmah*, as in "I shall teach you (*a'AL-EFekha*) wisdom" (Job 33:33). The Torah that comes from *hokhmah* is indeed bestowed on the needy, His mercy on *dalet*, as we taught. Therefore Scripture says [at the giving of the Torah]: "God spoke all these words, saying" (Exod. 20:1), on which the rabbis comment: "He spoke them all in a single utterance." Divine wisdom was concentrated there in such a way that Israel could not understand the Torah; it was all a *yod*, completely beyond revelation, a point hidden beyond all sight. All the words were there inside it. That was why Israel said: "You draw near and listen" (Deut. 5:24); "You speak to us" (Exod. 20:19). Moses represented the power of *da'at*, that which could bring that concentrated *hokhmah* forth to them so that they might receive it.

This then is A SPRING AMONG THE GARDENS: Abraham. The fact that the deep wellsprings of *hokhmah* flowed into the gardens was an act of *hesed*, compassion on the *dalet*. A WELL OF LIVING WATERS: Isaac, for he used his fear of God to dig until he reached this depth. FLOWING DOWN FROM LEBANON: Jacob, the mind drawing forth from the thirty-two and the fifty, as we have taught.[4] The passage in the Canticle continues: "Awake, O North, and come from the south." The rabbis have said that "he who seeks wisdom should go south, while one who seeks wealth should go north." Indeed these two things cannot come together; one who as-

---

4. Here the three patriarchs, usually associated with the second triad of *sefirot*, are each depicted as reaching up into the *sefirah* of the first triad that is parallel to their own: Abraham is *hokhmah*, Isaac represents *binah*, and Jacob *da'at*.

pires to wealth surely will not attain to that sublime wisdom which is the source of Torah. "Awake, O North" means that you should awaken from the north, shake that northerliness off yourself, that "north" of "Gold comes from the north" (Job 37:22), and come to the south, to the place of true wisdom.

The rabbis have also taught that "The son of David will not come until a fish is sought for a sick person and none can be found."[5] It is known, however, that fish are difficult for a sick person [to eat. The statement then requires further explanation]. The point is that there are two times at which messiah might come; either it will be "in its time" or else "I will hasten it" (cf. Isa. 60:22).[6] We prefer, of course, that it be hastened. But when can this happen? Only when we serve God in such a way that His purpose in revealing the Torah is fulfilled: *gimel dalet* as "bestowed upon the needy." The word "fish" (*DaG*) represents these letters in reverse, showing this fulfillment: By means of the Torah, in which the presence of *ḥokhmah* is concentrated, we recognize the reality of God. It has to begin from below, from the *dalet* who is in need, reaching out toward its source, toward that which can give to it. If Israel becomes sick, however, if their love turns sickly so that they lack the love to do this, then God says: "For My sake, for My sake, shall I do it" (Isa. 48:11). This is "in its time," at that time when messiah's arrival can be delayed no longer. . . .

How can we ever reach this point [of ourselves arousing the redemption]? Such great holiness is required for it, the holiness of "Make yourselves holy and be holy, for I am holy" (Lev. 11:44). We can, however, be helped by the Sabbath day. Without the Sabbath, reaching from the profane alone, we could indeed never reach that rung. But the great holiness of the Sabbath allows us to draw some of its sanctity into the weekday world as well. It is in this way that we can attain the level of *DaG*. And that is why it is considered a good deed to eat fish on the Sabbath, pointing to all that we have said.

May God put it in our hearts to serve Him truthfully and wholeheartedly.

---

5. A sign of bitter frost or extreme poverty.

6. Messiah will come, according to Talmudic tradition, either when his arrival is hastened by Israel's preparations, or else in God's own time. The goal here, as in much of Jewish spiritual writing, is to find the proper way to bring about the hastening. While some sought out theurgic or even mystical-revolutionary means toward this end, we should note that the counsel here is entirely orthodox and pietistic.

Amen Selah unto eternity. Blessed is the Lord forever. Amen. Amen.

IX

JACOB LEFT BEER-SHEBA . . .

The fulfillment of the entire Torah is rooted in faith, as we have been taught: "Along came Habakkuk and reduced all the commandments to one, as Scripture says: 'The righteous lives by his faith'" (Hab. 2:4). Faith includes full faith in the Creator, blessed be He, in His providence, and in every word that the sages have brought forth as well. This latter is called "faith in the sages." One who believes in this way surely will be able to hear words of chastisement and teachings of Torah, and will come to a life of proper action. The Torah tells us that: "they had faith in the Lord and in His servant Moses" (Exod. 14:31). Even though they were not sufficiently developed in their intellect to have true faith in God Himself, by means of their faith in Moses His servant they came to hear God's words and were thus brought to faith in Him. The great enemy of such faith is pride, that which makes you think: "I too am a servant of God, and I am just as great a scholar as he is." Better to be humble and to judge the other one more generously. This is what will bring you to: "I have gained insight from all my teachers" (Ps. 119:99). One who has faith, even if he have no great intellect of his own, can attain to a high rung. This is so even if it is "Night shining like day" (Ps. 139:12), by means of faith.[1] A word to the wise.

   In this way you can reach the rung of return to God, having your heart so pure and clean that the *shekhinah* can dwell there. Of this Scripture says: "Let them make Me a sanctuary that I might dwell in their midst" (Exod. 25:8); "I am sanctified amid the children of Israel" (Lev. 22:32). This was why the people Israel were chosen—so that they might be a chariot or throne for His glory. "The patriarchs are

---

1. Even if it does have to be mediated through another. The teaching is very central to Hasidism, and was one for which it was most criticized. The "sage" here is intended to refer to the Hasidic master, and the faithful disciple may through him attain to the highest rungs—even without understanding of his own.

the chariot"; they so emptied all their limbs, and especially their hearts, that they were able to draw God into themselves. But for this you first must turn aside from evil, casting out the evil urge from within yourself so that it does not hold you back. "A person cannot live in a cage with a serpent." You have to "turn from evil and do good" (Ps. 34:15); depart from evil with a whole heart, without any self-deception at all. Then you will "do good"; you will have made a place so that the good can dwell within you. This good is none other than God Himself, who is called "the good"; "God is good to all" (Ps. 145:9).

This return has to begin with a verbal confession before God, one held in absolute truth and wholeheartedness, one of full regret. Only then can you repair the harm that has been done. When you sin you do damage to the Torah, to those twenty-two letters through which heaven and earth were created. By sin you remove letters from the divine Torah: if you stole, transgressing "You shall not steal," you took those letters out of the Torah, and out of your own soul as well. Afterwards, when you confess by speech, again employing the letters, saying "I did thus-and-so and I hereby regret it"; as you mention that sin with your lips, the letters return to the Torah above, repairing the damage that you wrought.

This is "Return, O Israel, to the Lord your God" (Hos. 14:2), to which the Talmud adds: "Great is repentance, reaching to the very throne of glory." The return places you in a position to become a throne for the sublime glory, for God Himself. You are to return "to the Lord *your* God"; to the point where the Lord becomes *your* God. Until now He was Lord, but was not *your* God, as it were. This was because of sin, which placed an iron curtain between you and your Father in heaven. Now, in the course of true penitence and confession, your body and soul have become a chariot for His presence; indeed He has become *your* God.

In this way one becomes a "leg." The throne itself is far beyond us—"the King seated upon a high and elevated throne." What we then refer to here are the legs of the throne, those of which Moses spoke when he said "six hundred thousand *on foot*" (Num. 11:21). The divine throne, as it were, stands on these legs; the existence of the very universe depends on Israel's fulfillment of God's Torah. The verse "Return, O Israel, . . ." then goes on to say: "For you have stumbled in your transgression." Stumbling too refers to the feet; because of your transgression you were not a proper "leg." Scripture continues: "Take words with you and return to the Lord"—"words" refer to the confession of the lips, setting it forth in words and letters as you turn from sin. Such speech repairs the letters, and the heart is purified by its own regret. Then there is a place for the good, for God Himself to dwell, as the verse goes on to say "and take good."

This is what the Talmud meant in saying: "Whoever does not say 'true and firm' in the morning prayer and 'true and faithful' in the evening has not fulfilled his obligation."[2] The *zaddiq* is called "morning" or "dawn"; he is true and firm, bound to God's graciousness as in "to declare Your graciousness in the morning" (Ps. 92:3). "And Your faithfulness at night" refers to those who are on the level of "night," not having the intellectual power on their own and thus being "in the dark"; through faithfulness they too can attain it all.

This is JACOB LEFT; Israel are referred to as Jacob when they are not on the highest rung, when they are "heels." In such a state he LEFT BEER-SHEBA, strayed away from the well of living waters that sates all with goodness. HE CAME TO HARAN; he fell into the low state where he encountered divine anger and forces of judgment. HE STOPPED THERE FOR THE NIGHT, in that place of darkness whence the light of God had fled. But afterwards THE SUN HAD SET; (literally "had come"); he saw that "the Lord God is sun and shield" because HE CAME UPON A CERTAIN PLACE, which refers, as we have said, to prayer, to confession in words. Then TAKING SOME OF THE STONES OF THE PLACE, these are letters, as the *Sefer Yezirah* tells us, which had been cast into that place of darkness, HE PUT THEM AT HIS HEAD, he took the letters back to the head, to their root, and thus set straight the damage he had done. HE LAY DOWN, *wa-yishkav* hinting again at the twenty-two letters in that place. And then HE DREAMED, *halom* meaning *halim*, to restore health, he recovered from his weakness and became A LADDER SET UPON THE GROUND AND ITS TOP REACHED HEAVEN, because he brought the Creator into himself. Then BEHOLD ANGELS OF GOD, those representing the forces of judgment, the name *elohim*. Now they were GOING UP and being sweetened in their root, and DOWN, as the quality of judgment fell by the way. May God bring us to repentance of full heart and soul.

Amen Selah unto eternity.

---

2. The Talmudic reference is to the text of the redemption-blessing in the liturgy, placed between the *shema'* and the *'amidah*.

X

In the Midrash Tanḥuma:

"Rabbi Simeon ben Halafta was asked: 'In how many days did God create the world?' He replied: 'In six days.' 'And what has he been doing since then?' 'He has been making ladders, making one person poor and another rich, as Scripture says: "The Lord makes poor and rich; He casts down and raises high" (1 Sam. 2:7).' "[1]

Such is the case with the ladder that Jacob saw in his dream: It was set into the earth but its head reached heaven. There we are told that Jacob took some stones upon which to lie down. Had he had a pillow with him surely he would not have chosen stones.[2] When he returned, however, it says: "The man had grown extremely prosperous" (Gen. 30:43). God blessed him on his return with the blessing of Abraham: "The Lord blessed Abraham in all" (Gen. 24:1).

We have said earlier in interpreting the verse "The heavens are My throne and earth is My footstool" (Isa. 66:1) that this footstool has been given over to Israel; it is they who must redeem these "legs" of the lower rungs. They are to seek out the holy sparks; by means of all earthly things they are to ever draw themselves near to their Creator. Great joy will spread through all the worlds as God takes pleasure in the uplifting of lesser things to become a chariot for Him. Thus is the divine throne made whole, as all that had fallen away from it is restored. Jacob our Father did this, for "Jacob lifted up his feet" (Gen. 29:1).

Of this uplifting it is written: "Mine is silver and mine is gold, says the Lord" (Hag. 2:8). Why does the verse mention only silver and gold as belonging to Him? Has God not made the whole world? Is He not "owner of heaven and earth" (Gen. 14:19)? He said this because so much of the conduct of the world's business and acquisition to fulfill human needs takes place through the media of silver and gold. Every one of Israel must be especially careful to draw these near to His service; there is nothing in this world that does not contain His holy sparks. God's joy is especially great when these metals, coming from the depths of earth, right out of the soil itself, are dedicated to His

---

1. The Midrashic text is quoted from memory, resulting in several inaccuracies. The subject is Rabbi Yose ben Halafta; the source is not to be found in Tanhuma. See sources at end of section.

2. Indicating that he departed in poverty.

name. This may take place only by means of faith, and that faith must extend also into the realm of one's business practices. There we must deal in truth, for truth is the seal of God. In this we receive help from above, as we raise up the holiness to be found there by applying absolute truth to dealings in business. [That "help" indicates the] presence of God, so that the spark of divinity found in those business dealings (conducted truthfully and in accord with Torah) can be joined directly to Him. This is why the Hebrew term for business is *massa' u-mattan*, literally "lifting up and giving." You lift up the spark from the place where it had fallen and give it back to its source. This is why Israel were scattered among the nations: so that through dealing with them in such matters of business and even in conversation with them we would be able to bring forth those sparks. Thus is God's chariot formed of all things in the world; footstool and throne are set right and uplifted in an added way. It was in this sense that the Talmud interpreted "all of existence which is at your feet" (Deut. 11:6) to mean "a person's money, that which sets him on his feet." It is through money that one can set the footstool aright; faith must be applied to your possessions, and in this too you must conduct yourself truthfully and in accord with our holy Torah's law, for God is present, in reduced form, here too. Then you may truly become His chariot.

Our father Jacob did all this; he "lifted up his feet." He wrestled with the angel of Esau until "he saw that he could not best him" (Gen. 32:26). This struggle was over all that was to befall the later generations. By this battle, fought with all of Jacob's tremendous power, he established that the Other Side would not be able to do [ultimate] harm to his descendants at any time in the future. "You, children of Jacob, have not been destroyed" (Mal. 3:6). By being children of Jacob, who fought so hard for you and defeated the Other Side, it should be easy for you to serve God. That power will not be able to harm you in any of the ways it might have done had Jacob not defeated it. . . . This was what the struggle was about; when the Torah says "a man wrestled with him" it was for the sake of all his children, right down to messiah's times. This is why it says "until the dawn"; until that time of which it has been written: "Then shall your light break forth like the dawn" (Isa. 58:8), the days of the messiah.

"He saw that he could not best him and he touched his hip at the socket" (Gen. 32:26); "hips" have the same meaning as "feet," that of "all of existence that is at your feet."[3] It is there [in our attitude toward money] that the Other Side might find something to hold onto. Not only might one not be raising sparks to the good through money, but money itself might even draw one far away from God. Among its evil forces that Other Side has emplanted avarice, the lust after money. Using this object of the very highest divine service, one even greater than the study of Torah, that force has been clever enough (by the power of our sins) to do that which would keep us far from God.

How is this service greater than the study of Torah? He who studies Torah effects a unification [of God with] something that is already elevated; the divine joy is greater when holy life is found in the raising up of the lowly. In this sense such service is greater than that of study. One still has to study Torah in order to know how to go about this uplifting, as well as for various other reasons; Torah remains the root. But service of God through business dealings and other lowly things is also a form of Torah; without Torah one never would come to it. It is through Torah that one can come to the realization that Torah exists in these things as well. Torah exists in all things, since God and His Torah are one. Hold on to this, then, but do not let the other slip out of your hand.[4]

[How, then, does it happen that money becomes the object of desire and] keeps us far from God? All this is done by the evil urge, called the "thigh muscle,"[5] that which makes a person forget to serve his Lord (*NaSHeh/maNSHiy*). That is why Torah forbids the eating of this; it means that Israel should not earn their livelihood through this sort of money, money that comes through the evil urge. This is "on the socket of the hip," and would keep Israel from uplifting the "legs," needed to restore the footstool of which we have spoken. This is why the holy books make a point of telling us that *sulam* ("ladder") and *mamon* ("money") are numerically the same.[6]

And so "he had a dream: a ladder"—*ḥalom*, as we have said, refers to restored health or renewed vigor. Jacob strengthened himself in God's service with regard to the ladder of money. Even though it is "set upon the ground," tied to earthly things, "its top reaches to heav-

---

3. Classical Hebrew uses *regel* to denote both "leg" and "foot."
4. Serve God through both Torah study and the uplifting of wordly things.
5. That part of the animal which Jews do not eat, in remembrance of Jacob's struggle; see Gen. 32:33.
6. Money is a ladder, on which you can go either up or down.

en," its root is in heaven. The life-force that gives it being comes from a high and holy place. "Angels of God"—representing the various nations—"go up and down on it"—as we have said. By proper presence and sacred direction of mind one can bring the life forth from them; they have life only due to the sparks that dwell in their midst. Therefore they go down "on it"; read this word rather as "through him" (*bo*). The opposite is also true of the nations: As we turn far away from God, heaven forbid, we give strength to them and they "go up." Jacob then fulfilled God's intent: He took of the stones in that place, that which came out of the very earth, and placed them at his head, bringing them back to their source in the holy, in the Endless.

When he went to Aram Naharayim, Jacob continued to seek out holy sparks; from within the *qelipot* of Laban he brought forth the matriarchs, Rachel and Leah, and the twelve tribes. That was why the angel [of Esau] was not able to defeat him. This too is the meaning of these four exiles that Israel have been forced by God's decree to undergo. Now in this fourth exile, that of Edom, it is those sparks that we have to uplift and purify. The more they oppress us, the closer our redemption comes; it causes us to return to God, and that serves to hasten the end. We have explained this in connection with "a time when men ruled over men to do them harm" (Eccles. 8:9); in fact the nations do harm to themselves, for our suffering at their hands only helps to complete the purification. When the angel was defeated by Jacob, surely the power of Esau in this world was defeated as well. No nation does anything in this world except by the will of its angel above. As soon as the angel was defeated he agreed that there would begin an exile in Edom. Even if all the sparks were to be uplifted immediately, he had to agree to whatever would happen, without condition. That is why Essau said to Jacob: "Let us start on our journey" (Gen. 33:12); come to me and begin the exile, begin redeeming the holy sparks. "And I shall walk opposite you" (Gen. 33:12)—I shall oppose you insofar as I am able. Jacob answered: "My lord knows that the children are frail and that the nursing flocks and herds are a care to me; if they are driven hard a single day, all the flocks will die." If you oppress them all at once in their exile, they will not be able to stand the pain. Then exile will bear so heavily on them that they will not be able to gather up the holy sparks. Rather, "let my lord go ahead of his servant"—I shall not begin yet to lift out and purify the life that is in you—"while I travel slowly"—let the exile take a long time, but let the oppression not be so great that Israel lose their awareness of mind in the exile. Let it not start yet, but let it not be so heavy that it cause them to fall—otherwise "all the flocks will die." This will last "until I come to my lord in Seir"—until the days of messiah, when all the purifications are completed. Then "liberators shall march up on Mount Zion to wreak judgment on Mount Esau, and dominion shall be the Lord's" (Obad. 1:21). So long as the exile lasts, God has only indirect dominion (*mamlakhah*). The Creator has to lessen Himself in such a way that He can enter into the rule of the nations, giving them life for the sake of the holiness that dwells within them. "In all their troubles, He is troubled"[7] (Isa. 63:9). This is why He has only that indirect rule. In the future, however, there will be no further need for this. "We shall rejoice and exult in *His* salvation" (Isa. 25:9); no longer will He need to reduce Himself to have His presence flow through the nations, since there will be no more holy sparks among them. Then "dominion (*melukhah*) shall be the Lord's." All this will happen because "the Lord shall be King over all the earth" (Zech. 14:9); we shall restore to Him dominion over all earthly things.

Scripture therefore tells us that "Jacob arrived safe" (*shalem*; literally "whole") (Gen. 33:18), on which the rabbis said: "Whole in body, whole in Torah." Everything he did, bodily things and those dealing with money as well as Torah, was for the sake of bringing forth God's glory. Thus "Jacob journeyed to Sukkot" (Gen. 33:17), for the *sukkah* teaches us to leave our regular dwellings and live in a temporary and vulnerable one; this world should be but a temporary dwelling for us, all of our efforts being directed toward the world to come and the drawing of divinity into everything in this world.[8] There "he built himself a house" (Gen. 33:17)—by such intelligent service of God we will be able to build the heavenly Temple, constructed of that holiness which the righteous have uplifted. That is why students of Torah are referred to as "builders"; they build their portion of the heavenly Temple, the Jerusalem above, righteousness, the *shekhinah*. All they do is for the sake of the *shekhinah*'s redemption.

Now we understand why it was that Isaac sought to bless Esau. Did he not understand that this son was the wicked one? He wanted

---

7. God's act of *zimzum* in entering into the dominion of the nations is depicted as painful for Him, a suffering parallel to that of Israel in exile.

8. The author here shows how far he is from true otherworldliness; even directing one's efforts toward "the world to come" in fact is nothing other than working toward the manifestation of God's glory here on earth.

rather to bless him with the blessing of this world. True children of Jacob consider that to be no blessing at all, but only the necessary vehicle to reach the world to come that lies within it; the latter is hidden within the former, and without "this world" one cannot get to "the world to come."[9] The excesses of this world belong to the seed of Esau, lest they draw the seed of Jacob away from their Creator. Rebekah told Jacob to take the blessing [the one intended for Esau], but even then he postponed its taking effect until the end of days, as the *Zohar* teaches. He wanted there to be nothing that might distract him from the service of God.

Isaac said to Esau: "Your brother came with guile and took your blessing" (Gen. 27:35); the Targum renders "guile" as *hokhmah* (wisdom or cleverness). Indeed the *Zohar* tells us that it is precisely through wisdom that the process of uplifting takes place. Isaac meant to tell him that "in the end he will purify out of you any blessing that I give you," by means of *hokhmah*. That is why "you live by your sword" (Gen. 27:40), you live only through those souls and sparks that come from the world of destruction (*HaRBekha/HuRBan*). That is how you have life, just like the case that contains the *tefillin*. Jacob will lift that life out, bit by bit, until the process is completed (speedily in our day!). And so before Jacob left for Aram Isaac blessed him again, this time with the blessing of Abraham. Abraham, we will recall, was blessed "in all" (Gen. 24:1); he was able to serve God in all things. It was he who first brought this thought to light; he was the first of the faithful and the first to know his Creator. It was in this way that the patriarchs served as chariots for God. His throne was now made whole, and Jacob was given this blessing while the excesses were deeded to Esau.

And so the Midrash asked, "In how many days did God create the world?" The reply "in six" takes into account our interpretation of "that God created in making" (Gen. 2:3)—the world is still in the making, Creation is not yet complete. God created the world and gave it to Israel that Creation might be completed through this uplifting. When messiah comes, Creation will be completed; this too will of course be the work of God, by means of the life and the heavenly assistance that He gives to Israel. "And what has He been doing since

---

9. The quotation marks in the translation are meant to convey the entirely unconventional way in which the author is using these terms. "World to come" is here really the hidden essence of all things that exist, including, or perhaps especially, the most earthly.

241

then?" the Midrash goes on to ask; "what," it means to say, "is the process of redemption?" The answer refers to the making of ladders, ladders of gold and silver, as He makes one, namely the domain of evil, "poor," as He gives the "wealth" to the other, the domain of the holy. Thus are the bounds of the holy to widen in the days of our messiah.

Blessed is the Lord forever. Amen. Amen. May the Lord reign forevermore. Amen. Amen.

Sources: *Wa-Yeze*

I

In the house of Eber	Megillah 17a
He took a step outside	cf. Zohar 1:147a
There were twelve stones	Bereshit Rabbah 68:11

II

The four ells	Berakhot 8a
There are twenty-two	Tiqquna 70 (132b)

III

Drag him off to the house of study!	Qiddushin 30b
Seven names	Sukkah 52a

IV

The angels of Babylon and Greece	Wa-Yiqra Rabbah 29:2
The gates of prayer	Baba Mezi'a 59a
Ten journeys	Rosh Hashanah 31a
God did a good deed	Gittin 88a
Abraham grew weak	Mekilta Amalek 2

V

The four kingdoms	Wa-Yikra Rabbah 29:2
Does not fly upward	Tiqquna 10 (25b)
Mar 'Ukva sent	Gittin 7a
Can also refer to prayer	Berakhot 26b
The world to come was created by *yod*	Menahot 29b

WA-YEZE

VI
When he reached Haran   Sanhedrin 95b
From the Western Wall   Shemot Rabbah 2:2
More than the calf wants to suck Pesahim 112a
One who comes to purify   Yoma 39a
The smallest measure of distress Arakhin 16b

VII
The heretic who taught   Sanhedrin 39a
Elijah/Phineas   Targum Y. Exodus 6:18

VIII
The Midrash reads   Shir Rabbah 1:2
Rabbi Meir taught us   Avot 6:1
The following mnemonic   Shabbat 104a
He who seeks wisdom   Baba Batra 25b
Until a fish is sought   Sanhedrin 98a

IX
Along came Habakkuk   Makkot 24a
A person cannot live in a cage   Ketubot 72a
Reaching to the very throne   Yoma 86a
True and firm   Berakhot 12a

X
In how many days   Pesikta de-Rav Kahana 11b
At your feet   Sanhedrin 110a
That which makes a person forget Zohar 1:170b
Whole in body, whole in Torah   Shabbat 33b

WA-YISHLAḤ
Genesis 32:4–36:43

INTRODUCTION. The opening and essential theme of this section, the encounter of Jacob with Esau after his return from Aram, has already been dealt with in the final teaching of our preceding section, one that in fact more properly should belong with *Wa-Yishlaḥ*. It, along with the single teaching that is presented here, deals with the wrestling bout between Jacob and that being representing his brother Esau, the encounter through which Jacob is renamed Israel, "struggler with God."

In a larger sense, these teachings for the Hasidic author continue the theme of the *parashah* above: the ongoing battle of Jacob and Esau. This universal struggle, often depicted in the preceding section as that of Israel and the nations, is here presented in more internalized form, as the battle between the human will to do good and the power of the evil urge within every individual. Jacob's struggle is thus the human struggle, one that will continue until the time of redemption, when the knowledge of God will be so overwhelming that there will be no more need to do battle with evil. The teaching offers us a clear presentation of Hasidic messianism: a vision of the human condition in which the presence of God is so clear that all evil falls aside of its own accord, and man knows there is no truth but that of his oneness with the divine.

*　　　*　　　*

WA-YISHLAH

I

THAT IS WHY THE CHILDREN OF ISRAEL TO THIS DAY DO NOT EAT THE THIGH MUSCLE THAT IS ON THE HIP. (Gen. 32:32)

There is a well-known esoteric tradition concerning the parallels between cosmos, time, and the human soul. These are referred to (in the commentary of RABeD to the *Sefer Yezirah*)[1] by the acronym *'aSHaN* (*'olam, SHanah, Nefesh*), based on the verse "Mount Sinai was all in smoke" (*'ashan*; Exod. 19:18). Each of these three, it is taught, contains the same entire structure, that which is described [in man] as consisting of two hundred forty-eight limbs and three hundred sixty-five sinews.

The cosmos, time, and the human soul are all structured in the same way. Each of them contains the same constituent parts, described in the tradition as the two hundred forty-eight "limbs" and the three hundred sixty-five "sinews" of the body. The limbs of the body are to be found in the world, in cosmos, for Scripture refers to such things as "the navel of the earth," "the mouth of the earth," "the nakedness of the earth." The same is true for time: Each of the three hundred sixty-five days of the year represents a particular "sinew." We learn all this from *Sefer Yezirah*, as the commentary of RAVeD teaches concerning the word *'aSHaN* ("smoke"): He reads it as an acronym for *'olam, SHanah, Nefesh* ("cosmos, time, soul). Thus, he teaches, are we to understand: "Mount Sinai was all in smoke" (Exod. 19:18).

Among the days of the year, it is the ninth of Av that forms the "thigh muscle" in the bodily form of time. This is the rear point, the place where the forces of evil have their hold. It was on this day of their domain that both first and second Temples were destroyed, that Betar was defeated, that Jerusalem was ploughed under. This day is parallel to Yom Kippur, the most holy and sublime day of the year, a day on which Satan has no power to rise in accusation. "One parallel

---

1. The order of the original has here been slightly altered for the sake of clarity. The Yezirah commentary attributed to Rabbi Abraham ben David (RAVeD) of Posquieres is actually that of Joseph ben Shalom Ashkenazi, a Kabbalist of the fourteenth century.

to the other has God made" (Eccles. 7:14): The ninth of Av stands as the special day for the forces of the Other Side, the time when they are given more power. That is why these events took place on that day.[2]

It is in this verse, then, that the ninth of Av receives its mention in the Torah. THE CHILDREN OF ISRAEL ... DO NOT EAT. These words are followed by the particle 'eT, to be taken as abbreviating Tishe'ah 'Av, the ninth of Av. Israel fast on that day so as not to give strength, by their eating, to the forces of evil. This is why the Zohar teaches that "one who eats on the ninth of Av is the same as one who eats of the thigh muscle"; this day itself is that muscle, as we have said.

Thus we explain "a man wrestled with him until the dawn"—even today this wrestling goes on, as Satan in the form of the evil urge accuses Israel and seeks to keep them far from God. This will ever continue "until the dawn"—until the time (be it soon!) of our righteous messiah, when "I will remove the spirit of defilement from the earth" (Zech. 13:2). Of that day it is said: "The Lord holds a sacrifice in Bozrah" (Isa. 34:6); this refers to the wiping away of evil from the world and the ultimate purification of the holy. Then there will be no more battle with Amalek, no more of that "rear point." Israel and their Creator will be joined face to face, without any intervention by the accusing force. This will precisely reverse that which is said of the Temple's destruction: "He has drawn back His right hand" (Lam. 2:3) and "They went backward and not forward" (Jer. 7:24).

"He saw that he could not best him"—that God would not abandon Jacob to his hand. "And he touched his hip at the socket"—the rear point, the thigh muscle, the ninth of Av. There he touched him to do Israel harm, and he accomplished all that he did. It was through his power and his eternal war against Israel that exile has come about, both the collective exile and the exile of the individual, that of the soul in the hands of the evil urge. As its darkness covers over the light of understanding, the awareness of Israel's mind is diminished. No longer do we have that full presence of mind which we had at Sinai, by which we attained to the Torah. Thus it is that the secrets of Torah are handed over to the evil forces, as their darkness covers the

---

2. The balance of the universe must be maintained. If power is to be taken from the accuser on Yom Kippur, the day when Israel's judgment is to be sealed, it must be returned to him at some other time.

light and takes Israel away from God. All this goes on "until the dawn," when evil will be wiped out as the world is filled with the knowledge of God. Then "all of them shall know Me, from great to small" (Jer. 31:33). Of course then there will be no evil. Torah's wholeness will be restored, as all the forgotten bits of teaching will come forth from the clutches of evil and be returned to Israel. In this way will mind itself be redeemed from exile.

It was this that the rabbis meant when they said: "Every single acacia tree (*shittah*) that the nations have taken from Israel and Jerusalem, God will return to us." They refer to the Torah, which is written line (*shittah*) by line. All those lines of Torah or aspects of mind that the nations, the forces of evil, have taken, God will return to us as evil is wiped away. Then will mind be so fully present that there will be no more "rear," only the presence of God face to face, just as it was when the Torah was given. "Face to face the Lord spoke to your entire congregation" (Deut. 5:4/19). Thus will it be when the redeemer comes.

Amen Selah unto eternity. Blessed is the Lord forever. Amen. Amen. May the Lord reign forevermore. Amen. Amen.

Sources: *Wa-Yishlah*

The ninth of Av	Ta'anit 26b
One who eats on the ninth of Av	Zohar 1:170b
Every single acacia tree	Rosh Hashanah 23a

WA-YESHEV
Genesis 37:1–40:32

INTRODUCTION. The story of Joseph and his brothers, comprising the latter portion of the book of Genesis (and three full sections in the weekly reading), has exercised relatively little fascination on the minds of Jewish spiritual authors. *The Light of the Eyes* is not at all atypical of Hasidic works in having extended discussions in those chapters of Genesis through the adventures of Jacob, and then tapering off to a mere occasional remark. Perhaps these writers unconsciously sensed the relatively "secular" character of the Joseph narratives, in which the hand or voice of God plays rather little direct part. Perhaps also it is the exclusion of Joseph from place among the formally recognized "patriarchs" that makes him of less interest than he might intrinsically be.

Where Joseph does achieve mention, it is as prototype of the *zaddiq*; he is the single figure who is most regularly called by this title throughout both rabbinic and Kabbalistic literature. His particular claim to righteousness is related to his success in overcoming temptation in his refusal to submit to the charms of Potiphar's wife. It is with reference to Joseph as *zaddiq* that the one teaching in this section concludes, in the course of a striking reversal of the symbol of the "Coat of Many Colors."

Jacob's love and preference for Joseph is entirely unproblematic to this as to most premodern Jewish authors. While the modern reader approaches the Joseph story from a psychological point of view, aware of the dynamic of rivalry that Jacob's favoritism has created among his sons, the Hasidic author saw nothing but good in Jacob's special love for Joseph. If anything, the father of many children who singles out one for special affection was seen as paradigmatic, exemplifying in human terms God's particular love for Israel or for the *zaddiq*.

I

NOW ISRAEL LOVED JOSEPH BEST OF ALL HIS SONS, FOR HE WAS A CHILD OF HIS OLD AGE. HE MADE HIM A COAT OF MANY COLORS. (Gen. 37:3)

The Torah is eternal; it refers to all times and to every person. It existed before the world, and only afterwards took on the form of stories about events in time. While the patriarchs Abraham, Isaac, and Jacob lived, the Torah took on the stories of their lives. The same should be true of all times; Torah is so called because it teaches or points the way. Thus we have to understand in this verse what way is indicated for us.

We have been taught: " 'In the beginning God created'—for the sake of Torah and for the sake of Israel." The real purpose of all creation was so that God might do good for His creatures. Surely He had no need to create the world; a person who does something out of need is lacking in something. God is whole in every way, so much so that the term "lack" may not be applied to Him; surely we cannot say that He needed to create. Rather it is in the nature of the good to bestow goodness, and "the Lord is good to all" (Ps. 145:9). That was why He created the world: so that His creatures might enjoy His goodness. Now the true joy that Israel have in the world lies in fulfilling God's commandments; in this they find joy in Him. In this He too rejoices, as we have been taught: "Israel sustain their Father in heaven." A father takes pleasure in his delightful child.

Thus should we understand a statement in the Mishnah: "Be not like servants who serve the master in order to receive a reward; be rather like servants who serve him not in order to be rewarded." The statement certainly seems repetitious. If you are not to serve for reward, why do you again have to be told to serve as though not for reward? But the truth is that: The joy you should have in fulfilling a commandment is a true spiritual joy, something of the world-to-come. Your service should not be in order to receive some reward afterwards, something you anticipate for the future. Rather in that very moment, in the doing of the commandment, this joy from above should be aroused in you. This is "not in order to be rewarded"— your service should not be "in order" for anything, for that implies the future; your joy is in the act itself, and in that way do you find joy in God.

" 'In the beginning'—for Torah and for Israel"—but God is infinite; how then could He create a finite world? He did so through the Torah: "You have clothed Yourself in glory and beauty" (Ps. 104:1). He concentrated His presence in the Torah in order to create a finite world. He did this for the sake of Israel, that they might follow this Torah and hence receive His good. But why then did He begin His Torah with stories; why not begin it with the first of the commandments? We will best understand this by listening to the words of the Passover Haggadah: "It is a *mizwah* for us to tell of the Exodus from Egypt, and the more one tells of this Exodus, the more praiseworthy." Why "the more one tells"? Remember that "the ordinary conversations of the sages require study." You cannot always be studying Torah; there are times when you need to speak of worldly things. But "the righteous walk in them" (Hos. 14:10)— even when the righteous are speaking of worldly things they remain attached to God. Their very words are Torah, and they uplift souls with these words just as they do with words of Torah. Indeed there are some souls who are better uplifted by this talk than they are by Torah study. They have no power to join themselves to Torah, and it is only worldly speech that can reach them. This is the Exodus from Egypt (MiZRaYiM)— going out of the narrows of the sea (*MeZaR YaM*), going near the bounds of that Sea of Wisdom. That is why we must always speak of the Exodus; indeed *always*. Whatever it is that we speak of, the Exodus should be present in it. And that is why "the more one tells"— not only on Passover, but constantly.

And so ISRAEL LOVED JOSEPH. The Zohar refers to God as "the elder Israel," and Joseph is the *zaddiq*. He is called Joseph (yosef, literally "he adds") because the *zaddiq* is always adding something by his fear of heaven, always raising up yet another rung from below. FOR HE WAS A CHILD OF HIS OLD AGE—Onkelos translates this as "a wise child"; he raises up souls by means of his speech, and all of them are purified in wisdom. HE MADE HIM A COAT OF MANY COLORS: The *zaddiq* fashions garments for God, the gar-

ments in which He is clothed.[1] COLORS (*PaSsYM*): to be taken as an abbreviation for "the mouth that speaks of the Exodus from Egypt" (*Peh Sah Yezi'at Mizrayim*).
Blessed is the Lord forever. Amen. Amen.

Sources: *Wa-Yeshev*

Israel sustain	Zohar 3:16
Be not like servants	Avot 1:3
Ordinary conversations	Sukkah 21b
The elder Israel	Zohar 1:182b, 2:16a

---

1. By making mention of God as he discusses worldly things, the *zaddiq* makes those things into "garments" for God. This is another way of saying that he discovers (or, more dramatically, allows for) the presence of God in those worldly things. Simultaneous or identical with his "uplifting" of the lower world to God, then, is his bringing a sense of the presence down into the lower world, making divinity accessible to all, even to those who stand far from Torah.

MI-QEẒ

Including Homilies for Hanukkah

Genesis 41:1–44:17

INTRODUCTION. *Mi-Qeẓ* provides the only example we have in Genesis of the combined teachings on the weekly Torah portion with special homilies for a holiday that falls within that portion's week. While it was not *necessarily* the preacher's task to refer to both of these in one homily, to do so would have been considered both appropriate and a demonstration of the speaker's particular skills.

Our section begins with a teaching on the *zaddiq* and his powers in the world. While *Me'or 'Eynayim* does not yet speak of the *zaddiq* in dynastic or "professional" terms, the special powers of the holy man in the upper worlds as well as in the universe of history are clearly evident. Talk of the "righteous one" represents a subtle shifting of religious values in Judaism, one particularly worthy of note. The *shekhinah* dwells in the Temple not by virtue of an inherent holiness of the place and not by irrevocable divine decree. It is the righteousness of Israel that brings about God's presence, and their sin that causes Him to depart. Thus far a statement of religious values to which Jeremiah could in no way object. But the "righteousness" of Israel is here embodied in the "righteous one," the *zaddiq*, of whom the high priest Mattathias is said to be a perfect example. It was by *his* power (albeit through his teachings to Israel) that the presence was restored and the Temple purified. In this teaching the claims for the *zaddiq* are somewhat restrained, and the original values of moral rectitude are still clearly to be seen in him. It is a transitionary piece, however, as is

Me'or 'Eynayim as a whole: The movement from *zaddiq* as *example* of moral righteousness to *zaddiq* as *embodiment* of divine power has already begun to take place.

Opening the second homily is a bit of moral preachment, containing some sound psychological advice on the habit-forming character of life-patterns, including those of sin. The author defines Hanukkah as a time for return to God, using the symbol of the defiled oil that was once again made fit for use in His service. Since Hanukkah is a time for penitents, God sees fit to dwell with them in their lowly state, and the low and small Hanukkah lamp comes to represent His willingness to meet the penitent even at the humblest of rungs. From Hanukkah the same teaching turns back to the Torah portion, interpreting Pharaoh's dream with which this portion opens. The drama of the two sets of seven cows is read as that of the seven *sefirot*, here depicting as seven moral virtues, and their counterparts in the world of sin. While these seven sins and virtues have nothing historically to do with the list frequently discussed in Christian moralistic literature, the student of comparative morals might find it interesting to juxtapose the two.

In the third teaching Rabbi Nahum touches on a theme that is most common to Hanukkah homilies elsewhere in Hasidism: the distinction between Hanukkah and Purim. Haman, the enemy of the Purim story, sought to destroy the physical existence of Jewry; hence Purim is a time for bodily celebration, feasting and merrymaking. The Hellensitic enemy of Hanukkah was an enemy in the realm of spirit; the Syrians sought the acculturation of the Jews rather than their obliteration. Hence the appropriate celebration of Hanukkah remains in the realm of spirit: feasting is limited, but Psalms of thanksgiving (*hallel*) are recited. Here the author takes Hanukkah as a time of return to Torah, as a time for asserting spiritual loyalty to the traditions of Israel.

The final two teachings of *Mi-Qez* are both incomplete, but represent interesting lessons in the problem of studying written records of an essentially oral literature (see Introduction). The fourth teaching is a scattered series of reflections on various Biblical verses connected to the Sabbath. The thread that joined these pieces into a single sermon is, however, lost, as is whatever connection it may have had to this week's reading. It contains some interesting materials on the relationship between Sabbath and revelation as well as on the essentially practical character of Torah-study (hence the gentile student, whose reflections remain theoretical, is condemned), but it is incapable of being restored to wholeness.

The fifth teaching represents a problem of another sort. It is lacking at the end, as the editor of the Hebrew volume frankly admits, and the final section that is offered is nearly identical with a portion of a preceding homily. Does this repetition represent faulty editing, an editor having mistakenly appended a part of one written text to complete the missing ending of another? Or might the passage in fact be authentic to both homilies, reflecting the fact that the preacher's need to speak each year on the same portion sometimes exceeded the number of original thoughts he was able to offer on the same materials? Such questions, not essential to the reader of such a text in translation, are the bane of the scholar who would seek to construct a "critical" text in any of these necessarily fragmentary recollections of originally oral teachings.

$$* \quad * \quad *$$

I

"The rabbis taught: What is Hanukkah? . . . On the twenty-fifth day of Kislev . . . the Hellenists entered the sanctuary . . . "

It would seem that the sage is asking why these days are called Hanukkah.[1] If so, what answer is here offered? In fact the word Hanukkah is composed of *HaNu KoH* ("they dwell in 'thus'"). There is an aspect of divinity that is called "thus"; this is *malkhut*, the seat of divine rule. The king commands: "Thus will it be; thus will it be!" It is this aspect that issues commands through all the worlds and by which the universe is ruled. This is why the *zaddiqim* have within their power dominion over all the worlds: they bear within themselves this aspect of God's kingship. So the rabbis have taught us on the verse "the righteous one rules the fear of God (2 Sam. 23:3)"; "Who rules over Me? The *zaddiq*. The Holy One issues His decrees, but the righteous one may cancel them."

---

1. In fact the Talmudic question is not about the name, but about the meaning and origins of the celebration. For the Hasidic author, writing a millennium and a half later, Hanukkah is so much a part of the sacred calendar that he cannot imagine the Talmudic masters not knowing what it is.

On this tradition the *Zohar* asked: "Does the *zaddiq* then control God?" In fact it is God himself who cancels the decree. Several times we have taught that "in all their suffering, He suffers" (Isa. 63:9)—that the *shekhinah* is in exile. *Shekhinah*—so called because it dwells (*SHoKHeNet*) everywhere, is identical with this aspect of divine rule. It is also called "Community of Israel," for it includes all of Israel, since all of them have their origins here. "All Israel are the children of kings." Anything an Israelite suffers, then, has to do with the fall of the *shekhinah*, of this principle of rule. Scripture refers to it in "You weaken the rock that bore you" (Deut. 32:18). The righteous, by means of their good deeds, raise up the *shekhinah*, as in "Give strength to God!" (Ps. 68:35). The rabbis comment: "Israel add strength to the 'family' above."[2] This aspect of divinity is called "family," for it gathers within itself all those divine potencies that stand above it; all of their powers flow into the *shekhinah*. As she is raised up from her fall or exile, all evil decrees and forces of judgment are overcome.

The world was created for the sake of Torah and for the sake of Israel; all of Creation took place in order that He might be known and recognized by His creatures. But what means exist by which we can know Him? Only by cleaving to His ways do we know Him: "Just as He is merciful, so you be Merciful" and all the rest; it is in this way that we approach Him. Now when the Hellenists came into the sanctuary, the *shekhinah* was in a fallen state, as it were; the powers of evil had triumphed. Then Mattathias the High Priest, who was a great *zaddiq*, taught people again how to cleave to God's ways. The *shekhinah* was then uplifted and the forces of judgment set aside. It was in this way that the Hellenists were defeated. The Talmud indeed teaches us that "when the Hellenists came into the sanctuary . . . all the oils were defiled." Wisdom is called "oil"; all wisdom was defiled, even that of Torah, for people studied it with pride and for the wrong reasons. The Talmud goes on to tell that "when the Hasmoneans overcame them . . . they found one container of oil." The letters of 'eHaD ("one") are numerically thirteen: They held fast to the thirteen attributes of God. When the Greeks invaded they made thirteen breaches in the Temple wall—for then Israel had not been faithful to these thirteen. Thus did divine rule fall and evil triumph. Now, how-

---

2. The term *"famalia shel ma'alah"* is used by the rabbis to refer to God in the context of His array of powers and His angelic retinue; it should not be interpreted over-literally.

ever, that they had returned to God's thirteen ways, evil fell apart of its own accord. Understand this.

II

AFTER TWO YEARS' TIME, PHARAOH DREAMED THAT HE WAS STANDING BY THE NILE, WHEN OUT OF THE NILE THERE CAME UP SEVEN COWS, HANDSOME AND STURDY, AND THEY GRAZED IN THE REED GRASS. BUT PRESENTLY, SEVEN OTHER COWS CAME UP FROM THE NILE BEHIND THEM, UGLY AND GAUNT, AND STOOD BESIDE THE COWS ON THE BANKS OF THE NILE; AND THE UGLY GAUNT COWS ATE UP THE SEVEN HANDSOME STURDY COWS. AND PHARAOH AWOKE . . . IT WAS A DREAM. (Gen. 41:1–7).

The Torah as we have been given it teaches that man is a part of God above; by means of the Torah he can draw himself near to God. Of this Scripture asks: "For what has the land been destroyed?" And God Himself answers: "Because they have forsaken My Torah" (Jer. 9:11). Even if "seven courts of rabbis were to worship idols, so long as they did not forsake the Torah"—and the light of Torah could lead them to repent—"they would not be punished." When they do leave the Torah, however, they are punished for all their sins; they no longer have any means by which they can return to God.

Scripture tells us: "Let your clothes always be freshly washed, and your head never lack ointment" (Eccles. 9:8). Every commandment we fulfill creates a garment for us; this is called "the cloak of the rabbis."[1] Sins also make a garment, but a soiled one. Thus "one sin causes another." Scripture seems surprised when it speaks of "a soul that sins . . ." (Lev. 5:1). A holy soul should after all long for the service of God. What is it that brings the soul to sin? "No person sins unless he is possessed by the spirit of folly"—this is the unclean garment [created by his former sins], by which the evil urge grabs hold and leads him to sin again. Of Joseph we are told that "she grabbed

1. The cloak is the raiment of the soul in the world-to-come, woven of the good deeds one has performed while alive in this world.

256

him by his garment" (Gen. 39:12). Joseph saw that he had become an important person and he used to curl his hair; it was by means of that "garment" that she was able to grab hold of him. Joseph realized what had happened, saw that it was in this way she had achieved power over him. Therefore "he left his cloak in her hand and ran outside" (Gen. 39:13). He stripped off that garment and returned to God. "If a scholar should sin during the night," it has been taught, "think no ill of him the next day, for perhaps he has repented." "There is no one so righteous in the world that he does good and never sins" (Eccles. 7:20). He considers what he has done, however, regrets his actions, and sets aside that soiled garment before it leads him into further sin.[2] "One good deed causes another" in the same way, and weaves the soul's proper garment. Jeroboam too was caught by his garment. God also uses this, however, to lead you on to another *mizwah*. And so "let your clothes"—your spiritual garments "always be freshly washed"— may they always be clean and not soiled. "And your head never lack ointment"—this refers to fine oil, that of wisdom, for "olive oil makes one wise." If you have these proper garments, God will grant you wisdom and understanding, "for the Lord grants wisdom from His own mouth, knowledge and understanding" (Prov. 2:6).

Of course there are people who perform the commandments without any awareness of mind or understanding; "even the most empty among you," we are taught, "are as filled with *mizwot* as a pomegranate is with seeds." Such performance, however, cannot bring forth wisdom from above. This is why God has given us the commandment of the Hanukkah candles. As the time for each of the *mizwot* comes along, that very power which was present in the event commemorated is aroused once again. On Passover we came out of bondage, out of enslavement to the great power of defilement, but out of physical bondage as well. Now, as Passover time comes around again, each of us can be liberated from his own forces of evil; this is why we burn the leaven, representing the forces of evil. On Shavu'ot we receive the Torah, that which guides us for the rest of the year in God's service. On Sukkot we are enveloped in the clouds of glory, the

---

2. The author offers a very realistic and down-to-earth vision of the *zaddiq* here: He too sins, but knows enough not to let the pattern created by sin grab hold of him and keep him in its clutches. This contrasts sharply with much more idealized notions of *zaddiq*, as a person untainted even by the *thought* of sin, that are to be found elsewhere in Hasidism.

love of God that surrounds us. Purim represents the fall of the wicked among the nations, so that we might be able to survive this bitter exile. Now Hanukkah is the time for a person to return to God by means of the Torah, just as happened in the days of Mattathias the High Priest. The Hellenists had defiled all the oil; all of wisdom had been corrupted. There remained but a single container of wisdom, that of Torah. There too there was but a drop, hardly enough for one day, yet it burned for eight. The world is built on cycles of seven days; once a seven passes there begins another. These are called "the seven structural days."[3] Now Mattathias served God on a very high contemplative level: he was indeed a High Priest. He was able to bring forth the light of an eighth day, beyond the seven, that of *binah*, giving light to the eight candles.[4]

This is why the Hanukkah candles have to be elevated from the ground by at least three handbreadths, so as not to appear as set in the ground, and lower than ten handbreadths, "for the *shekhinah* has never come lower than ten." God searches for ways that man not be utterly cut off from Him; He miraculously brings Himself down lower than the ten handbreadths,[5] right to where man is, so that he might repent and come back to Him. The oil of the candles refers to wisdom, and "God grants wisdom from His own mouth, knowledge and understanding," teaching man how to serve him in a higher contemplative way. All this comes about through the *mizwah* of lighting the Hanukkah candles. Just as it was then, so it is in every generation when the time of this commandment arrives.

The rabbis have taught that "wicks and oils that may not be used for the Sabbath lights may be used for kindling the lights of Hanukkah." The Sabbath is called "a special gift that I have among My treasures," given to man in order to bring him close to God. "A person who observes the Sabbath, even if he be as thoroughly idolatrous as was the generation of Enosh, is forgiven, for Scripture says: 'He keeps the Sabbath from desecration' (*Me-HaLeLo*) (Isa. 56:2)—read rather 'he keeps the Sabbath and is forgiven' (*MaHal Lo*)." But the holiness of Sabbath is difficult to enter; Sabbath is very high and sublime, the name of God Himself. How can a person enter into

---

3. A common term for the seven lower *sefirot*, to be outlined in detail below.

4. His worship was so high that it transcended the ordinary cycle of time, bringing to that cycle a new light from the higher world that remains timeless.

5. In connection with the *sukkah* it is taught that "the presence never came down lower than ten." In the miracle of Hanukkah the *shekhinah* overcomes this stated limit.

something so high as Sabbath? On Hanukkah, however, God brings Himself down, lower than the ten handbreadths, right down to where the person is, in order to draw him near. And so wicks and oils forbidden for the Sabbath may be used on Hanukkah: Just as a wick is set in place first and then the oil is poured around it before it is lighted, so man is God's wick, wisdom is His oil, and His intent is that light shine forth from a person's deeds and service. This includes even those "wicks" that cannot be used on the Sabbath, people who would not catch onto the Sabbath light. On Hanukkah God has brought himself down to them; He *gives* them the light by which they may come back to Him, a light that may even lead them to the high and most ecstatic form of His service. This happens every year when the time for Hanukkah lights comes around. Before Mattathias[6] there was no need for this commandment; only in his day were all the oils defiled, leaving none but that of Torah, and that studied but by few and in a lowly manner. He, however, was a "priest"—one who serves God, and a "high" priest—one who serves Him in an elevated manner. It was he who brought about the miracle of the eight lights, and thus were the enemies defeated.

As for miracles, they exist both hidden and revealed. God is both hidden and revealed, and so is His Torah. "The hidden things belong to God, but the revealed are for us and our children" (Deut. 29:28). God performs many miracles in ways we cannot see; indeed "there is none besides Him" (Deut. 4:35). Other miracles also exist, of the sort that are obvious to us. But all of these come about through our study of Torah: When we study the esoteric or hidden Torah, a hidden miracles is brought forth; when we study the revealed Torah, an open miracle is wrought. The "single cruse of oil" refers to the Torah that was studied in those times: there was only a bit of it, and in its smallest form. Only the High Priest worshiped God in an enlightened way.

It is taught in the holy writings that the name Pharoah comes from a root (*PR'*) that refers to revelation. "The day of Pharoah's birth" (Gen. 40:20) is thus the day of revelation. But Scripture admonishes us: "How long will you lie down, O lazy one; when will you rise up from your sleep?" (Prov. 6:9). This "sleep" comes about because man is too burdened to maintain full presence of mind. A person can

---

6. He seems to ask why, if this quality inheres in a particular moment of the calendar year, it was made manifest only so late as the time of the Hasmoneans.

even be studying Torah or observing the *mizwot* in a mindless way and remain asleep all the while. Then his study has no power to bring about miracles; only after he studies in an attentive and mindful way can the miracles happen.

Now we may understand our passage:

AFTER TWO YEARS' TIME: "Two years" refers to sleep (*SHeNatayim/SHeNah*); when the period of sleep is ended and a person is aroused to study with real attention and awareness, then

PHAROAH: revelation

DREAMED: was healed (for the root can also have that meaning), for then miracles began to be revealed again,

HE WAS STANDING BY THE NILE, that is, Torah,[7]

WHEN OUT OF THE NILE THERE CAME SEVEN COWS, HANDSOME AND STURDY: Man is compared to beast, as in "You save both man and beast, O Lord!" (Ps.36:7). Some people are so cunning that they make themselves like beasts. Man on his own is nothing; whatever good he has in him is a gift of God, for "the Lord grants wisdom from His own mouth." The seven handsome cows thus represent the seven attributes or qualities that come to man from the seven *sefirot*:

Love—to love the Lord;

Fear—to fear Him or stand in awe of Him;

Glory—to glorify Him;

Victory—to vanquish the evil urge, for "a person should always get his good urge aroused against the evil";

Beauty—appreciation and gratitude toward God;

Foundation—the sense of being bound to all these qualities at once;

Dominion—granting power and dominion to God, making Him King over all the world.

These seven qualities are referred to as COWS, for a person must make himself as passive as cattle.

THEY GRAZED IN THE REED GRASS: The term *aḥu* ("reed grass") is rendered by the Targum as *aḥewa*, "brotherhood": they grazed in brotherhood. The reason people hate one another is most generally pride or jealousy, the feeling that "I should have gotten the

---

7. Torah is frequently compared to water or a body of water.

good or glory that went to him." If a person makes himself like cattle, he loves the entire world and has no hate for his fellowman.

BUT PRESENTLY, SEVEN OTHER COWS CAME UP: The evil urge strives to lead us into sin by his own version of the seven qualities:

Love—the love of money and pursuit of pleasures;

Fear— the fear of punishment;[8]

Glory—the glorification of self;

Victory—defeating one's enemies;

Beauty—appreciating oneself alone;

Foundation—being bound to all *these* qualities;

Dominion—to rule on one's own.

THE UGLY GAUNT COWS ATE UP THE SEVEN STURDY COWS: Within the good deeds we do, some power is always given to the forces of evil. Those forces "eat up" the good that we do in Torah study and the performance of *mizwot*.

"No one could tell that they had consumed them" (Gen. 41:21): Therefore we are told that when we repent, our "intentional sins are turned into merits"—the merits that we had are then rescued from the hands of evil.

AND PHAROAH AWOKE ... IT WAS A DREAM! When a person wakes from the sleep of time, he is restored to true health.

Now we understand why this section is read on Hanukkah: The Torah offers counsel on how to return to God and serve Him.... And that is why "the Hanukkah candles may not be used"—one should have no intent but that of serving God alone, nothing for the sake of this world, nothing for the sake of the world-to-come.

III

Hanukkah candles must be kindled by the time that "footsteps cease in the market."

"He who regularly kindles the Hanukkah lamp," the Talmud also tells us, "will have scholarly sons." Such scholars, of course, will

---

8. The author is unusual, but not unique, among Jewish moralists in seeing the fear of punishment as a negative factor in the religious life, one created as a smokescreen by the evil urge to keep one from true worship.

not be walking about the market, but will be busy studying Torah; this is the reference to "footsteps cease in the market." The Talmud says that these are the footsteps of the kindling-dealers.[1]

Now we know that when the time comes for each of the *miẓwot* assigned to a special season, there is awakened at that time the very quality that abounded when the original event took place. It was on Passover that we came forth from Egypt. The chief liberation was that from the great depths of defilement; on each of the holidays we children of Israel come forth from one or another of the evil forces. Were there not a Passover every year, it would seem impossible that a person could have the strength to be close to God. On Shavu'ot each of us receives the Torah, an indication of what approach we should have in our minds in serving God during that year. On Sukkot we are again surrounded by God's love; love envelops us as it did in those days, when we were surrounded by God's clouds of glory. Purim is the time of the fall of Amalek: now too, as in each generation, the wicked among the nations have their fall. Hanukkah is a time when the enemies of our religion wanted to take us away from Torah and the life according to God's law. By dint of miracle we were able to stand fast and hold onto Torah and the practice of our religion. So it is every year, that this is a proper time to gain strength in holding fast to Torah and to our laws. Whatever strength we have in doing so comes from our ancestors, those in early times who prayed for us.

The patriarchs prayed in their time for all future generations, right down to the messiah, may he come soon. Of Abraham Scripture says: "He pursued them until Dan" (Gen. 14:14). It is taught that there he felt weak [because God showed him that his offspring would one day worship idols in that place—cf. Judg. 18] and prayed for his descendants. Abraham also hinted at Hanukkah when he said: "You stay here with the ass while I and the boy go to *KoH*" (Gen. 22:5), the numerical value of which is twenty-five, referring to the twenty-fifth of Kislev; he prayed that in the time of Mattathias they might defeat the Hellenists on that day. Joseph the righteous too was concerned about this matter when he said to Benjamin, "May God be gracious (*yeḤoNeKH*) to you, my son" (Gen. 43:29); the word is the same as *Ha-NuKKaH*. He prayed for miracles and wonders on that day. Every year the wicked and the enemies of Torah fall, until finally they will be completely wiped out and our righteous messiah will arrive. This

---

1. Lit.: Palmyreans. The point is that they would be the last to leave the market.

is: "I have prepared a lamp for My anointed one" (Ps. 132:17): The Hanukkah lamp serves as preparation for that anointed messiah. Then will all evil be defeated; there will be no more "footsteps of the Palmyreans," as Scripture refers to "Palmyra among the mountains."[2]

IV

"For [1] thus says the Lord: 'As for the eunuchs who keep My Sabbaths . . . and hold fast to My covenant, I will give them . . . sons and daughters . . . which shall not perish' " (Isa. 56:4–5).

Why is it the Sabbath in particular that they will need in order to have sons and daughters, and not some other commandment?[2] It is said of the nations that "their flow is like that of horses" (Ezek. 23:20) [i.e., they are steeped in sexual excess]. Israel have no part of this; their portion is rather in God, and their coupling is in holiness. "Male and female He created them, and He called them humans" (Gen. 5:2); He gave to them the power of generation and said to them: "Be fruitful and multiply and fill the earth" (Gen. 1:28). Why "fill the earth?" For it has been taught that "the son of David will not come until all the souls in the *guf* are used up." RaSHI tells us that this *guf* is a chamber that is the source of all souls; it is thus that messiah's arrival awaits our fulfillment of "be fruitful and multiply." When messiah comes, God willing, "earth will be filled with knowledge of the Lord." . . .

*   *   *

"Heaven and earth were finished" (Gen. 2:1). The Targum says "perfected." Sabbath is the covenant above; all of Israel collectively are called the Community of Israel, as in "The community of Israel said

---

2. There is no such verse in Scripture, and Palmyra is in fact in the desert. He seems to have confused Palmyra (*Tadmor*) with *Tabor* in Jer. 46:18.

1. Here are preserved only loosely related fragments of what was originally a long homily on the Sabbath. Its point of departure seems to have been the plural use ("Sabbaths") in this verse and elsewhere.

2. The plain meaning of this verse is here completely distorted. Scripture assures the eunuchs of a memorial more faithful than that of offspring, not that they will become child-bearing. This distortion has an earlier history; see Zohar 1:187b and R. Margaliot ad loc., n. 4.

to God."[3] It is she who unites with her lover. This is why the Sabbath was given in secret;[4] the *mizwah* of coupling must be performed in private.

*   *   *

"You shall keep my Sabbaths, for it is holy unto you" (Exod. 31:13–14). The holiness enters into you, as is explained in the Zohar.

*   *   *

"The major categories of labor [forbidden on the Sabbath] are forty less one." Why did they not say "thirty-nine"? The point is that on the Sabbath we consider all our labors to be finished. A person who labors at something shows that he has some lack; he does this labor to make up or attain what he needs. Sabbath is the name of God; it is, as it were, complete in every way, needing no labor because it is lacking in nothing. "Is anything lacking in the royal household?" And Sabbath is called "Queen." So labor is needed only when we are "less one," lacking in something; if we are "less one," lacking the One, indeed that Sabbath cannot be complete.[5]

*   *   *

If you make those two Sabbaths into one, then they are called "labors."[6] Thus the rabbis said: "If Israel were to keep two Sabbaths, they would be redeemed forthwith." Why "forthwith"? You might think that this refers to two separate Sabbaths, and that Israel would have to wait from one Sabbath to the next to be redeemed. "Forthwith" tells you otherwise, for in one Sabbath there are two.

*   *   *

---

3. "The community of Israel said to God: 'Who will be my partner?' And God replied: 'Israel will be your partner.' " Here Sabbath is depicted in masculine terms (*berit*), opposed to *zirmat susim* above, and Israel is his beloved.

4. At Marah, before Sinai, where all the world was present.

5. The reading here is uncertain, based on a guess as to the missing links in this teaching. He may also mean (see below) that if one of the two aspects of Sabbath is missing, that Sabbath is considered violated.

6. His reading of the word *mel'akhot* remains unclear.

The Sabbath command was given at *Marah* (literally "bitterness"). They were so sad that they would not be able to receive the Torah, the World of Joy. "They came to Marah" (Exod. 15:23), they came to a state of melancholy. "And they were unable to drink the waters of Marah"—they were unable to receive the waters of Torah. That is why they were there given the Sabbath; with the Sabbath they would be lacking in nothing, and then they could receive the Torah.[7]

*   *   *

"On the seventh day He ceased and was refreshed" (Exod. 31:17). *Wa-yinafash* can also consonantly be divided as *wey [avedah] nefesh*: "Woe! The soul is lost! On the Sabbath we lack for nothing, so that the woe the soul had felt beforehand is now lost.

*   *   *

Sabbath is called "covenant" and Torah is called "covenant." Concerning both study of Torah and Sabbath observance it is taught that a gentile who partakes of them deserves death. If he cannot keep the Sabbath, surely it will not be possible for him to reach Torah.[8]

*   *   *

"A gentile who studies Torah is like a high priest." But how is this possible if Torah is forbidden to them? The answer is that he is to study the seven commandments of Noah, which were given to everyone. The main thing is the deed; "study is greater only because it leads to deeds." That is why he is not to study outside the seven commandments; it is those that he is to live by, and study must be for the sake of fulfillment in action. Other *mizwot*, those that he does not observe, it is forbidden him to study.

We too should learn a lesson from this, especially those who study in a way that is not "for its own sake," for the sake of fulfillment in the deed. Of the one who does study for its own sake we are

---

7. It is a state of fullness, rather than one of emptiness and depression, that best prepares us to hear God's word.

8. For Israel too had to be given the Sabbath to uplift them from the ordinary human condition of anxiety before they could receive the Torah.

told that he "merits many things (*devarim*) . . . that it clothes him in humility and awe." By studying Torah you merit to speak of it to others (for there are some who understand Torah but cannot teach it to others). This is the promise of *devarim*, the ability to speak words of Torah and to teach others.

The most important thing is that you not consider yourself a *zaddiq*; "even if all the world tells you that you are a *zaddiq*." The study of Torah for its own sake leads you toward righteousness; this can work only if you believe that you are not yet there.

"Clothes him in humility and awe"—in the name of our teacher the *hasid* Israel of Polotzk: Sometimes a person has to act without awe for the sake of heaven. Awe itself can keep him from coming too close, and his duty to attain to perfect union. The same with humility: Sometimes you have to cast it aside for the sake of heaven. This is the meaning of "clothes him" in humility and awe—like a garment, sometimes you wear it, and sometimes you lay it aside. "The words of a wise man are gracious" (Eccles. 10:12).

V

IT SHALL BE AS YOU SAY (Gen. 44:10).

But the brothers had suggested that the one in whose goods the cup might be found would die, while Joseph, after saying this, then ordered only that he be kept as a slave. When they were returned he said to them: "Do you not know that a man like me practices divination?" (Gen. 44:15). Have not we learned that "there is no divination in Jacob" (Num. 23:23)? Could Joseph have been lying? And how could a lie be recorded in the Torah of truth?

The point is that God set up through Joseph a series of events leading to Jacob's arrival in chains in Egypt. This had to happen so that the debt of "your offspring shall be strangers in a land not theirs" (Gen. 15:13) might be eliminated.

It was by means of Torah that God created the world. Since the power of the creative force remains evident in its creature, Torah is ever present in the world. This has been true since creation: Adam studied Torah, and after him Noah, Shem, and Eber. In the generations of Enosh, the flood, and Babel, however, evil reached such heights—unlike the wickedness of other generations, in which people were merely drawn by their passions—that the world and Torah were cut off from God. Their spiteful cry of "What is God that we should worship Him!" had a real divisive power to it, separating the cosmic One from the *shekhinah*, as Scripture says: "A whisperer separates familiar friends" (Prov. 16:28; *aluf/alef*). Then the Torah fell into the evil clutches of Egypt. Thus spoke the holy lips of our teacher the *ḥasid* Rabbi Dov Baer, and the same is to be found in the Lurianic writings. This is why the toil of Egyptian bondage was in "mortar and bricks" as explained in the Zohar. "Mortar" (*ḥomer*) refers to the principle of inference from minor to major, *qal wa-ḥomer*. "Bricks" (*levenim*) refers to the clarification (*libbun*) of the law. Because they labored at the pressing of *ḥomer*, they were able to rescue the *qal wa-ḥomer* from Egyptian spiritual bondage; thus was one of the thirteen principles that rule Torah's interpretation uplifted. The same is true of *levenim*, as the Zohar explains.

That is the meaning of "Jacob saw that there was produce (*shever*) in the land of Egypt" (Gen. 42:1). Even though the shekhinah had departed from him [after Joseph's disappearance], he understood that the broken vessels—those that remained from the prior worlds that God had created and destroyed, for the sake of free will—existed as fragments (*shever*) in Egypt. Torah lay in the hands of the evil forces. Scripture says of Torah: "She has hewn out her seven pillars" (Prov. 9:1); there are also "seven bowls for the lamps" (Zech. 4:2.)[1] These have to be joined together, the process that the Zohar calls "subsuming the left under the right." "The commandment is a lamp and the Torah, light" (Prov. 6:23). This is the *shever* that was there in Egypt, the essential *seven* in a fragmented state: we are to *love* God, to *fear* Him, to *glorify* Him, to be *victorious* over the evil urge, to be *grateful* to Him, *binding* all these qualities together and giving Him *dominion* over us. But love turned instead to pleasure, fear to things external, glory to self-centeredness, victory to the defeat of fellowmen, and gratitude to the arbitrary. Of this [back side of the divine qualities] the Ba'al Shem Tov spoke when he said, interpreting a verse of Scripture: "A man who takes his sister—that is *ḥesed*" (Lev. 20:17). A person who seeks out a forbidden sexual liaison (God protect us!) does so because of the love that is in him. That love is *ḥesed*; it comes from one of

---

1. Of the Temple candelabrum that the prophet sees in his vision. That chapter is read as the *haftarah* for the Sabbath of Hanukkah. The seven branches of the Temple candelabrum are presently to be identified with the seven *sefirot*.

267

the attributes of God. Now he has taken that and done ill with it, bringing love down, as it were, into a defiled place. Joseph "gathered up all the *kesef*" (Gen. 47:14); read *kesef* here as "love" rather than as "money" (*kasaf* elsewhere means "to long for"). He ordered that *this kesef* be returned "to each man in the mouth of his bag" (Gen. 44:1), to show his father that there was someone in Egypt gathering up the bits of love that had fallen into the hands of the evil forces there. Love had fallen so far primarily at the hands of that one who rode astride the snake when he went to seduce Eve. This is the meaning of Joseph's divination, for "divination" and "snake" are the same word (*naḥash*): Joseph set right that which the snake had damaged.

Joseph was able to see that once [the fragments] that had fallen into Egypt were uplifted, a Temple was going to be built. This would take place in Benjamin's portion of the land, and for this reason Joseph said of Benjamin: "He will be a servant to me" (Gen. 44:17), meaning that the service of God would be in his inheritance. "And you shall be free from sin,"* the verse continues, since the morning offering each day atoned for the sins of night and the evening offering for sins committed during the day. In this way "you shall be free from sin"; [Jerusalem was called, when the Temple stood,] "righteousness dwells in her" (Isa. 1:21).[2] The brothers said: "We shall be servants" (Isa. 1:16), telling him that the Temple would also be partially in Judah's territory, but he told them that the true service would be in the portion of Benjamin. "As for you," he added, "go in peace up to your father"—your Father in heaven. . . . [3]

Sources: *Mi-Qeẓ*

I

What is Hanukkah?	Shabbat 21b
The righteous one rules	Mo'ed Qatan 16b
Does the *zaddiq* then control God?	Zohar 1:45b
The children of kings	Shabbat 128a

---

2. For no sin ever lasted the night.
3. There follows a short string of associations between Hanukkah and the patriarchal narratives, virtually identical to that found at the end of III.

Israel add strength   Ekhah Rabbah 1:33; Zohar
                                                 2:32
Just as He is merciful   Sotah 14a
When the Hellenists came   Shabbat 21b

II
Man is part of God above   Cf. Shefa' Tal, introduction
Because they have forsaken   Nedarim 81a
One sin causes another   Avot 4:2
The spirit of folly   Sotah 3a
He used to curl his hair   Tanhuma wa-yeshev 8
If a scholar should sin   Berakhot 19a
Jeroboam   Sanhedrin 102a
Even the most empty   Eruvin 19a
Never lower than ten   Sukkah 5a
Wicks and oils   Shabbat 21a
A special gift   Shabbat 10b
A person who observes   Shabbat 118b
Some people are so cunning   Hullin 5b

III
Footsteps cease   Shabbat 21b
He who regularly kindles   Shabbat 23b
There he felt weak   Mekilta Amalek 2
Palmyreans   Shabbat 21b

IV
The son of David will not come until   Yebamot 62a
The Community of Israel said   Bereshit Rabbah 11:8
Categories of labor   Shabbat 73a
Sabbath is the name of God   Zohar 2:88b
Sabbath is called Queen   Shabbat 119a
If Israel were to keep two Sabbaths   Shabbat 118b
Given at Marah   Sanhedrin 56b
The soul is lost!   Bezah 16a
A gentile who partakes of them   Sanhedrin 58b, 59a
A gentile who studies Torah   Sanhedrin 59a
Because it leads to deeds   Qiddushin 40b

THE LIGHT OF THE EYES

Merits many things	Avot 6:1
Even if all the world tells you	Niddah 30b

V
Jacob's arrival in chains	Shabbat 89b
Mortar and bricks	Tiqquney Zohar 147b
The shekhinah had departed	Targum Y. to Gen. 45:27
In Benjamin's portion	Zevahim 53b
The morning offering atoned	Shir Rabbah 1:9

WA-YIGGASH
Genesis 44:18–47:27

INTRODUCTION. We have already noted the sharp decline of interest that the Hasidic authors evince in the Genesis narrative as it reaches the Joseph story. While the preceding section of *Mi-Qez* was sustained by the Hanukkah association (and the Sabbath of Hanukkah was a common time for disciples' visits—hence the increase in homilies for that occasion), this present section is represented only by a single teaching, and the last weekly reading of Genesis, *wa-yehi*, is lacking altogether.

Seeming to sense the secularity of the Joseph narrative, our author straightforwardly poses the question that lies at the root of so much of Biblical exegesis, particularly that emerging from circles of mystics and pietists: Can the Bible be *merely* that which it appears to be? The claims that the tradition has made for Scripture, and for Torah in particular, far outstrip that which certain parts of the text itself seem to offer. Thus the medieval exegetes ask whether "the sister of Lothan was Timna" (Gen. 36:22) can really have been part of God's primordial esoteric self, or whether the names and genealogies of ancient rulers—particularly the Edomite ones!—are really fitting matter for a text that is said to be sublime.

The Kabbalists are especially strong-minded about this issue, calling down curses on anyone who sees the surface meaning alone as the true content of Torah. "Were the Torah to speak only of ordinary matters," says the Zohar, "we could compose a better one in our own day." Of course it is this principle that urges on the great homiletical creativity that we find in the mystical and Hasidic literature: It is the inadequacy of the plain meaning to the truth that forces the thinker or preacher to seek out a meaning of his own, in the case of Hasidism often one related to the spiritual questions of his own time. This assumption also serves to limit the power of true exegesis, however. If the text may not be "mere" story, the narrative structure and content of the tale quickly pale into nothingness, and it may as well be the numerical values of two isolated words in the text that inspire the homily as the story of Joseph itself. This will of necessity make for a certain sameness in the homiletical collection, a trend evident nowhere more than in these sections. No matter that the weekly subject is the tale of Joseph; The task of the Hasidic preacher remains unchanged. No wonder, then, that our single incomplete homily here deals in fact with a theme familiar to us from the very beginning of this volume, the presence of God in all things and the ultimate oneness of God and self.

*   *   *

I

THEN JUDAH WENT UP TO HIM AND SAID: "PLEASE, MY LORD, LET YOUR SERVANT APPEAL TO MY LORD, AND DO NOT BECOME ANGRY WITH YOUR SERVANT, YOU WHO ARE THE EQUAL OF PHARAOH. (Gen. 44:18)

Why is this recorded in the Torah? Surely it could not simply be a story; the holy Zohar curses those who say that the Torah is merely a book of stories! Scripture tells us, after all, that "You are clothed in glory and beauty" (Ps. 104:1), and that Torah is God's glory and beauty is well known. "Grant your beauty to the heavens!" (Ps. 8:2), but God caused the Torah to be clothed in garments.[1] The Torah is called "fire"; "Are not my words like fire?" (Jer. 23:29). Just as no one can hold onto fire without something in between, so can the Torah not be held without some intermediary. This is the reason for the garbing of Torah in various forms. Sometimes the Torah is also called "water";

---

1. The garbing of Torah in stories makes its heavenly truths accessible to those who dwell on earth; in such garb Torah is more appropriate to humans than to the heavenly hosts.

"O All who are thirsty, go to water" (Isa. 51:1). But how can Torah be both fire and water—are not the two opposite to one another? This could not be but by the hand of God Himself, the One who "makes peace in His heavens" (Job 25:2). We have learned that the heavens too are made of fire and water (*SHaMaYiM/'eSH-MaYiM*) and God holds them together. He remains as intermediary between the two, ever joining them to one another.

What are "water" and "fire"? They are nothing other than the love and fear of God, those qualities that form the basis of the entire Torah. "Without love and fear, nothing flies upward." Fire represents fear; just as we are afraid to approach a fire, so too God Himself, the Fire who consumes all fires. Water represents love; just as all kinds of pleasurable things grow in the water, so does water stand for all of the world's loves. This is why the rabbis tell us that the word Torah has a numerical value of six hundred eleven, even though the commandments number six hundred thirteen. The two *mizwot* of the love and fear of God are the root of all Torah; they must be present in every *mizwah* we perform. That was why, at Sinai, we heard the first two commandments from the mouth of God Himself.[2] The root of the entire Torah was given us by God. "I am the Lord your God" stands for love—"who brought you out of the Land of Egypt"—and therefore you shall love Me. "You shall have no other gods"—no other powers [shall be objects of your fear].

Scripture says: "The Lord your God will circumcise your heart . . . to love the Lord your God with all your heart and soul, for the sake of your life" (Deut. 30:6). But why should God seemingly want us to love Him for an extraneous reason, "for the sake of your life"? The point is that we must have full faith that all our strength, the very life within us, is God. The person is a microcosm, containing all the universe in miniature, and God holds them all together. "It is You who connect and unite them all." Thus said the *ReMa*,[3] that the blessing that praises God for "doing wondrously" refers to the fact that matter is joined with spirit. Now God has taught us how to love Him: "for the sake of your life"—for the sake of that God who is your very life! All your strength, all your life, is nothing but God; it is He

---

2. While all the others came through Moses.

3. Rabbi Moses Isserles, a legal authority and an important religious thinker of the sixteenth century. The blessing referred to is usually taken as one of thanksgiving for the workings of the human body.

who brings together and gives unity to all the worlds that lie within you, holding spirit and flesh together. Move any limb of your body— it is God who is moving it. This is why Scripture said: "Fear the Lord your God" (Deut. 10:20): God the powerful, God the all-capable, Master of all strength, Master of your own strength! "You shall have no other gods," as the Ba'al Shem Tov understood it. On the verse "lest you turn aside and worship other gods" (Deut. 11:17)—as soon as you turn aside from Him, He who is your life and your strength, you are worshiping other gods.

Several times we have mentioned that "the *zaddiq* rules over the fear of God" (2 Sam. 23:3); God says that the *zaddiq* has authority over Him, for He may issue a decree, but the *zaddiq* will annul it. The Zohar questioned this, and we have explained it on the basis of the distinction between *bi*, "in Me," and *'alay*, "over Me" . . .[4]

(The homily is incomplete)

Sources: *Wa-Yiggash*

Merely a book of stories	Zohar 3:152a
The heavens are made of fire and water	Hagigah 12a
Without love and fear	Tiqquney Zohar 25b
Six hundred eleven	Makkot 23b
Thus said the ReMa'	Orah Hayyim 6:1
The *zaddiq* rules	Mo'ed Qatan 16b

---

4. The Talmud has God saying: "Who rules over Me? The *zaddiq*." The preposition used for "over," however, is *bi*, more literally translated as "in"; the *zaddiq* rules "in" God. This same *bi* form is in our opening verse, here translated as "please," but supraliterally "in me." The oral homily certainly went on to say that the *zaddiq* is one who recognizes that God dwells within him and is the source of all his powers, and that this is the meaning of his seeming authority "over" the divine will. Judah here represents the *zaddiq*, coming before Joseph as before God, to negate the decree of the ruler. See above, Hayyey Sarah 2, n. 12.

SUGGESTIONS FOR FURTHER READING

There is available a wide variety of published materials on the Hasidic masters and their teachings, ranging from works of the most impeccable scholarship to popular materials of many sorts and of varying quality. The list that follows is the editor's selection of works that would be helpful either to the beginning student or to the scholar of mysticism/popular religion in another context who would like access to Hasidic sources for purposes of comparison.

There is no adequate history of Hasidism available in any language, and none at all in English. The German reader may turn to Simon Dubnow's *Geschichte der Chassidismus* (also available in Hebrew and Russian), sorely outdated but still a basic work in the field. Lacking a full history, the English reader should be reminded that there are many excellent articles on various aspects of Hasidism in the *Encyclopedia Judaica*.

Primary sources in Hasidism fall into two essential categories: 1) homilies, tracts, and devotional instructions, and 2) tales of the Hasidic masters. Very little in the former category is available in English. *Tanya*, the major tract of *HaBaD* Hasidism, has been translated in several volumes and is available through the Kehot/Lubavitch Press in Brooklyn, as are several other *HaBaD* treatises. The *Tract on Ecstacy*, another early *HaBaD* source, was published under that name by Louis Jacobs (London, 1963); this is a very important text on inward states in prayer and contemplation. The present editor has also, together with Barry W. Holtz, contributed a small anthology of Hasidic prayer instructions, entitled *Your Word Is Fire* (Paulist, 1977).

By contrast, a great deal of the tale literature is accessible to the English reader. It should be noted that Hasidic tales were committed to writing at a late date, are hagiographical rather than historical in purpose, and thus should not be seen as entirely reliable historical sources. Nevertheless, as a literary genre of latter-day Hasidism and an embodiment of its spirit they are of first rank. The earliest collection of such tales has appeared in English as *In Praise of the Ba'al Shem Tov* (Bloomington, 1970). Fine latter-day anthologies of tales are Martin Buber's classic *Tales of the Hasidim* (New York, 1947–48), Jiri Langer's *Nine Gates* (London: 1961; a particular favorite of this reader), and Elie Wiesel's *Souls on Fire* (New York, 1972).

Historical and critical studies of Hasidism have been undertaken, particularly since the Second World War, both in Israel and the diaspora. While most of this scholarship is conducted in Hebrew, there is a good variety of studies available in English. Full-length books include Samuel Dresner's *The Zaddik* (London, 1960), Louis Jacobs' *Hasidic Prayer* and *Seeker of Unity* (London, 1972, 1966), and my own *Tormented Master: A Life of Rabbi Nahman of Bratslav* (New York, Schocken, 1981). Of first rank among scholarly articles in English are those of Joseph Weiss, published over the course of several years in the *Journal of Jewish Studies,* London. These uniformly rich and interesting papers cover such topics as "Contemplative Mysticism and 'Faith' in Hasidic Piety" (1952), "Via Passiva in Early Hasidism" (1960), and several others. It is hoped that these will soon appear in collected form. Rivka Schatz-Uffenheimer's "Contemplative Prayer in Hasidism" (*Studies in Mysticism and Religion Presented to Gershom G. Scholem;* Jerusalem, 1967) offers the reader a sampling of her longer and very important book in Hebrew on Hasidic mysticism. Gershom Scholem, while he has dealt rather little with Hasidism in his writings, is author of a summary chapter, the final lecture in his *Major Trends in Jewish Mysticism* (New York, 1954). There are also two important essays, one on "Devekuth, or Communion with God" and the other on "The Neutralization of Messianism in Early Hasidism," both to be found in his collection *The Messianic Idea in Judaism* (New York, 1971). A collection of essays on the early history of Hasidism by the late Abraham Joshua Heschel, originally published in Hebrew and Yiddish, has now been prepared for English publication by Samuel Dresner and should soon make its appearance.

INDEX TO PREFACE
INTRODUCTION & NOTES

INDEX

Day of Atonement, 199 n 6.
Day of Judgment, 198 n 3.
Days of Awe, 90.
Demiurge, 152.
Deuteronomy, 4:25–26, 214 n 3; 6:8, 94 n 2; 22:6–7, 71.
De Vidas, Elijah, 33 n 10.
Diaspora, 20, 135 n 1, 202.
Din, 12, 12 n 13, 27, 42 n 41, 119 n 9, 122 n 12, 124 n 1, 218 n 4.
Dov Baer, Maggid of Miedzyrzec, 5–6, 6 n 8, 7, 9, 15 n 17, 17–18, 21, 24 n 37, 25, 179 n 4, 202, 204.
Dresner, Samuel, 2 n 3, 18 n 20, 276.
Dualism, 19, 35 n 17, 155 n 8, 173.
Dubnow, Simon, 275.

Eber, 205 n 1.
Ecstasy, 178 n 3, 179 n 4, n 5, 198 n 2.
Edels, R. Samuel, 154 n 4.
Eiger, Yehudah Leib, 9.
Elijah, 228 n 3.
Elijah ben Ze'ev Wolf of Yurevich, 24.
Elimelech of Lezajsk, 18.
Emanations, 10–12, 41 n 36, 80, 161 n 1.
Enoch, 162 n 4.
Ephraim of Sudilkov, 25.
Esau, 19, 96 n 8, 171, 174 n 1, 194 n 3, 196 n 6, 198 n 3, 244.
Esther, 55 n 8.
Eve, 55 n 8, n 9.
Evil, 14, 14 n 16, 15, 19, 32 n 4, 42 n 41, 52 n 6, 72 n 3, 83 n 7, 96 n 8, 138 n 1, 172–173, 193 n 2, 194 n 3, 199 n 6, 223 n 10, 244.
Eyn Sof, 14 n 16.
Exodus, 156 n 11; 14:19–21, 156 n 10; 18:1, 55 n 10; 19:2, 66 n 2; 31:3, 11 n 12; 34:6–7, 149.

Fatalism, 16.

Genesis, 72 n 2; 1:6, 56; 1:27, 186 n 2; 4:26, 38 n 28; 5:1, 186 n 2; 17:1, 118 n 8; 18:1–3, 136 n 1; 18:9, 168 n 7; 19:30–38, 116 n 5; 24:1, 148, 149; 25:28, 196 n 6; 33:4, 168 n 7; 36, 194 n 3; 36:22, 271; 50:25, 156 n 11.
Gevurah, 62 n 3, 108 n 2, 119 n 9.
Gittin, 88a, 214 n 3.
Gnosticism, 2 n 2, 79, 161 n 1.
God, acts of, 10, 64 n 4; and being, 65, 134 n 1; children (people) of, 4, 15, 109 n 4, 230 n 3; and creation, 13–14; fear of, 90, 100 n 1, 101 n 3, 172, 178 n 1, 203, 217 n 2, 230 n 3; finding of, 48, 50 n 4; gifts of, 18, 175 n 3, 182 n 11; immanence of, 35 n 17; and Israel, 4, 12, 15, 54 n 7, 57, 109 n 4, 174 n 1, 249; judgment of, 62 n 3, 89, 98 n 2, 100 n 2, 108 n 3, 160 n 1, 171, 194 n 4; kingdom of, 100 n 1, 120 n 10, 143 n 4; knowledge of, 36 n 19, 56, 112 n 6, 124 n 1, 244; left hand of, 12, 194 n 3, 199 n 5, 230 n 3; light of, 15, 132, 161 n 1; love for, ix, 54 n 7, 57, 79, 101 n 3, 104, 163 n 5, 178 n 1, 203, 217 n 2; love of, 4, 54 n 7, 57, 90, 101 n 3, 115 n 4, 131, 157 n 2, 178 n 2, 194 n 3, 249; mercy of, 108 n 2, n 3, 149, 157 n 2, 171, 178 n 1, 191 n 4, n 5, 194 n 3, 209 n 7, 215 n 5; mind of, 11; names of, 37 n 20, n 22, 47, 68 n 5, 83, 98 n 2, 108 n 2; nearness to, 9–10; power of, 55 n 10, 154 n 4, 163 n 5, 172, 255 n 2; presence of, x, 4, 6, 12–13, 15, 17, 36 n 19, 38 n 26, 47–48, 55 n 8, 56, 70 n 6, 79–80, 84, 115 n 3, 132, 137 n 2, 148, 155 n 7, 172, 185 n 1, 227 n 6, 244, 251 n 1, 252; right hand of, 12, 104, 209 n 7; service of, 48, 238 n 4, 253; is Torah, 84, 152 n 3; transcendence of, 35 n 17, 38 n 26, 40 n 32; transgression of, 56; union in, 37 n 20, 57, 79–80; union with, 15, 54 n 7, 70 n 7, 80, 157 n 12, 172, 190 n 3, 204, 244, 272, 274 n 4; withdrawal of, 14, 14 n 16, 15, 137 n 2, 161 n 1, 227 n 6, 252; word of, 47, 84, 168 n 9, 204, 265 n 7; and world, 4, 13–15, 47, 64 n 4, 79–80, 108 n 3, 173, 230 n 3; worship of, 10, 32 n 4, 34 n 14, 204, 258 n 4, 261 n 8.
Green, Arthur, xi, 1 n 1, 5 n 6, 15 n 17, 17 n 19, 18 n 20, 22 n 25, 257.
Gries, Ze'ev, 3 n 5.

HaBaD, 1 n 1, 5, 8, 11, 15, 157 n 12, 275.
Halakhah, 8, 178 n 2, 210 n 1.
Haman, 195 n 5, 199 n 6, 253.
Hanover, Nathan, 31 n 3.
Hanukkah, 253, 254 n 1, 258 n 5, 267 n 1, 268 n 3, 271.
Hasidism, communities (schools) of, x, 4–5, 5 n 6, 8, 18, 21, 21 n 22, 23, 89; and God's presence, x, 36 n 19, 47–48, 50 n 4, 70 n 6, 79, 132, 148, 175

278

INDEX

n 3, 186 n 3, 244, 272; and homilies, 1,
1 n 1, 2–3, 3 n 5, 4, 8–9, 26, 48, 70, 90,
148, 203, 204, 253, 271–272, 275; and
inwardness, 10, 12, 14 n 15, 16, 18, 48;
and Judaism, x, 3, 6, 12 n 13; and
Kabbalah, 2 n 2, 4, 7, 9, 11–14, 14 n 15,
n 16, 15, 34 n 15, 38 n 25, 56–57, 104,
135 n 2, 148–149, 161 n 1, 173, 197 n 1,
198 n 2; and mysticism, ix, x, 4–5, 10,
13, 15, 48, 57, 79, 203–204, 271, 276;
and non-Jewish world, 16, 19, 172–173;
and oral tradition, x, 1–2, 5; and
prayer, xi; and Psalms, 7 n 10; and
return to God, 132, 253; and Scripture,
7, 7 n 10, 26, 70, 89–90, 103, 202, 248,
271–272; and tales, 1–2, 2 n 4, 3, 3 n 5,
5, 275; and Torah, x, 7, 7 n 10, 8, 13,
18, 22, 34 n 15, 47, 90, 104, 202–203;
and transformation, 172, 193 n 2; and
union, 57; and word, 65, 204; and
zaddiqim, x, 1–3, 16–18, 18 n 20,
64–65, 103–104, 186 n 3, 211 n 2, 233 n
1, 257 n 2; and Zohar, 6–7, 9.
Hasmoneans, 259 n 6.
Healing, 6, 33 n 12, 148, 154 n 4, 157 n
12, 228 n 2.
Hersey, 4, 47, 155 n 8, 227 n 1.
Heschel, Abraham, ix, x, 27, 276.
Hesed, 12, 12 n 13, 104, 108 n 2, 115 n 4,
119 n 9, 122 n 12, 124 n 1, 135 n 2, 175
n 3, 209 n 7.
Hillman, James, 14 n 15.
Hirsch, R. Zevi, 22.
Hokhmah, 11, 13, 80 81 n 2, 82 n 5, 84,
124 n 1, 131, 132, 134 n 1, 135 n 2, 165
n 3, 168 n 8, 203, 217 n 2, 230 n 1.
Holiness, 31 n 2, 203–204, 252; sparks of,
19–20.
Holtz, Barry W., 1 n 1, 275.
Homilies, collected, 2, 4, 24; and
Hasidism, 1, 1 n 1, 2–3, 3 n 5, 4, 8–9,
26, 48, 70, 90, 148, 203–204, 253,
271–272, 275; and Judaism, 7; and
Scripture, 4, 6, 8, 26, 70–71, 89–90,
148, 202, 248, 271; and Talmud, 3, 8;
and Torah, 7–8, 23–24, 47–48, 252.
Horodezky, S.A., 21 n 23, 22 n 26, 25 n
40.
Hosea, 6:2, 22 n 29.
Humility, x, 148, 155 n 7, 253.
Hurwitz, Siegmund, 14 n 15.

Isaac, 77 n 6, 94 n 4, 108 n 1, 131,

171–172, 185 n 1, 191 n 4, n 5, 194 n 3,
196 n 6, 215 n 4, 231 n 4.
Isaiah, 32:17, 23 n 35; 41:10, 23 n 30.
Ishmael, 174 n 1.
Ishmaelites, 174 n 2.
Israel, and Canaanites, 122 n 11; and
creation, 79; and exile, ix, 15, 90, 96 n
8, 213 n 1, 214 n 3, 240 n 7; and God,
4, 12, 15, 54 n 7, 57, 109 n 4, 174 n 1,
249; land of, 212 n 3; love for, 104;
merits of, 199 n 6, 252; and nations,
19–20, 173, 174 n 1, 193 n 2, 196–197 n
7, 202, 240 n 7; sins of, 19, 64 n 4, 92 n
2, 142 n 3, 198 n 3, 252; strength of, 52
n 5.
Isserles, R. Moses, 273 n 3.

Jacob, 12, 77 n 6, 94 n 4, 96 n 8, 108 n 1,
131, 171–172, 185 n 1, 191 n 5, 202–203,
205 n 2, 208 n 6, 213 n 1, 215 n 4, n 5,
231 n 4, 238 n 5, 244, 248.
Jacob Joseph of Polonnoye, 17–18.
Jacob Samson of Shepetovka, 24 n 37, n
40.
Jacobs, Louis, 14 n 16, 15 n 17, 16 n 18,
275–276.
Jared, 162 n 4.
Jeremiah, 252.
Jeremiah, 46:18, 263 n 2.
Jeroboam, 98 n 3.
Jethro, 55 n 10.
Joseph, 50 n 3, 55 n 8, 156 n 11, 248,
271–272, 274 n 4.
Joshua, 212 n 3.
Judah, 274 n 4.
Judah ha-Nasi, 192 n 1.
Judah Leib ha-Kohen, 24 n 37.
Judaism, and charism, 17; and exegesis,
7; and Hasidism, ix, 3, 6, 12 n 13; and
Kabbalah, 4, 12 n 13, 31 n 3; and
moon, 56; and morality, 12 n 13, 31 n
1, 261 n 8; and mysticism, ix, 3, 5–6, 9,
17, 18 n 20, 37 n 20, 64, 79, 83, 98 n 3,
131, 232 n 6; rabbinic-, 3–4, 8, 19, 48,
71; spirituality of, 6, 131, 232 n 6, 248;
and theology, 4, 6.

Kabbalah, 43 n 43, 81 n 2, 157 n 2, 198 n
2, 199 n 5, 209 n 7, 213 n 1, 245 n 1;
and creation, 49 n 1; and dualism 19,
173; and gnosticism, 2 n 2, 9; and
Hasidism, 2 n 2, 4, 7, 9–15, 14 n 15, n
16, 34 n 15, 38 n 25, 56, 104, 135 n 2,

279

INDEX

INDEX

INDEX

Torah, 72 n 2, 93 n 1, 185 n 1, 187 n 5, 204, 205 n 2, 217 n 2, 238 n 4, 251 n 1, 253, 264 n 8, 272; broken, 50 n 3; and creation, 47–48, 79, 82 n 5, 84, 104, 148, 152 n 3; and *da'at*, 11 n 12, 12; and Hasidim, x, 7, 7 n 10, 8, 13, 18, 22, 34 n 15, 47, 90, 104, 202–203; and homilies, 7–8, 23–24, 47–48, 252; interpretation of, 149; and Kabbalah, 34 n 15, 42 n 42, 47, 83–84, 118 n 8, 134 n 1, 271; and love, 178 n 1; source of, 203; study of, 48, 84, 90, 253; two-, 83–84; words of, 124 n 3, 125 n 1, 126 n 3, 132; and worship, 34 n 14.
Transformation, 4, 6–7, 10–11, 52 n 6, 56, 72 n 3, 100 n 2, 101 n 3, 157 n 12, 167 n 5, 172, 175 n 4.
Twerski, A.D., 21 n 23, 24 n 40.

Vilna Gaon, 24 n 40.
Virtues, 253.

Walden, A., 24 n 37.
Weiss, Joseph, 6 n 7, 9 n 11, 276.
Wender, M., 2 n 3.
Wiesel, Elie, 276.
Wisdom, of God, 84, 131, 164 n 2; lower-, 79–80; and Torah, 47; upper-, 80.
World, "to come", 240 n 8, 241 n 9, 256 n 1; and creation, 13–14, 49, 79, 108 n

3, 131, 163 n 5; diminishment of, 64 n 4; of Emanation, 161 n 1; and God, 4, 13–15, 47, 64 n 4, 79–80, 108 n 3, 173, 230 n 3; lower, 15, 79, 82 n 5, 135 n 2, 149, 179 n 5, 251 n 1; outer-, 13; of Thought, 11 n 12, 220 n 5; and Torah, 134 n 1, 180 n 6, 206 n 4; upper-, 252, 258, 4.

Yaari, A., 24 n 37.
Yesod, 41 n 37.
Yom Kippur, 43 n 43, 199 n 6, 246 n 2.
Yoma, 23a, 42 n 40.
Yose ben Halafta, 236 n 1.

Ẓaddiqim, x, 1–3, 16–18, 18 n 20, 25, 39 n 29, 64–65, 70 n 7, 89, 103–104, 124 n 3, 132, 139 n 2, 143 n 4, 157 n 12, 181 n 9, 186 n 3, 203, 210 n 1, 211 n 2, 248–249, 251 n 1, 252–253, 257 n 2, 274 n 4.
Zadoq ha-Kohen of Lublin, 9.
Ẓimẓum, 14, 14 n 16, 15, 15 n 17, 161 n 1, 172, 240 n 7.
Zohar, 6, 9–10, 12 n 13, 19, 32 n 7, 35 n 17, 37 n 20, 89, 149, 198 n 3, 271; 1:1b, 40 n 32; 1:65b, 39 n 31; 1:87b, 263 n 2; 3:25a, 35 n 17.
Zoroastrianism, 227 n 1.
Zusya of Anipol, 5, 24, 24 n 40.

INDEX TO
TEXTS

INDEX

INDEX

INDEX

INDEX

INDEX

INDEX

87, 93, 125–126, 140, 152–153, 183, 186, 212, 221, 234, 249–250, 255, 266; is eternal, 249; and evil, 79, 213, 262, 266–267; fallen-, 49, 94, 267; forsaking of, 256; fulfilling of, 133, 135, 233–234, 237, 262; giving of, 58–60, 62, 73, 81, 96, 102, 116–117, 120, 127, 133, 166, 174, 187, 231, 247, 257, 262, 265; and God, 49, 84, 94, 96, 107, 114, 152–153, 178, 187, 193, 229, 232, 237–238, 250, 256, 258–259, 261, 272–273; higher-, 206; and *hokmah*, 81, 133–134, 165, 216–217, 229–232; interpretation of, 164, 166, 168, 267; letters of, 154, 160–161, 170, 177–178, 207, 219–220, 234–235; and life, 49–51, 73, 107, 152, 212; and love, 177–179, 183–184; and mind, 63, 247; oral-, 206, 208, 210; perfection of, 95, 97, 121; revealed-, 85, 120, 205–207, 209, 216–217, 229, 232, 259; root (source) of, 164–165, 205–207, 216–217, 219, 232, 235, 273; secret (hidden), 84–85, 96, 133, 139, 206–207, 209–210, 216–217, 219, 231, 246, 259; service of, 113, 138; study of, 33–34, 51, 61–62, 72, 75, 77–79, 81–85, 95–96, 113, 117, 121, 125, 151, 179, 185, 212, 217–218, 221, 230, 238, 240, 250, 259–262, 265, 266, 269; written-, 206, 210; and *zaddiq*, 66, 78, 85, 97, 140.
Transformation, 37, 42, 52, 55, 63–64, 72–74, 77–79, 98, 100, 159, 167, 198–199, 217, 219, 221–223, 226.

Vanities, 37, 150.

Wa-Yiqra Rabbah, 242.
Wisdom, ascent to, 52; and evil, 189; and fear, 31, 33, 178, 180, 200; of God, 35, 122, 134, 168–169, 185, 187, 231, 259; and life, 35; light of, 166, 168–169; lower, 81–83; and man, 164–165, 170; paths of, 230; rungs of, 82; supernal, 35, 49, 81, 229; and Torah, 166, 178, 185, 216–217, 219, 229, 255, 258; upper, 82–83, 165.
World, of action, 74; -to come, 91,

222–224, 240–242, 249, 261; of Contemplation, 39; creation of, 35, 38, 41–42, 48–49, 65–66, 72, 74, 80–81, 84, 93, 108–110, 125–126, 134, 140, 152, 154, 155, 157, 162, 174, 176–177, 183, 222, 236, 241, 249, 255, 266; as fallen, 223; foundation of, 66, 68; and God, 35, 61, 81, 108, 134, 137, 139, 174, 177, 223, 236, 240–241, 249, 260, 266; hidden-, 146, 156–157; higher, 35, 161; of Joy, 197–198, 265; of Love, 114, 116–117; lower, 35, 37, 39–41, 68, 81, 94, 100, 127, 152, 161, 205; raising of, 68; revealed-, 146, 157; of Speech, 125–126, 216; of Thought, 37, 185–186, 216–220, 223; and *zaddiq*, 65–67, 119, 254.

Yalqut Ovadiah, 201.
Yebamot, 130, 200, 269.
YHWH, 34, 36–37, 50, 80–81, 100, 108, 110–111, 126, 133, 151, 210, 215, 221, 227.
R. Yohanan ben Zakkai, 35, 65, 69, 156, 169.
Yom Kippur, 245.
Yoma, 65, 86–87, 129–130, 146–147, 200–201, 243.
R. Yose, 145, 147.

Zaddiq, and chastisement, 91; cosmic, 39; and creation, 65–66; and holiness, 98, 210–211, 225–226, 255; and love, 68; and rungs, 66–67, 76, 91, 107, 146, 225, 250; and sparks, 39; and Torah, 66, 78, 85, 97, 140; and wisdom, 250.
Zechariah, 2:17, 123; 4:2, 267; 13:2, 190, 193, 246; 14:9, 224, 240.
Zephaniah, 3:9, 94, 106.
Zevahim, 270.
Zimzum, 82, 110–111, 152, 177, 179–180, 184.
Zohar, 36, 42, 50, 53, 75, 77, 82, 85–88, 108, 120–121, 129–130, 132, 136, 140, 145–147, 154, 169, 195, 198–199, 201, 207, 217, 222, 241–243, 246–247, 250–251, 255, 267–269, 272, 274.